Sir James Whitelocke's
Liber Famelicus 1570–1632

Damian X. Powell

Sir James Whitelocke's *Liber Famelicus* 1570–1632

Law and Politics in Early Stuart England

PETER LANG
Bern · Berlin · Bruxelles · Frankfurt am Main · New York · Wien

Die Deutsche Bibliothek – CIP-Einheitsaufnahme

Powell, Damian X.:
Sir James Whitelocke's Liber famelicus 1570–1632 : law and politics in early Stuart England / Damian X. Powell. – Bern ; Berlin ; Bruxelles ; Frankfurt am Main ; New York ; Wien : Lang, 2000
ISBN 3-906764-48-6

British Library and Library of Congress Cataloguing-in-Publication Data:
A catalogue record for this book is available from *The British Library*, Great Britain, and from *The Library of Congress*, USA

Cover design: Thomas Jaberg, Peter Lang AG

Cover image: The first folio of Sir James Whitelocke's Liber famelicus (British Library Additional MS 53725), reproduced by permission of the British Library.
John Bruce, who edited the manuscript for the Camden Society in 1858, has scored the areas he omitted from his printed edition.

ISBN 3-906764-48-8
US-ISBN 0-8204-4637-8

Printed in Germany

For Dieni

Contents

Acknowledgements

This book began life as a doctoral dissertation completed in the University of Adelaide, and my principal guide and mentor in the studies that led to its completion has been Professor Wilfrid Prest, who deserves first thanks for his assistance and kindness along the way. Professor John Morrill of the University of Cambridge, and Dr John Reeve of the University of New South Wales examined the thesis, and have provided constant support and advice during the process of revision that has reached its conclusion in the publication of this book. Professor Donald Kennedy of the University of Melbourne provided the initial and crucial inspiration to study British history. The staff and students of the history departments of the Universities of Melbourne, Adelaide and Canterbury provided intellectual and social support from which to contemplate Stuart England, and their libraries provided the logistical support to research its historical treasures. In Melbourne, Professor Robin Sharwood kindly read and commented upon the material relating to ecclesiastical law. In New Zealand, Dr Marie Peters kindly read and commented upon the entire text. In the United Kingdom, I benefited from the assistance and kindness of the staff and libraries of Universities of London, Cambridge, Oxford and their colleges, the libraries of the inns of court, the British Library, and St Dieniol's Library Wales. Conversations with Professor Conrad Russell of the University of London and Professor Kevin Sharpe of the University of Southampton have greatly stimulated my thinking on the causes of the Civil Wars. The History of Parliament Trust allowed me to consult and cite from an as yet unpublished piece on James Whitelocke's parliamentary career. The Marquess of Bath kindly allowed me to consult and reproduce material from the Whitelocke family papers held at Longleat House. I am grateful to the Editors and Syndics of Cambridge University Press for allowing me to draw upon my piece on 'Sir James Whitelocke's advice to the Crown in 1627', *Historical Journal* 39 (1996), pp. 737-42. In Adelaide, Melbourne and Britain, Mr Anthony Page has been a fellow traveller and great supporter throughout the entire process. The Warden of Trinity College Melbourne, Professor Donald Markwell, encouraged and supported the completion of the book. Professor Alan Powell, my father, provided important assistance with the technical aspects of publication. My greatest debt remains to my parents, for their support and encouragement in life. I dedicate this book to my wife, Dieni, who through her love puts all that is above into proper perspective.

All dates are given in the old style; the year is taken to begin on 1 January. Any errors or omissions are my own.

Damian X. Powell
Melbourne
Maundy Thursday 1999

Introduction

Liber Famelicus.

This book I began to write in, the 18 April 1609, *anno* 7 *Jacobi regni sui Angliæ, et Scotiæ* 42.

In it I entend to set downe memorialls for my posterity of thinges most properly concerning myself and my familye.

Stuart England has vanished in the years since a thirty-nine year old lawyer, James Whitelocke, committed these words to a small paper notebook, inviting his descendants to reflect upon his part in their family's history. Now deposited among the manuscript collections of the British Library, the *Liber Famelicus* invites its reader to abandon their preconceptions and immerse themselves in an investigation of the historical past, as it draws one ever deeper into James Whitelocke's changing perception of the world.[1]

1 BL Additional MS 53725 ('Liber Famelicus'), fol. 1; *Liber Famelicus of Sir James Whitelocke, A Judge of the Court of King's Bench in the Reigns of James I and Charles I. Now First Published from the Original Manuscript*, ed. John Bruce, Camden Society Old Series no. 70 (London 1858), p. 1 [hereafter cited as *Liber Famelicus*]. In 1791 Lieutenant-General John Whitelocke had an elaborate manuscript copy of the *Liber Famelicus* prepared out of private interest. John Whitelocke's copy ended up in the possession of the Royal College of Music, from where it is now on loan to the Bodleian Library. The original manuscript subsequently passed to family members in Ireland as ties dissolved with the Buckinghamshire region in which James Whitelocke had built up his estate. In 1858, John Bruce recorded the *Liber Famelicus* as in the possession of the grandson of Carleton Whitelocke, one of Bulstrode Whitelocke's sons by his third

While Whitelocke's descendants were responsible for the preservation of the *Liber Famelicus* over three centuries, its status among historians derives from the scholarship of John Bruce, who edited the manuscript for the Camden Society in 1858. Despite a dated historical introduction, Bruce's edition of the *Liber Famelicus* warrants only minor correction. A dearth of candid political commentary in the early Stuart era has made the *Liber Famelicus* popular with historians, who draw upon Bruce's edition with confidence in search of contemporary opinion on law, religion, education, and politics.[2]

Throughout a long and controversial career as a parliamentarian and judge, Whitelocke offered candid insights on the personalities and issues that shaped the early Stuart age. His condemnation of Sir Thomas Ellesmere as 'the greatest enemye to the common law that did ever bear office of state in this kingdom', written in bitter epitaph to the acerbic Lord Chancellor, contrasts with praise of Sir Edward Coke as 'the most just, honest, and uncorrupt judge that ever sate on benche' to provide colorful evidence of legal and political tensions within the Jacobean state. Whitelocke denounced the earl of Salis-

---

wife. By 1930 the *Liber Famelicus* was in the possession of Percy Whitelocke-Lloyd in Dublin, who passed it to a family friend. In 1965 Ruth Spalding tracked down the *Liber Famelicus* and persuaded its final owner to sell the manuscript to the British Library, making it available for general inspection. *Liber Famelicus*, p. xix; *The Diary of Bulstrode Whitelocke 1605-1675*, ed. Ruth Spalding (Oxford 1990), p. 67 [hereafter cited as *Diary*]; Bodleian MS Dep. d. 804; Ruth Spalding, *The Improbable Puritan: A Life of Bulstrode Whitelocke 1605-1675* (London 1975), p. 257. Spalding provides a engaging account of her location of James Whitelocke's original manuscript as a postscript to *Improbable Puritan*, pp. 244-61.

2 See n. 4 below, and cf., for example, David Lemmings, 'Ritual and Law in Early Modern England' in *Law and History in Australia: A Collection of Papers presented at the 1989 Law and History Conference*, ed. Susan Corcoran (Adelaide 1991), p. 7; Roger Lockyer, The *Early Stuarts: A Political History of England 1603-1642* (London & New York), p. 111; James McConica, 'The social relations of Tudor Oxford', *Transactions of the Royal Historical Society*, 5th series (1977), pp. 124-6; J.H. Baker, *The Legal Profession and the Common Law: Historical Essays* (London 1986), p. 210 [hereafter cited as *Legal Profession*].

bury, who as treasurer introduced the unpopular fiscal innovation of impositions, as one who had 'rotted above ground', while the earl of Northampton was considered 'a verye rot, and left the world suspected of ill dealing toward the state'. Kinder words were reserved for Sir Ralph Winwood, secretary of state from 1614 until his death in 1617, whom Whitelocke had known since his student days at Oxford and was praised as a 'worthye frende'.[3]

Such private reflections as these have provided generations of historians with food for thought, and Whitelocke's own historiography is, in part, a microcosm of the interpretative differences that affect our understanding of the early Stuart era. At issue is the character, and effect, of the 'common law mind', articulated by John Pocock as lying in partial resistance to advocates of an unbridled royal prerogative. In particular, Whitelocke's famous 1610 declaration of parliamentary rights, and his equally important opinion on the Crown's right to check parliamentary excess in *Eliot's Case* (1630), suggest the need for careful consideration of the relationship between individuals, their writings, and the emergence of political theory that could serve the ends of parliamentarians in eventual resistance to Crown policy.[4]

---

3 See *Liber Famelicus*, pp. 39, 47, 48, 49, 51, 53, 56, 61.

4 For contrasting interpretations of Whitelocke's legal, political, and religious views and impact cf., for example, Robert Ashton, *The English Civil War: Conservatism and Revolution 1603-1649*, 2nd ed. (London 1989), p. 12; *Constitutional Documents of the Reign of James I*, ed. J.R. Tanner (Cambridge 1930), pp. 245-6; J.P. Sommerville, *Politics and Ideology in England 1603-1640* (London 1986), pp. 153-4; Christopher Brooks & Kevin Sharpe, 'History, English Law and the Renaissance' in Kevin Sharpe, *Politics & Ideas in Early Stuart England: Essays and Studies* (London and New York), p. 177; *idem*, *Sir Robert Cotton 1566-1631* (Oxford 1979), p. 23; W.R. Prest, *The Inns of Court Under Elizabeth I and the Early Stuarts 1590-1640* (London 1972), p. 207; J.S.A. Adamson, 'The Diary of Sir Richard Hutton 1614-1639' (book review); *Cambridge Law Journal* 51 (1992), p. 552; Glenn Burgess, *The Politics of the Ancient Constitution: An Introduction to English Political Thought, 1603-1642* (London 1992), pp. 143-4; Richard Cust, *The Forced Loan and English Politics, 1626-1628* (Oxford 1987), p. 152. For the 'common law mind' see J.G.A.

In 1989 Kevin Sharpe observed that a 'particular reason for the lack of interest in the relationship between ideas and events' in early Stuart history was because 'revisionist scholarship has widened the gulf between intellectual and political history'. This book attempts, through an examination of Whitelocke's life and times, to bridge this gap. It argues that the political controversies of the early Stuart era are best understood with concern to the discursive constraints, and possibilities, at work in private life and public debate. In their search for a coherent political outlook in men such as Whitelocke, historians have failed to see that certain voices are privileged in certain settings. The *Liber Famelicus* suggests, in its voices and silences, why men such as Whitelocke, deferential in private request for patronage and support, could express open opposition to the wishes of the king in a widely circulated public speech. By relating the textual traces of James Whitelocke's life back to the broader ideological investments of the early Stuart period, this book exposes confusions and contradictions within his universe of discourse, suggesting inconsistencies which have a bearing upon the collapse of the Stuart regime.[5]

Pocock, *The Ancient Constitution and the Feudal Law, A Reissue with a Retrospect* (Cambridge 1988); Ian Maclean, *Interpretation and meaning in the Renaissance: The case of law* (Cambridge 1992), p. 9; W.R. Prest, *The Rise of the Barristers: A Social History of the English Bar 1590-1640*, rev. ed. (Oxford 1991), p. 257; Glenn Burgess, 'Common Law and Political Theory in Early Stuart England', *Political Science* 40 (1988), pp. 4-17; L.L. Peck, 'Kingship, counsel and law in early Stuart Britain' in *The Varieties of British political thought, 1500-1800*, ed. J.G.A. Pocock, G.J. Schochet & L.G. Schwoerer (Cambridge 1993), p. 91, C.W. Brooks, 'The Place of Magna Carta and the Ancient Constitution in Sixteenth-Century English Legal Thought' in *The Roots of Liberty: Magna Carta, Ancient Constitution, and the Anglo-American Tradition of Rule of Law*, ed. Ellis Sandoz (Columbia and London 1993), pp. 57-9; Alan Cromartie, *Sir Matthew Hale 1609-1676: Law, religion and natural philosophy* (Cambridge 1995), pp. 107-9.

5 Sharpe, *Politics and Ideas*, pp. 3-4, and compare his comments on Quentin Skinner, John Pocock and Johann Sommerville on pp. 4-7, 283-8; Conrad Russell's comments on Sommerville in *The Causes of the English Civil War* (Oxford 1987), pp. 144-6; John Morrill's observations on Sommerville *in The*

Unusually, Whitelocke learnt the rhetoric and logic both of civil and common law in preparation for public life. We begin, as does he, with recollections of an Elizabethan childhood. Thereafter, we shall follow him from Oxford University to the inns of court, and from there into political life as a barrister-MP and judge, concluding with an assessment of his social and familial connections within the county community.

Charles I and the Road to Personal Rule (Cambridge 1989), p. 4, and Michael Walzer's comments upon the relationship between action and ideology *in The Revolution of the Saints* (Cambridge, Mass. 1965), p. 66.

Part I
Learning and Law

Chapter 1

Childhood and university education

James Whitelocke's *Liber Famelicus* provides 'the best single account of early education' in the early modern period, surviving as one of the more fascinating products of what Lawrence Stone dubbed an 'educational revolution', which saw unprecedented expansion of enrolments at the universities and the inns of court in the later sixteenth and early seventeenth centuries. His virtually unprecedented achievement of a dual training in civil and common law reflects a window of opportunity that existed, for young men whose academic ability was coupled with limited means, within the essentially scholastic design of the formal curriculum and the humanist vision of the Oxford colleges.[1]

Whitelocke's childhood reflections were written to stress his subsequent achievement, yet ring true in their suggestion of a less than idyllic beginning to life. His father, Richard, fell ill and died on a trading expedition in Bordeaux on 7 November 1570, three weeks before James Whitelocke's birth. His mother, Joan, remarried less than a year later, and Whitelocke's admiration for her comes through in his tale of her struggle with his 'unthrift' and 'unkinde' stepfather, Thomas Price, to preserve the children's inheritance and to 'finde meanes to bring them up in lerning and civility'.[2]

---

1 McConica, 'Social relations of Tudor Oxford', p. 124; Lawrence Stone, 'The Educational Revolution in England, 1560-1640', *Past & Present* 28 (1964), pp. 41-80 [and cf. Elizabeth Russell, 'The influx of commoners into the University of Oxford before 1581: an optical illusion?', *English Historical Review* 92 (1977), pp. 199-225]; *The History of the University of Oxford*, ed. James McConica (Oxford 1986), vol. 3, p. 282; Prest, *Rise of the Barristers*, p. 111.

2 *Liber Famelicus*, pp. 5-6; 13-14; *The Parish Register of St. Dunstan in the East, London 1558-1654*, ed. A.W.H. Clarke, *Harleian Society* 69 (1939), pp. 11, 97.

In his reflections upon his early life, Whitelocke stressed the pains taken by his mother to ensure that her four sons were educated

> in as good sort as any gentleman in England wulde do, as in singing, dancing, playing on the lute and other instruments, the Latin, Greek, Hebrew, and Frenche tongues, and to write fair; everye on of them to that he was likelyest to do good in, but all wear by her appoynted and directed to the best course, that is, of lerning, and to have been professed scholers...[3]

The youngest twin of four brothers, Whitelocke's own experiences in early life may well have encouraged him to look to education, rather than social connections, as a conduit to social progress. Of his three brothers the eldest, Edmund, seems to have held most promise, winning a place at Christ's College, Cambridge, from Merchant Taylors' School. Edmund's natural ability for languages, Whitelocke recalled, was developed at Cambridge as he was 'grownded in the liberall sciences', after which Edmund went to study common law at Lincoln's Inn. At the inns of court Edmund's professional ambitions took a back seat to his social life. A tour of the continent 'to redeem his mispent time' led him to a dozen years of travel without academic gain. Upon return to England, Edmund depended upon the charity of powerful patrons for his financial security – but associations with the earls of Essex, Northumberland and Percy led to his incarceration on suspicion of treason before an early death in the 'mirthe and good companye' of the earl of Northumberland in 1608.[4]

If Edmund's misfortunes served as a warning to James Whitelocke about squandering his educational potential, then the fate of his two other brothers was equally sobering. His twin, William, abandoned

---

Whitelocke once mentions his step brother, George, but it appears that in light of his strained relations with his step-father Thomas Price, their own relations were not strong. For the difficulties facing men in Whitelocke's position cf. Joan Thirsk, 'Younger Sons in the Seventeenth Century', *History* 54 (1969), pp. 358-77; Linda Pollock, 'Younger Sons in Tudor and Stuart England', *History Today* 39/6 (1989), pp. 23-9.

3 *Liber Famelicus*, p. 6.

4 *Liber Famelicus*, pp. 7-10.

his studies for a life at sea, serving with Sir Francis Drake, and was killed 'in a conflict withe the Spanyards' at the age of twenty-seven. Whitelocke considered him 'exceedingly wastfull in expence, and carelesse of all worldly matters that tended to thrift'. The surviving brother, Richard, followed in the footsteps of their father and left school at sixteen to travel and trade, eventually taking a Danish wife. According to James Whitelocke, Richard 'tasted many varieties of fortune, sumtime good and sumtime bad, and hathe travayled over many countries, and by the uncerteynty of trafique hathe susteyned great losses in his estate'. It appears that the uncertain lives led by the other Whitelocke boys encouraged James to stay at home and channel his energy into a bookish existence less fraught with adventure.[5]

I

'I was brought up at school under Mr. Mulcaster,' James Whitelocke recounted in the *Liber Famelicus*, 'in the famous school of the Marchantaylors in London, whear I continued untill I was well instructed in the Hebrew, Greek, and Latin tongs.' Given their importance to his subsequent professional success, the pride he expressed in his school and his educational achievements there was entirely appropriate. Merchant Taylors' School had been established in 1561, with the provision of one hundred scholarships to be given on 'genuine promise of usefulness' to students of the 'middling sorts'. Whitelocke was to prove an exemplar of the school's ideal (expressed in the words of his headmaster, the noted humanist Richard Mulcaster) that education provided the means 'to bring forth the student who will serve his country best'.[6]

---

5 *Liber Famelicus*, pp. 11-12.

6 *Liber Famelicus*, p. 12; F.W.M. Draper, *Four Centuries of Merchant Taylors' School* (London 1962), pp. 5, 10, 241-51; Joan Simon, *Education and Society in Tudor England* (Cambridge 1966), pp. 306-7; Richard Mulcaster, *Elementarie* (London 1582) in *The Educational Writings of Richard Mulcaster (1532-1611),*

James Whitelocke's son Bulstrode was later to testify that his father's 'abilities in learning were extraordinary', an assessment which centred upon the fact that James Whitelocke was 'expert in the Latin and Greek and well versed in the Hebrewe, when he went to Oxford' and 'deeply studyed in divinity'. During his stay at Merchant Taylors' School, James benefited from the help of the London linguist John Hopkinson, an 'obscure and simple man for wordly affayres', whose fluency extended to 'the lefthand tongs' such as 'Chaldean' (Aramaic), Syriac and Arabic. In his desire to emulate Hopkinson, Whitelocke pursued a daily study routine lasting until midnight, which brought on 'a dangerous disease' in his legs only cured through 'violent exercise' and blood-letting in the winter before he took up residence at Oxford University. By concentrating upon the Book of Job, the Psalms and sections of Genesis, Hopkinson's tutoring provided Whitelocke with a solid theological foundation that was further developed at university. Singing and music provided a welcome relief from studies, and also the chance to act in plays presented before Queen Elizabeth to demonstrate 'good behaviour and audacitye'.[7]

At every level of early modern education, students were encouraged to read, write, think, and speak in Latin. For the better students at Merchant Taylors' there was added incentive to show a good command of spoken Latin, as it was upon this basis that one or two students were selected, 'meteste as well for learninge, personage, poverty, and years, to be presently preferred' to St John's College, Oxford. In the presence of the president and other senior members of the Company of Merchant Taylors, as well as the president and two senior fellows of St John's, students displayed their knowledge of the language and style of reputable classical authors in an annual exercise known as the oration. Selected for an oration in his seventeenth year, it appears that James Whitelocke's gift for languages and love of public performance

---

ed. James Oliphant (Glasgow 1903), pp. 21, 66. For more on Mulcaster's educational philosophy see S.L. Collins, *From Divine Cosmos to Sovereign State* (Oxford 1989), pp. 86-8.

7 *Diary*, pp. 47, 66; *Liber Famelicus*, pp. 12-13.

did not let him down. On the Feast of St Barnabas (11 June) 1588, he was elected to study for the Bachelor of Civil Law. Though the summer of the Spanish Armada was, in Whitelocke's understated words, 'a little distemper to the quiet course of studyes', he thus began earnestly preparing himself for the rigours of university life.[8]

II

J.M. Fletcher has noted the intellectual tensions present in a 'strange situation' by end of the sixteenth century in which 'an influential body of Oxford students was following a course that had little connection with that prescribed by the statutes'. James Whitelocke's Oxford was shaped by the impact of lay, humanist ideals upon the essentially medieval system of learning embodied in the formal statutes of the late sixteenth century. His reflections upon Oxford in the *Liber Famelicus* are brief, but provide a fascinating glimpse of collegiate university life, stressing lay influence in the universities, and the importance of a vigorous collegiate system of instruction alongside the formal syllabus.[9]

---

8 H.F. Fletcher, *The Intellectual Development of John Milton*, 2 vols (Urbana 1956), vol. 1, pp. 210-11; Mulcaster *Elementarie*, pp. 46, 183; C.M. Clode, *Memorials of the Guild of Merchant Taylors' of the fraternity of St. John the Baptist in the City of London* (London 1875), pp. 405-8; Guildhall Library Microfilm 326, Merchant Taylors' Company Court Minute Book, fol. 211v; W.H. Stevenson & H.E. Salter, *The Early History of St. John's College Oxford* (Oxford 1939), p. 147; *Liber Famelicus*, pp. 12-13. John Brinsley, writing on this exercise in his *Ludus Literarius; or the Grammar Schoole* (1612), suggested that in such circumstances, the 'ancient scholar' asked to 'make an Oration to entertaine a Benefactor, or other person of note' should, 'excusing themselves by their tender yeeres, want of experience and of practice in that kinde', proceed to employ a 'variety of choice phrases' to show their mettle.

9 *History of the University of Oxford*, vol. 3, pp. 180; M.H. Curtis, *Oxford and Cambridge in Transition 1558-1642* (Oxford 1959), p. 50. For some general criticisms of Curtis see Kenneth Charlton, *Education in Renaissance England*

The Bachelor of Civil Law was 'the most easily gained of all degrees offered at Oxford in the sixteenth century'. The Elizabethan Statutes placed almost the entire measure of assessment for the degree of BCL on a single public disputation, based upon two questions drawn from Justinian's *Corpus Juris Civilis*, the key text of civil law. The BCL required attendance over five years at the lectures of the Regius professor, Albericus Gentilis, largely drawn from Justinian's *Corpus*. The statutes also required attendance at Faculty disputations held every second term, alongside college lectures by St John's dean of law, Edward Sprott, which supplemented those of the regius professor. That Whitelocke makes no mention of the formal teaching regime in his recollections of Oxford is instructive. It is known that in his time Gentilis pursued his professional obligations in lack-lustre style and frequently delegated the chore to a deputy. St John's College minutes for 28 May 1592, in which the president and the seniors demanded that the weekly disputations between the law students be duly observed, suggests that Sprott's teaching also met with a certain amount of inertia on the part of the students, who knew full well that such exercises had no formal bearing on their degree.[10]

Whitelocke's own discussion of his university education stresses the importance of college tuition in his intellectual formation, noting the influence of Rowland Searchfield, his college tutor (and later bishop of Bristol). It was not law, but the arts which Whitelocke later recalled as under Searchfield he 'continued the study of logique and the artes, but above all of historye; in whiche I toke great delite'. Beyond a reference to 'Titus Livius' in whom he considered himself 'verye perfect', Whitelocke also recalled that under the guidance of his tutor he 'red Aristotle in Greek'. In directed and undirected reading, Whitelocke undoubtedly benefited from the rapid expansion

---

(London 1965), pp. 167-8; Christopher Hill, *The Intellectual Origins of the English Revolution* (Oxford, 1965), pp. 300-14.

10 *History of the University of Oxford*, vol. 3, pp. 274-6, 292, 358, 647; B.P. Levack, *The Civil Lawyers in England 1603-1641: A Political Study* (Oxford 1973), pp. 16-18; Stevenson & Salter, *Early History of St. John's*, pp. 271, 285.

of St John's library, during his time as a scholar, into probably the largest library in Oxford.[11]

The extension of Whitelocke's knowledge of the classics during his college years is demonstrated in a personal commonplace book that survives from his time as a student at Oxford. Whitelocke divided the book 'into two parts: in it first, there will be a discussion of life and manners, in it second, of nature and her hidden laws'. He arranged the first part under alphabetical headings starting with 'absona' and ending with 'zona'. Under headings, Whitelocke gathered information from standard works: Varro's *De Lingua Latina*, Plato's *Respublica*, Cicero's *De Inventione (rhetorica vetus)* and *De Oratore*, Livy's *Epitomae*, Aristotle's *De Anima*, and so on. Headings such as 'academia', 'disputatio', and 'lingua (Graecia/Latina)' suggest the vast range of topics on which an educated man was expected to be able to talk with authority, and a significant number of headings received no addition, suggesting that Whitelocke's ambitions outstripped his reading (or his common-placing, at any rate).[12]

In a smaller and subsequent section treating 'points that will be unravelled which deal with natural and theoretical knowledge', Whitelocke's ambition to fill his headings was again excessively optimistic; what little information he did accommodate came principally from Cicero, Aristotle or Plato. Towards the end of the notebook, Whitelocke constructed a rudimentary grammar as a supplementary organisational device, which he divided into 'orthographical' categories such as etymology, syntax, dialectic, and authority. Mostly blank, headings contain intermittent references to Socrates, Plato, Ovid and others. Of course, once constructed, this common-place book served as a ready reference source to be added to at will, and Whitelocke ended the book with an alphabetical list of headings, citing the folios whence he had compiled his information.[13]

---

11 *Liber Famelicus*, pp. 76, 13; *History of the University of Oxford*, vol. 3, p. 460.

12 CUL MS Dd. 9.20, fols 1, 3, 7, 114, 218, 470 (translated from the Latin). I am greatly indebted to Professor Baker for making me aware of this manuscript.

13 CUL MS Dd. 9.20, fols 250-6, 479-570.

James Whitelocke's commonplace book invites reflection upon the ways in which the humanist objectives of early modern education presaged the formation of the legal mind. Education in the *Corpus Juris Civilis* presupposed and encompassed all the elements of the trivium; indeed, Richard Holdsworth's 'Directions for a Student in the Universitie' (1596) suggested that a 'smattering tast' of Justinian was 'of great use' to a general education in the arts. By expanding upon the principles of the *Corpus*, the lectures of the regius professor (however lack-lustre) encouraged the development of a philosophically-educated mind beyond any practical training in law. During his course of formal studies, Whitelocke would have acquainted himself with legal-humanist authors, such as Alciatus and Cujas, as a matter of routine, as well as medieval commentators like Baldus and Bartolus. In placing the weight of expectation upon proficiency in logic and rhetoric, the university syllabus aligned its demands with the aims of college tuition and exercises, in which much read or written work was, in the final instance, delivered orally.[14]

III

A distinguishing feature of university colleges has always been the opportunity for lifelong friendships to flow from a shared life of study. James Whitelocke's unclear theological orientation in the 1590s mirrors a formative but 'ill-defined' period for English Arminianism. At St John's, branded to posterity as a nursery of Catholicism through association with two of its most famous sons, Edmund

14 T.K. Shaller, 'English Law and the Renaissance: the Common Law and Humanism in the Sixteenth Century' (1979 Harvard University PhD thesis), pp. 34-7; Maclean, *Interpretation and meaning*, p. 68; Richard Holdsworth, 'Directions for a Student in the Universitie' in Fletcher, *Intellectual Development*, vol. 2, p. 646 (for a discussion of the limitations of Holdsworth's 'Directions' see Hill, *Intellectual Origins*, pp. 307-8); William Fulbecke, *A Direction or Preparative to the Study of the Lawe* (London 1600), p. 26v; Levack, *Civil Lawyers*, pp. 16-18.

Campion and William Laud, James Whitelocke formed friendships with a group of ambitious clerics whose patronage was to play an important role in his later professional success. His ties with an 'Arminian nucleus' including John Buckeridge and William Laud are conspicuous. Given the poverty of material on Laud's own time at Oxford, Whitelocke's relationship with him adds something to our understanding of the context in which Laud began his climb to prominence.[15]

Whitelocke has left a tantalizingly brief account of his association with Laud – the man who, it has been claimed, fractured the delicate theological consensus of the English Church almost single-handedly during his time as prelate. References throughout the *Liber Famelicus* suggest a very close relationship between Whitelocke and his 'loving frend and ancient collegue' during their long mutual association with St John's. Unfortunately Whitelocke offers no view on Laud's religious formation at Oxford, which remains largely obscured, and while both benefited from the support of John Buckeridge in the 1590s, Tyacke considers it a mistake to assimilate Buckeridge's position during this time to that of Arminianism.[16]

Whitelocke and Laud both owed their start in professional life to the overwhelmingly mercantile, urban social complexion envisaged in the endowment of St John's, creating a societal composition which

---

15 Hugh Trevor Roper, *Catholics, Anglicans and Puritans* (London 1987), pp. 46-8, 57, *idem*, *Archbishop Laud 1573-1645* (3rd ed., London 1988), pp. 34, 39; Charles Carlton, *Archbishop William Laud* (London & New York 1987), pp. 11-15; *History of the University of Oxford*, vol. 3, pp. 411-23.

16 *Liber Famelicus*, p. 77; Michael Hawkins, 'The Government: Its Role and Its Aims' *in The Origins of the English Civil War*, ed. Conrad Russell (London 1973), pp. 60-1; Patrick Collinson, *The Religion of Protestants: The Church in English Society 1559-1625* (Oxford 1982), p. 90; Ashton, *English Civil War*, p. 110; Nicholas Tyacke, *Anti-Calvinists: the Rise of English Arminianism c. 1590-1640* (Oxford 1987), p. 17. For the development of Buckeridge's religious views see Peter Lake, 'Lancelot Andrewes, John Buckeridge, and avant-garde conformity at the court of James I' in *The Mental World of the Jacobean Court*, ed. L.L. Peck (Cambridge 1991), pp. 113-33.

was 'probably unique in the two universities'. Laud entered St John's a year after Whitelocke, and from this time onwards social and intellectual similarities may have cemented their friendship. Both were relatively poor, and equally determined to make their way in the world, particularly in relation to those gentry lads who had entered university 'to get such learning as may serve for delight and ornament'. Laud made few friends during his undergraduate years at St John's, yet enjoyed the companionship of Humphrey May, who would later share lodgings with Whitelocke at the Middle Temple. It seems fair to conclude that intellectual prowess may have served, for these scholarship lads, as a way to compensate for social insecurity.[17]

For the large numbers of men drawn to St John's from the merchant classes, a university degree opened two doors for advancement. While the majority of St John's graduates took orders, up to a third of the scholars went on to a career in the law, medicine or commerce, many of whom withdrew from ecclesiastical training. Whitelocke's mention of colleagues such as Humphrey May, who graduated Bachelor of Arts in March 1591 and left St John's to become his room-mate at the Middle Temple, and Walter Pye (whom Whitelocke tells us 'was my collegue in St. John's colledge in Oxon, and came to the Middle Temple a little before me'), reinforces the impression that this career path was frequently travelled by the end of the Tudor period. Yet while Whitelocke's desire to graduate as a layman was not unusual, his desire to 'joyne the study of the common law withe the civill' was remarkable, and resulted in an equally remarkable subterfuge.[18]

---

17 Carlton, *Archbishop William Laud*, pp. 6-7, 11-13; *Liber Famelicus*, p. 21; Tyacke, *Anti-Calvinists*, pp. 67-72; Holdsworth, 'Directions for a Student in the Universitie' in Fletcher, *Intellectual Development*, vol. 2, p. 647, and cf. Lawrence Stone, 'The Size and Composition of the Oxford Student Body 1580-1910' in *The University in Society*, ed. Lawrence Stone, 2 vols (Princeton 1974), vol. 1, pp. 3-37.

18 James McConica, 'Scholars and Commoners in Renaissance Oxford' in *University in Society*, vol. 1, pp. 156-67; *Liber Famelicus*, pp. 14, 21, 90; *History*

James Whitelocke was one of only eight scholars who proceeded to the inns of court from the degree of Bachelor of Civil Law between 1571 and 1603, and the sole BCL to progress to the bench of the Middle Temple before the Civil War. In the *Liber Famelicus*, Whitelocke confessed that during his study for the BCL his ambition 'had a farther reatche, for I ever had a purpose to ayme at the study of the common law'. In Michaelmas term 1590 Whitelocke enrolled himself at an inn of chancery (New Inn) and 'went into commons thear for a while', returning to St John's to continue his studies without arousing the suspicion of the college fellows. Whitelocke's audacious pursuit of simultaneous training in common and civil law underlines the declining popularity of the BCL at the end of the sixteenth century; it suggests, also, that college statutes could be extremely flexible. Sir Thomas White's original provisions allowed probationers thirty days of absence from the college each year, while fully-admitted scholars could take up to sixty days of leave over this time. In practice, there were numerous ways to extend this period, as Statute 32 granted two additional periods of sixty days to a scholar who gave the rather vague assurance under oath that his absence was *ex causis promotionis*. With six months potentially available for purposes outside the domain of study each year, Whitelocke eventually left New Inn and entered the Society of the Middle Temple on 2 March 1592.[19]

---

of the University of Oxford, vol. 3, p. 155; McConica, 'Social relations of Tudor Oxford', pp. 116-17; Levack, *Civil Lawyers*, pp. 50-85; *idem*, 'The English Civilians' in *Lawyers in Early Modern Europe and America*, ed. W.R. Prest (London 1981), pp. 108-28.

19 *History of the University of Oxford*, vol. 3, p. 282; Prest, *Rise of the Barristers*, p. 111; *Liber Famelicus*, pp. 13-14; Stevenson & Salter, *Early History of St. John's*, p. 290; *Middle Temple Records*, ed. C.H. Hopwood, 4 vols. (London 1904), vol. 1, pp. 333, 345 [hereafter cited as *Middle Temple Records*]. The legal terms of the inns were divided into Michaelmas (October 17 to November 28), Hillary (January 23 to February 20), Easter (which began seventeen days after Easter and ended the Monday after Ascension Day), and Trinity (which lasted for nineteen days after Whitsunday).

By this time, Whitelocke's peripatetic wanderings from Oxford to London were common knowledge among the fellows of St John's. John Barton has noted that colleges reserved scholarships for the BCL 'primarily to enable those fellows who felt no vocation for the clerical life to postpone the moment when they would be obliged to take orders or leave the college'. It seems unlikely, however, that Whitelocke would have been able to maintain his scholarship without the support of Ralph Hutchenson, the college president, and the support of John Buckeridge may also have been of crucial importance. Despite heated debate on the necessity of candidates for the BCL progressing to clerical orders in 1594, Whitelocke peregrinated between Oxford and London, and 'kept in commons... at all sutche times as I coulde have dayes, by ordinary licence, by grace, or for furthering of the colledge businesse, to be absent from thence'.[20]

In 1594 Whitelocke fulfilled the single disputation required by the university for admission to the BCL. It was only after pressure was placed upon St John's to reform its lapsed regulations in 1598 that the college finally requested that Whitelocke vacate his place along with eleven other scholars. The eight years in which Whitelocke had been allowed to dispatch college business between London and Oxford presaged his subsequent employment as college steward in October 1601, a post which he held until his appointment as chief justice of Chester in 1620.[21]

IV

James Whitelocke's experience of the collegiate university indicates that a pragmatic assessment of the syllabus allowed him to exploit the loosely-articulated educational offerings of Faculty, college and tutor. In a sense, he recognised an opportunity for professional advance-

20 *History of the University of Oxford*, vol. 3, p. 277; *Liber Famelicus*, pp. 14-15.

21 Stevenson & Salter, *Early History of St. John's*, pp. 193, 249, 286; *Register of the University of Oxford*, ed. M.A. Clark, 4 vols (Oxford 1889), vol. 3, p. 186.

ment at Oxford squeezed between the traditional design of the university as a theological training school and an emerging receptiveness to lay, humanist ideals. There is no reason to doubt, however, that he took his studies seriously. He stated that the 'hunting of the hare on foot' was his single relief from the academic regime, 'but never so as that I detracted my times of study or scholasticall exercises by it' – although this comment may have been written for his son Bulstrode, who later complained that because of his father's small allowance he could not afford a horse for hunting during his own time at Oxford, and whose academic progress was a constant worry to his father. It appears that unlike his son, Whitelocke always enjoyed his intellectual pursuits. For the rest of his life, private conversation and public performance of an intellectual nature provided an important part of his identity, and college life gave him the opportunity to make lasting friendships with like-minded young men.[22]

'At its best', James McConica has written, sixteenth-century Oxford education 'matched mastery of style and a broad classical culture with a tested dialectical skill that was a formidable instrument in debate and exposition'. By acquiring expertise in the accepted methods of argumentative persuasion, James Whitelocke developed an ability for public speaking that was essential to his success as a barrister. One sees the formative influence of his university education in Whitelocke's later speeches in parliament, his jury charges, and his legal rulings. His life-long love of languages was expressed, for example, in a charge he (somewhat pretentiously) delivered in Latin as a judge for the benefit of a group of foreigners at the Oxford assizes.[23]

Whitelocke's grounding in classical history was founded upon this command of Latin, yet he also drew upon a knowledge of the Septua-

---

22 *Liber Famelicus*, p. 14; *Diary*, pp. 44-8. Bulstrode reflected that the 'wisdom of the father would discend to discourse with his boy, for which this age was ripe and delightfull', and later that his father worked 'by example and solid instruction, to heighten the mind and encourage the industry of the son'.

23 *History of the University of Oxford*, vol. 3, p. 731; *Diary*, p. 66.

gint based upon a mastery of classical Greek, a knowledge of Jewish history based upon conversance with Hebrew, and a considerable familiarity with English history, which Bulstrode tells us he knew 'exactly'. His thorough command of classical languages created a polyglot comprehension of the past that flavoured his activities from the House of the Commons to the Society of Antiquaries. It was in a form befitting the best traditions of university collegiate life that Bulstrode remembered his father as a man 'full of witt and pleasantness especially att meales, and as there was occasion his discourse was mixed with excellent learning'. For James Whitelocke, education was more than a technical apparatus. As a significant life experience, it nurtured qualities required for a place on the Jacobean public stage.[24]

24 *Diary*, p. 66; cf. Bulstrode Whitelocke, *Memorials of the English Affairs from the Beginning of the Reign of Charles I*, 4 vols (Oxford 1853), vol. 1, p. 50.

Chapter 2

Education at the inns of court and chancery

Some years after his admission to the Middle Temple, James Whitelocke prepared a paper on the historical development of the inns of court and chancery for the Society of Antiquaries. He did not elaborate upon the social and educational arrangements of his own time, 'because no man here but understandeth it, and, I suppose, our meetings are to afford one another our knowledge of ancient things, and not to discourse of things present'. Whitelocke's omission is unfortunate, because the political prominence of common lawyers such has himself has led historians to speculate widely about the intellectual impact of the inns of court and chancery.[1]

The relationship between the law and Stuart politics has been debated in the years since F.W. Maitland proposed an intellectual conflict between common lawyers, wedded to the 'ancient constitution', and civilians promoting 'absolutist' traditions received, through James I, from continental law. As the single holder of a BCL to process to a common-law judgeship under the early Stuarts, James Whitelocke offers an unusual and instructive case from which to test the relationship between common and civil law. As this chapter traces Whitelocke's progression through the inns of court and chancery, it

1 *A Collection of Curious Discourses written by Eminent Antiquaries upon several heads in our English Antiquities*, ed. Thomas Hearne, 2 vols (London 1771), vol. 1, p. 79 [hereafter cited as *Discourses*]; Hill, *Intellectual Origins*, p. 256; Stone, 'Educational Revolution in England', p. 78; J.H. Baker, *Legal Profession*, pp. 7-9; Prest, *Inns of Court*, pp. 220-1.

explores, through him, the social and intellectual context of the 'common law mind'.[2]

The *Liber Famelicus* tells us little about Whitelocke's early years at the inns, and it may be that this was, for him, a difficult stage of life, as he lost the educational status afforded to a scholar of St John's. While his journal stated simply that he 'became admitted into New In in Michaelmas term 1590, and went into commons thear for a while', an examination of his financial records suggest that fiscal, rather than educational or social concerns, guided his entry into New Inn. Enrolling for one year at this 'nursery' inn of chancery allowed him to pay a reduced admission fee of 20s. to enter the Middle Temple, whereas much higher fees were required from someone who could show no prior association with the 'parent' inn of court. New Inn also offered Whitelocke a practical training in the handling of plea rolls and writs, qualifying him for casual work as a 'common solicitor of causes' while pursuing his way to the bar at his inn. Mention as an attorney in a case listed in the Exchequer Appearance Books in 1597 shows that Whitelocke was supplementing his income with legal work fully three years before his call to the bar.[3]

---

2 F.W. Maitland, *English Law and the Renaissance* (Cambridge 1901); Levack, *Civil Lawyers*; *Law and Politics in Jacobean England: The Tracts of Lord Chancellor Ellesmere*, ed. L.A. Knafla (Cambridge 1977); M.A. Judson, *The Crisis of the Constitution: an essay in constitutional and political thought in England 1603-1645* (New York 1964), W.J. Jones, *Politics and the Bench: The Judges and the Origins of the English Civil War*, (London 1971); Wilfrid Prest, 'Predicting Civil War Allegiances: The Lawyers' Case Considered', *Albion* 24 (1992), pp. 225-236.

3 Prest, *Rise of the Barristers*, pp. 111-13; *Liber Famelicus*, pp. 5-7, 14; *Middle Temple Records*, vol. 1, pp. 164; 171; *Reports of Sir John Spelman*, ed. J.H. Baker, 2 vols, Selden Society 93 & 94 (1977 & 1978), vol. 2, p. 128; *Early Records of Furnival's Inn: Edited From a Middle Temple manuscript*, ed. D.S. Bland (Newcastle upon Tyne 1957), pp. 10-11; T.G. Barnes, 'Star Chamber Litigants and their Counsel, 1596-1641' in *Legal Records and the Historian*, ed. J.H. Baker (London 1978), p. 24 [hereafter cited as *Legal Records*]; PRO E2/2 (unfoliated) E. 39. No lists survive for fees at New Inn survive from this period, which have been calculated upon the basis of fees due at Clement's Inn for a

From the time of his admittance into the Middle Temple in March 1593, Whitelocke faced the prospect of finding at least £30 a year to maintain residence, and he clearly struggled for money in his early years at the inns. From 1594 he lived with his Oxford friend Humphrey May 'in the middle chamber of the house late belonging to Thomas Dashe, gardener of the Middle Temple', receiving May's brother Thomas into these somewhat lowly chambers in 1600. As at Oxford, application to the educational regime drew him towards the serious students, and away from the young 'gallants' who sought to polish their education with a stay at the inns. He was fortunate that his room mate and lifelong friend Humphrey May was a 'towardly student, and a principal reveller', as he undertook what he later described as a 'long and tedious course of study' to ensure his own social progress.[4]

I

Brian Simpson has suggested that it would be difficult to conceive of a less systematic code than English common law. Its subtleties demanded an appreciation of a complex tangle of rights, obligations and exceptions passed down in the year books, reports, and statutes, and often retained locally from 'immemorial custom'. As it lacked an authoritative text, the 'essentially shadowy' character of the law was supported by reference to the twin pillars of reason and custom. Whatever strain his financial situation must have caused Whitelocke, it was almost certainly compounded, in his early years at the inns of

slightly later period; *Pension Book of Clement's Inn*, ed. Sir Cecil Carr, Selden Society 78 (1960), p. xxxiii. For the relationship between the greater and lesser inns see Christopher Brooks, *Pettyfoggers and Vipers of the Commonwealth: The 'Lower Branch' of the Legal Profession in Early Modern England* (Cambridge 1986), pp. 151-81.

4 *Liber Famelicus*, pp. 21, 82; *Middle Temple Records*, vol. 1, pp. 330, 333, 345, 401; Prest, *Inns of Court*, pp. 27-9, 41; H. Rashdall, *Universities of Europe in the Middle Ages*, 3 vols (Oxford 1936), vol. 3, pp. 453-4.

court, by the difficulties of acquiring an education in the common law.[5]

In the absence of a tutor, the quality of training at the inns of court varied widely in Whitelocke's time and depended largely upon the motivation of the student. In his *Direction or Preparative to the study of the Lawe* (1600), William Fulbecke argued that by 'very diligent and earnest search' of sources ranging from standard medieval authorities, such as Bracton and Glanville, to a range of commentators such as Fitzherbert, Brooke, Lambarde and Crompton, students could 'sift out the reason of the Law'. Common lawyers often quoted 'reason' as the basis of their art. In fact, such 'reason' was poorly defined; Sir Edward Coke's argument that one acquired an understanding of it through 'long study, observation, and experience' was hardly of help to the struggling student. As he undertook the 'extraordinary pains' required to obtain 'exquisite knowledge in the lawes', Whitelocke was fortunate that his university training assisted his understanding of common law by providing specific tools of analysis, and by placing the law into a broader intellectual context.[6]

---

5 A.W.B. Simpson, 'The Common Law and Legal Theory' in *Legal Theory and Legal History* (London 1987), pp. 362-81; Barnes, 'Star Chamber Litigants', p. 23; Prest, *Inns of Court*, pp. 27-9, 116-7, 143-9, 221; Shaller, *thesis*, p. 109; Brooks, 'The Place of Magna Carta', p. 60.

6 Fulbecke, *A Direction*, pp. 27-9; D.J. Seipp, 'The Structure of English Common Law in the Seventeenth Century' in *Legal History in the Making: Proceedings of the Ninth British Legal History Conference*, ed. W.M. Gordon & T.D. Fergus (London 1991), p. 61; *idem*, 'The Reception of Canon Law and Civil Law in the Common Law Courts before 1600', *Oxford Journal of Legal Studies* 13 (1993), p. 410-11; Sommerville, *Politics and Ideology*, pp. 92-5; Edward Coke, *The First Part of the Institutes of the Laws of England, or, A commentarie upon Littleton* (London 1628), p. 97v; *The Diary of Sir Richard Hutton 1614-1639*, ed. W.R. Prest, Selden Society Supplementary Series 9 (1991), p. 21; D.J. Ibbetson, 'Common Lawyers and the Law Before the Civil War', *Oxford Journal of Legal History* 8 (1988), p. 147; R.J. Schoeck, 'Lawyers and Rhetoric in Sixteenth-Century England' in *Renaissance Eloquence*, ed. J. Murphy (Berkeley 1983), pp. 274-7; Prest, *Rise of the Barristers*, pp. 108-9.

While the common law was 'inherently corrigible' and subject to modification, the notion that law should enjoy its status because of its continued reception was in many ways emphasised in its transmission through the inns of court and the courts of Westminster Hall. Seipp has asserted that common lawyers 'maintained their own body of law as a living oral tradition, a common learning passed down to new entrants through courtroom attendance, lectures on statutes, and moot courting exercises'. In the absence of prescribed texts, the erudition of the law was selectively acquired by sifting through the voluminous reports, case books and commentaries, by court watching, and by noting the oral wisdom presented at the inns in *post-prandial* discussion, in moots, and in the law readings, at which an appointed senior expounded upon a particular parliamentary statute over several days.[7]

The personal legal records compiled by Whitelocke over the course of a long career in the law suggest that the workings of common law were typically associated, in the minds of its students, with a personal exposure to the knowledge and reasoning of those seniors who instructed them in the courts and in their learned societies. In such personal observations as a note that 'Cooke, the Queen's Attorney, argued in the affirmative but was so confused through lack of method that I could commit nothing to memory' during *Slade's Case* (1596-1602), Whitelocke emphasised the value of, and limitation upon, court-watching as part of the heuristic regime of the inns. By cross-referencing cases which had already appeared in court, such as '*William v. William*', first noted in Michaelmas term 1597, which returned to the King's Bench through a writ of error in Hilary term 1598, Whitelocke began to trace the complex patterns of litigation employed by the more successful barristers at Westminster. Note taking at the exercises at the inns of court and the courts of law

7 Simpson, 'The Common Law and Legal Theory', pp. 375-7; Prest, *Inns of Court*, pp. 124-34; Seipp, 'Reception of Canon Law', p. 411; Barnes, 'Star Chamber Litigants', p. 23.

gave him a feel for the business of the bar, and allowed him to work out what counted for good legal argument and what did not.[8]

While men of higher social standing might advance '*ex gratia* or for favour', it was the ability shown by Whitelocke in moots and other learning exercises that marked him as a man with a future in the law, and presaged his call to the bar of the Middle Temple. Whitelocke twice assisted in moots conducted during the 'Grand Vacations' at the inns of chancery in 1599, the year before his call to the bar. In his role as a moot-sitter, Whitelocke served as *de-facto* judge in moots held under the supervision of Nicholas Overbury, a senior barrister who served as Chancery Reader. Whitelocke must have been aware that this distinction marked him as a worthy candidate for advancement, and in August 1600 Overbury called Whitelocke to the bar, confirmed by the benchers on 24 October 1600.[9]

---

8 Ibbetson, 'Common Lawyers and the Law', p. 151; Prest, 'Legal Education of the Gentry', p. 23; *idem*, *Inns of Court*, p. 131; J.H. Baker, 'Criminal Justice at Newgate 1616-27: some manuscript Reports in the Harvard Law School', *Irish Jurist* 8 (1973), p. 311; J.S Cockburn, 'Trial by the Book? Fact and Theory in Criminal Process 1558-1625' in *Legal Records*, p. 74. For Whitelocke's record of exercises at the inns of court and chancery see CUL Ms Dd. 5.7, for his records of cases during his time as an assize lawyer see Longleat Papers, miscellaneous parcel 9, and for an ongoing record of legal principles seemingly compiled during his final years of practise as a judge see CUL MS Dd. 3. 69. I am grateful to John Baker for making me aware of the Cambridge University notebook. There are clear parallels between the techniques employed by Whitelocke's in CUL MS Dd.3.69 and, for example, the John March's 1651 printed translation of Brook's Abridgement, 'methodised and reduced under their proper heads and titles'; *English Reports*, vol. 73, p. 847.

9 Prest, *Inns of Court*, pp. 56-58, 133-4; *The Lives of the Right Hon. Francis North, Baron Guilford; the Hon. Sir Dudley North; and the Hon. and Rev. Dr. John North*, ed. Augustus Jessop, 3 vols (London 1890), vol. 1, p. 21; CUL MS Dd. 5. 7., fol. 218v (reversing); *Pension Book*, pp. xxvii-xxviii, xxx; *Middle Temple Records*, vol. 2, pp. 407, 536, 624; *Readings and Moots at the Inns of Court in the Fifteenth Century*, ed. S.E. Thorne and J.H. Baker, 2 vols, Selden Society 71 & 105 (1954 & 1989), vol. 2, p. lxxi [hereafter cited as *Readings and Moots*].

As a barrister, Whitelocke acquired a more active role in the educational life of the Middle Temple, most notably in the 'Grand Vacations' which formed the academic highlight of the year. On such occasions he was required to moot before the benchers and to take a leading role at readings held before the whole house – but a fine of 20s. for 'absence and being out of commons' during the August reading in 1604 testifies to Whitelocke's occasional absence. In 1611, Whitelocke was one of those appointed to provide the reader's feast, and on 6 February 1617 the benchers ordered him to 'stand at the Cupboard' (thus leading the debate) for Walter Pye, the Lent reader for that year. As the society held only two readings a year (one in Lent and one in August), and as the Middle Temple restricted full membership of the bench of the society to readers, even ambitious barristers such as Whitelocke could expect to wait twenty years or more before progressing to the bench. Whitelocke was almost certain to have cried foul if the benchers ignored his seniority, and was probably gratified to note that 'the untimely death of Mr. Stirrell' prompted the benchers to nominate him, twenty-two years after his admission, as Autumn reader on 29 January 1619.[10]

At his 1619 reading, Whitelocke employed his new status within the society to push for his fourteen-year-old son's admission, manipulating the vague requirement that a student have eight years of 'learning and continuance' before his call to bar at a time when 'continuance was coming to be interpreted in the sense of membership of the society, rather than residence in commons'. Whitelocke's

10 Prest, *Inns of Court*, pp. 60-2, 117; 128-9; H.H.A. Cooper, 'Promotion and Politics Among the Common-Law Judges of the Reigns of James I and Charles I' (Liverpool University 1964 MA thesis), p. 24; *Liber Famelicus*, p. 70; William Dugdale, *Origines Juridiciales* (London 1663), pp. 194-5; *Middle Temple Records*, vol. 2, pp. 407, 449, 546, 624, 629, 634, 638. Exactly what is meant by the cupboard is open to speculation; Dean suggests that it was a small table for the Reader to sit at which 'fulfilled the function of the Chair on ceremonial occasions', and is still given this name and function at the Middle Temple today; John Dean, *Middle Temple Hall: Four Centuries of History* (London 1970), p. 7.

readiness to employ the letter of the law to push his son's career forward shows inconsistency with a professed desire to uphold the 'ancient formes' of the society, and Bulstrode Whitelocke was entirely absent from the inn for three years. In these years James Whitelocke's servant Richard Oakely lodged in his master's chambers, completing his own period of residence to qualify for call to the bar. By this time, Whitelocke's once humble lodgings had grown to include a large study, a bedchamber, and two separate smaller studies. Indeed, his son was granted residence without fine because his father had 'spent money in building and enlarging the chamber and studies'. Through a characteristic combination of pragmatism and sheer hard work, James Whitelocke had turned a humble beginning at the Middle Temple into an unqualified professional success.[11]

III

The *Liber Famelicus* provides the most detailed description of the progression of a reading to survive from the early Stuart era. Beyond its intellectual merit, Whitelocke's 1619 reading also reflects upon an 'era of collective defiance and disobedience' at the Middle Temple that continued intermittently until the end of the seventeenth century. Referring to masques and Christmas revels in the opening remarks of his 1619 reading, Whitelocke commented that the Middle Temple's reputation 'of late hath been impayred in the exercises of young gentlemen which touch gentry and honour, and would soon be so in the exercises of the Ancients which touch learning and proficiency if good affection to the publick did not prevent it'. Given that groups of barristers were protesting against the compulsory observance of fast days by this time, there is a hint of desperation in Whitelocke's reflection that over the course of his reading he 'went to churche

11 *Liber Famelicus*, p. 14; *Middle Temple Records*, vol. 2, pp. 574-5, 640; Prest, *Inns of Court*, pp. 133-4; *Diary*, p. 49. Whitelocke expressed his desire to uphold the 'ancient formes' of the society in the opening remarks of his 1619 reading.

everye morning and evening the whole reading, accompanyed withe sutche benchers, cubberdmen, and senior barristers as wolde goe withe me'. Unfortunately for Whitelocke, lack of interest in the ceremonial aspects of his reading reflected a general apathy towards the exercise.[12]

As part of his preparation before his own election to read, Whitelocke served as an assistant at the readings of John Forde and William Rives. As he was keen to press his own claim to read before the society he gladly played his part, noting that in 'August, 1618, being on of the cubberdmen of the Middle Temple, I went up to argue at the reading, the reader being Mr. Ford of Devonshire, to whome I gave a buck and 14s'. It must have been a great disappointment to Whitelocke when Forde and Rives failed to obey the benchers' request to assist at his own reading, forcing him to invite George Shurley (Autumn Reader for 1615) and Richard Hadsor (Autumn Reader for 1617) in their place. If not for the work of Hadsor and Shurley, and the vigorous participation of John Hoskins (whom Whitelocke would support at his reading in Lent 1620), Whitelocke's celebrated reading would probably have been little more than an embarrassment to him before a range of eminent guests.[13]

On 1 August 1619 Robert Tounson, Dean of Westminster, preached before the Middle Temple at Whitelocke's invitation after which Whitelocke circulated the statute for his reading among the benchers. After breakfast on the following day, Whitelocke recounted,

> I went to the cubberd, and thear, before all the house, toke the othe of supreamacy, then went to my place, the northe end of the long table, whear

12 Prest, *Inns of Court*, pp. 101, 105, 112-3; *Liber Famelicus*, p. 74; Lincoln's Inn MS (misc.), fols 1-2; except where otherwise stated, all references to his reading are taken from Lincoln's Inn Library MS (unnumbered) reprinted in *English Legal Manuscripts*, ed. J.H. Baker.

13 *Middle Temple Records*, vol. 2, pp. 585, 619, 629, 634, 638, 646; CUL MS Ee. 6. 2, fols 192-225v, *passim*; *Liber Famelicus*, pp. 62, 74. Bruce has incorrectly identified these cupboardmen as 'Sturly' and 'Hudson'; see BL Add. MS 53725, fol. 110.

> Mr. Palmer, a Londoner born, my sublector, red my statute, 21 Henry VIII. ca. 13. After which I began, first made a speeche, and then went on to the statute, proposed my divisions, and put upon the division of that day ten cases, of whiche the puisne cubberd man chose on[e], and began *pro* and so *contra, alternatim.*[14]

As the reading progressed, Whitelocke opened the statute to debate with a detailed point-by-point analysis of cases arising from his ten 'divisions', each considering an aspect of law derived from the chapter of the statute at hand. John Hoskins, George Shurly, John Tynte and Thomas Trist, his cupboardmen, then took up and elaborated upon his interpretations. The other barristers, benchers, and judges who were present at the reading then further discussed and debated upon this erudition. Notes taken by an observer at the reading indicate that Richard Hadsor, who was pressing his own claim for admission to the highest ranks of the society, questioned Whitelocke's interpretation of his fourth and fifth cases and met with reply from Whitelocke.[15]

Two weeks after the reading began, Whitelocke concluded with a speech thanking the society, after which those assembled reflected upon the points that they had clarified in the course of the reading. Summing up, Whitelocke restated his ten divisions and six cases, which Hoskins and Shurly then reassessed. Whitelocke had the last word, 'breefly opening the poynts only, whiche being done, I uttered my conceites'. These 'conceits' consisted of the principal points arising from the reading, and they were open to clarification. As the senior bencher who presided over the reading now moved to end the discussion, he informed Whitelocke that 'they wold expect my opinion the next term'.[16]

Law readings of the early seventeenth century have been almost totally overlooked by scholars. Historians have hailed James White-

---

14 *Liber Famelicus*, p. 75.

15 Prest, *Inns of Court*, p. 123; CUL MS Ee. 6. 2, fols 192-225v, *passim*; *Liber Famelicus*, p. 74.

16 *Liber Famelicus*, pp. 74-5; *Mannual of law French*, ed. J.H. Baker, 2nd ed., (London 1990), p. 75

locke's 1619 reading, in which dual expertise in ecclesiastical and English law informed his interpretation of 21 Henry VIII c. 13, as a 'classic' and 'notable' example, but they have yet to investigate it in any detail. Given its preoccupation with the minutiae of an area of law O'Day has characterised as 'of almost labyrinthine complexity', such reluctance is understandable. What follows here is a summary of the Whitelocke's discussion of the thirteenth chapter of Henry VIII's 1531 statute on benefices, which formed a central part of his reformation of the clergy. The pluralities act set out to restrict the multiple holding of benefices to the more learned clergy, redefining advowson, or right of presentation, held by lay patrons, and ensuring that clerics were in close enough proximity to their beneficed parishes to make pastoral care feasible.[17]

The criteria for holding benefices were under constant revision over the course of the sixteenth century. In general, it was the responsibility of the bishops to pursue inquires into the vacancy of a church, to question whether the right to present a new cleric was undisputed, whether the cleric was properly ordained, innocent of crime, and at least 24 years of age. Bishops were also responsible for admitting qualified clerics to their churches, but the right of presentation remained with the patron unless the church had been left vacant for six months and no candidate put forward, in which case the right of presentation reverted to the bishop.[18]

---

17 Baker, *Legal Profession*, p. 445; *idem*, 'The Inns of Court and Legal Doctrine' in *Lawyers and Laymen: Studies in the History of the Law presented to Professor Dafydd Jenkins*, ed. T.M. Charles Edwards, M.E. Owen and D.B. Walters (Cardiff, 1986), p. 281; W.C. Richardson, *A History of the Inns of Court: With Special Reference to The Period of The Renaissance* (Baton Rouge 1980), p. 117, Prest, *Inns of Court*, p. 120; 226-7; Lemmings, 'Ritual and the Law', p. 7; Rosemary O'Day, 'The Law of Patronage in Early Modern England', *Journal of Ecclesiastical History* 26 (1975), pp. 247, 250; R.N. Swanson, 'Universities, Graduates and Benefices in Later Medieval England', *Past & Present* 106 (1985), p. 38, n. 49. The thirteenth chapter of 21 Henry VIII is reprinted in Statutes at Large, vol. 2, pp. 133-137.

18 Seipp, 'Reception of Canon Law', pp. 399-400.

Despite a vague rubric in the thirteenth chapter of the statute that prohibited 'any profit or medling' with leases and grants, patrons often saw an advowson as a commodity to be sold or granted on a conditional basis to 'other laymen or clergymen... anxious to become patrons *de facto*'. Lay and ecclesiastical patrons also contested control of benefices for a combination of religious and financial reasons, and this led to frequent challenge of the candidates and the rights of presentation. As property law did not easily cope with changes in the structure of local parishes, demographic shifts also prompted disputes. In his reading, Whitelocke even allowed that a benefice with cure might remain 'when there is neither church nor inhabitant'.[19]

The issue of pluralism was already contentious in the early decades of the seventeenth century. It would become increasingly heated as the Arminian push to improve the status of the clergy gathered momentum. While the civil lawyers who trained alongside Whitelocke at Oxford emphasised the provisions made in the statute of 21 Henry VIII 'for Church and Crown dignitaries, peers, and men of learning', many of his associates at the bar sought to restrict the financial and social powers of the church. In 1610, for example, 'divers utter barristers' of the two Temple societies had circulated a petition against an increase in the stipend of their preacher, William Crashawe, complaining that he drew income from a Yorkshire benefice held *in absentia*. In the face of general controversy, Whitelocke's reading presented a moderate appeal for the rights of the clergy.[20]

---

19 O'Day, 'Law of Patronage', p. 247; 21 Hen. VIII, c. 13, iii; Rosemary O'Day, *The English Clergy: The Emergence and Consolidation of a Profession* (Leicester 1979), p. 105; N.L. Jones, 'An Elizabethan Bill for the Reformation of the Ecclesiastical Law', *Parliamentary History* 4 (1985), pp. 171-89; M.M. Steig, *Laud's Laboratory: The Diocese of Bath and Wells in the Early Seventeenth Century* (Lewisburg 1982), p. 100; Christopher Hill, *Economic Problems of the English Church* (Oxford 1956), pp. 55-6; Lincoln's Inn MS, fol 10.

20 Levack, *Civil Lawyers*, p. 173, 188; Steig, *Laud's Laboratory*, p. 95; Christopher Hill, *Society and Puritanism in Pre-Revolutionary England* (London 1964), p. 495; *idem*, *Economic Problems*, p. 316; R.G. Usher, *The Rise and Fall of the*

While a benefice or 'living' was always attached to an ecclesiastical office, the patron presented to the benefice and the office separately, after which the beneficed clerk held a freehold for life, unless excluded for certain offences such as felony, simony, or plurality. The English church did not consider the sale of the right of next presentation to constitute simony, and it was relatively easy for a prospective patentee to find someone to purchase the right of presentation and then present him. It was thus common for a patron to sell the right to next presentation. Whitelocke's reading demonstrated that ambiguities existed 'where two patrons present severally to one church and either hath a distinct glebe and a distinct rate of the tythes and doe agree to officiate in turne'. He suggested that if one patron chose to relinquish his control of one advowson, there was nothing to stop the other patron from acquiring the moiety. If other parties made allegations of simony, the onus was upon the court to prove that the patron's choice of an incumbent was motivated by payment of money. Whitelocke argued that if a cleric was removed from a benefice by writ of *quare impedit*, the ruling entitled him to seek another living while the issue was still pending in the courts, and to remain in possession of the first living until the matter was fully resolved. If he successfully overturned the *quare impedit* by writ of error, Whitelocke suggested, then he was free to retain the living of his choice.[21]

At the heart of 21 Henry VIII c. 13 were the issues of pluralism and non-residence. Whitelocke's discussion of the laws of *commendam* noted the exemptions granted by the statute to restrictions on plurality,

---

High Commission (Oxford 1913), pp. 180-221; *Middle Temple Records*, vol. 2, pp. 514, 516; Prest, *Inns of Court*, p. 198. Of course arguments against plurality of benefices continued apace until the eve of the civil war, and are evidenced in such colourful works as the anonymous *A Purge for pluralities shewing the unlawfulnesse of men to have two livings, or, The downe-fall of double benefices: being in the clymacterial and fatall yeare of the proud prelates: but the yeare of iubilee to all poor hunger-pinch'd schollers* (London 1642).

21 Steig, *Laud's Laboratory*, pp. 92-4; Hill, *Economic Problems*, pp. 50-1; O'Day, *English Clergy*, p. 82; Lincoln's Inn MS, fols 7-13, 24-5. For what constituted simony see 21 Hen. VIII c. 13, iii-viii (*Statutes at Large*, vol. 2, p. 133).

which had led to widespread charges of abuse among the 'court clergy', whom Hill considered the 'worst pluralists, and probably the most numerous'. He acknowledged that the original effect of the statute on the laws of *commendam* was to delegate a vacant benefice 'to a learned man to see the cure served untill a fitt man could be provided', and noted the 'good advice' of the judges in the *Bishop of Lichfield's case* that the bishop should find a pastor and fill the office rather than retaining the living for his own profit. He concluded strongly in support of the clergy nonetheless, suggesting that while it 'was not reasonable in many respects' for a bishop to hold on to a living which he left vacant, a benefice '100 miles distant... is as good in law as if it were 20 miles[,] for the power of the grantor is not qualified by the situation but discrimination'.[22]

In the course of his reading, Whitelocke supported the rights of the Crown, the largest holder of benefices in England. By Whitelocke's time, a bureaucracy attached to the Lord Keeper's office controlled the majority of livings below £20 in the name of the Crown. The Crown also controlled many larger livings, which reverted to it by default if patron and bishop failed to fill the living within eighteen months. If the king promoted a cleric to the office of bishop, Whitelocke suggested, he was entitled to his former livings until the time of consecration. Proposing that an unlimited right of presentation was 'a flower of the Crown and annexed to the king's person', Whitelocke suggested that 'there hath been noe question but for 40 yeares and above the Crowne hath presented upon avoidance by promotion', although he acknowledged that the law in 'former times took no notice of this prerogative'. Whitelocke also upheld (with some slight reservations) the right of the Chancellor to present clerics to any benefice below the value of £20 as the 'gift of the king', and argued that where a benefice was acquired by royal donation it should not be held against a cleric as a second living. Whether this endorsement of

22 Hill, *Economic Problems*, p. 227; 21 Hen. VIII c. 13, xiii-xxi, xxiii, xxix (*Statutes at Large*, vol. 2, p. 1(3)5); Lincoln's Inn MS, fols 69, 71-2.

prerogative rights was politically motivated is hard to say, but it cannot have hurt Whitelocke's reputation among the numerous courtiers he invited to his reading, and may have presaged his subsequent promotion as serjeant-at-law and then chief justice of Chester.[23]

The laws relating to benefices were a fairly common topic for readings in the early seventeenth century, when little printed material on the topic was available. Whitelocke noted that the issues raised in the first three cases of his reading, which treated rights of presentation, were 'matters ordinary and in use yet seldome handled by Readers', and he was in little doubt 'that the comoditys we shall find there will be usefull for our law'. He indicated that the questions raised in the second week of the reading, which dealt with rights of inheritance, qualifications to rights of advowson, and requirements of residency, 'hath not been handled heretofore by any Reader that I can learn'. In his introduction, he professed a desire 'to comprehend variety yet with propriety... that we may... rather apply ourselves to debate that thoroughly which wee have in hand then to wander upon matters of another nature'. By concentrating upon the issue of pluralities, Whitelocke's reading digested, collated and informed a wide range of examples from the statutes, law books, trusted authors such as Fortescue and Littleton, newer sources such as Coke's *Reports*, and more recent and topical cases in the courts of law.[24]

Whitelocke's choice of a topic and selection of cases had a relevance which underlined the value of his reading to the legal profession. Whitelocke expressed a familiarity with benefices derived from his professional associations with the University of Oxford. He

---

23 O'Day, *English Clergy*, pp. 78, 113-18; Lincoln's Inn MS, fols 49, 115-20; Bodl. MS Hargrave 91, fol. 289v.

24 Steig, *Laud's Laboratory*, p. 93; Lincoln's Inn MS, fols 7, 78. Whitelocke admitted that he was 'on the heel of my predecessor', William Rives, who lectured on the giving of benefices in the Statute of Westminster 2 c. 1 in the Lent 1619 reading; Lincoln's Inn MS, fol. 2. For a fuller discussion of the techniques employed by readers to handle their sources see Baker, '*Inns of Court* and Legal Doctrine', p. 276.

undoubtedly observed many of the cases cited in his reading first hand, such as a contested right of presentation brought before the King's Bench in 1597, while he was still a student at the Middle Temple. In his reading, Whitelocke noted that he had 'seen visitations in Windsor by the Chancellor of England and in St Martyns le Grand by the Chancellor assisted by divers judges of the common law', while as steward of St John's, he observed courtroom battles over the control of donated benefices, 'a matter of great consequence and hath been very lately notably debated'. It was this personal experience that lent authority and practical relevance to Whitelocke's analysis.[25]

Given its emphasis upon relevant cases and practical arguments, Whitelocke's reading had obvious significance for those who sought to understand legal reason on the issue of pluralities. A student could check the cases provided in a manuscript of Whitelocke's 1619 reading against the opinions of those who contributed to the subsequent discussion upon each point of law, thus allowing him to establish a range of opinions and references on the topic. At the conclusion of the reading, Whitelocke drew together the principal points, or 'conceits', arising from the reading, whether those of reader, his assistants or guests. A list of the authoritative points raised from each division, compiled by a student of the reading as 'Conceipts sur le Stat de 32 Hen 8 c. 5 & c. 13', indicates the processes through which a law reading helped to establish what stood as 'good law'.[26]

The fact that at least nineteen manuscript copies of Whitelocke's 1619 reading have survived testifies to the interest in which it was held among lawyers of the day. Common lawyers had a particular

---

25 Lincoln's Inn MS, fols 3, 55, 65; CUL MS Dd. 8. 48, fol. 15, 'Gerard's Case'. This relevance is in contrast to the 'conundrums' thrown up at many readings that were of little practical use at the bar; see Baker, 'Inns of Court and Legal Doctrine', p. 275; cf. *Readings and Moots*, vol. 2, p. lxxii.

26 BL Hargrave MS 91, fols 296-319v; *Manual of Law French*, ed. J.H. Baker (2nd ed., London 1990), p. 75. The contributions made by various lawyers at Whitelocke's readings are noted in CUL MS Ee. 6. 2, fols 192-225v, which also lists its 'Conceyts' (conceits) in the last three folios.

interest in the laws regarding benefices, as they litigated in many disputes over advowsons, but also acknowledged that the rights of presentation represented 'the start of a long process conducted mainly by canonist rules'. It was Whitelocke's conversance with canon law and his ability to present this knowledge with an eye to the ambiguities of the law that characterised what Bulstrode Whitelocke called 'the solide law, and excellent and unusuall learning' of the 1619 reading. It is somewhat ironic that the contribution of the better law readings, such as Whitelocke's, helped to shift the 'hypothetical debate of the year books to the distinct rulings and judgments of the age of Coke', and so by 'giving a new meaning and force to precedent', they unwittingly contributed to the downfall of the system of readings itself.[27]

IV

In the speech he gave upon leaving the Middle Temple in 1619, Whitelocke paid tribute to 'those whome I may call my *coætanei*, for we began togeather in the universitye, came hether togeather, and

27 Seipp, 'Reception of Canon Law', p. 399; *Diary*, p. 47; Baker, '*Inns of Court* and Legal Doctrine', p. 278; *Reports of Sir John Spelman*, vol. 2, p. 124; cf. Barnes, 'Star Chamber Litigants', p. 23; Simpson, 'Source and Function of the Later Year Books', pp. 92-3. I have inspected BL Hargrave MS 91, fols 196-295v; BL Hargrave MS 237, fols 5-95v; BL Hargrave MS 198, BL Hargrave MS 91, fols 296-319v; CUL MS Ll .3.12, fols 326-477; CUL MS Ee .6.3, fols 192-225v; Bodl. MS Dep. d 746; Bodl. MS Rawlinson C. 207, fols 62-96v; MS Rawlinson C. 207, fols 245-270, Bodl. MS Ashmole 1150 (1), fols 1-83; Lincoln's Inn MS Miscellaneous 486 (8); Lincoln's Inn MS Law 14. Ii; Lincoln's Inn MS Maynard 79, fols 329-80; Middle Temple (uncatalogued copy, Muniments Room). Other copies revealed in my checks of major repositories include Trinity College MS 853 (4) and Trinity College MS 733 (3); Professor Baker has also located additional copies including Harvard Law School MS 1077; William Andrews Clark Library Selden-Hale Collection MS 586; and University of Pennsylvania Law School MS 1206.

have lived togeather ever sithence'. He thanked also those men he had met at the inn, whom he said

> may be called collegues, for we have lived togeather ever sithence in participation of studyes, in doing of exercises, in taking our degrees, and for 28 yeares, almost compleat, have been *collaterales*, and sat on by the others side.

Whitelocke emphasised the professional solidarity of the inns of court, advising the treasurer 'and the rest of this worthy societye' that

> it wolde be verye uncouthe to me to be cut of from these contentments, and to lighte upon new men and manners. It is not my meaning so to do... and my remove shall cawse only seperation of our bodyes, not a divorce of our mindes.

Unfortunately, while historical understanding of the relationship between the professional formation of lawyers and their political outlook has reached an impasse, this marriage of minds is obscured by the lack of records for the private conversation of the inns of court and chancery – conversation that Coke called the 'life of studie'.[28]

In recent times, tensions between the courts of common law and the equity courts in the Jacobean period have been seen less as part of broader political debate and more as the product of occupational rivalry. While Ibbetson has suggested that one 'can hardly separate the almost obsessive onslaught of the common lawyers on the prerogative courts from their historical and philosophical attitudes to the nature of

---

28 *Liber Famelicus*, pp. 21, 82 (I have corrected Bruce's use of 'thesaurer' from the original); Coke, First Institute, sig. qq^2 quoted in Prest, *Inns of Court*, p. 158. For the impact of lawyers and the Inns of Court on early Stuart society cf., for example, Derek Hirst, 'The Place of Principle' in T.K. Rabb & Derek Hirst, 'Revisionism Revised: two perspectives on early Stuart parliamentary history', *Past & Present* 42 (1981), pp. 83-9; Prest, *Rise of the Barristers*, p. 257; Burgess, 'Common Law and Political Theory' pp. 4-17; Brooks, 'The Place of Magna Carta', pp. 57-9; C.C. Weston & J.R. Greenberg, *Subjects and Sovereigns: The Grand Controversy over Legal Sovereignty in Stuart England* (Cambridge 1981), pp. 1-34; J.P. Kenyon, *Stuart Constitution*, 2nd ed. (Cambridge 1987), p. 75; *Biographical Dictionary of British Radicals in the Seventeenth Century*, ed. R.L. Greaves & R. Zaller, 3 vols (Brighton 1982), vol. 1, p. 156 [hereafter cited as *Biographical Dictionary*]; Sharpe, *Politics and Ideas*, pp. 38, 64.

the common law', Burgess has seen common-law rhetoric as 'a pretence' designed to protect 'professional isolation and status', regarding political debate in the period as concerning 'not so much the relationship between royal sovereignty and the law, as the relationship between legal and non-legal definitions of authority'. Burgess is right to state the insularity of the law, but he fails to emphasise that legal definitions of authority had explicit political overtones.[29]

The *Liber Famelicus* recounted that Whitelocke's own desire to study the common law was

> encouraged mutche thearunto by a book set out by Dr. Cosins... intituled, 'An Apologye of the Ecclesiastical Proceedings'... in whiche I saw how great use he made of his knoledge of the common law to upholde the authority of his owne profession, and to direct others of his place.

In light of Sir Edward Coke's argument that John Cosin would 'obtrude upon the world' with his claims for the jurisdiction of the courts spiritual, Whitelocke's irenic outlook provides an interesting point of comparison. Yet in a parliamentary speech of 1610, Whitelocke demonstrated that his professional surroundings had reconfigured his public voice, warning 'any churchmen' who might

> endeavour by application of the text of Scripture, to overthrow the antient law and liberties of the kingdom... to be admonished by the ill success of the cardinal [Wolsey]... and the miserable catastrophe of his whole life and fortunes.

As Whitelocke fused English law and English liberties together in public opposition to ecclesiastical discourse, he asserted a view reinforced by the social and educational life of the inns of court.[30]

---

29 P.G. Burgess, 'Custom, Reason and the Common Law' (1988 University of Cambridge PhD thesis) 'Introduction'; pp. 71-3, and see his *Absolute Monarchy and the Stuart Constitution, passim*; Ibbetson, 'Common Lawyers and the Law', p. 152; J.P. Kenyon, *Stuart Constitution*, 2nd ed. (Cambridge 1987), p. 75.

30 *Liber Famelicus*, p. 14; Edward Coke, *The Twelfth Part of the Reports of England* (London 1655) in *English Reports*, vol. 77, p. 1319; *A Complete Collection of State Trials*, ed. T.B. Howell, 34 vols (London 1809-28), vol. 2, col. 485 [hereafter cited as *State Trials*].

A revealing passage in the *Liber Famelicus* suggests Whitelocke's growing awareness of the political impact of a political outlook framed by eulogistic belief in the virtues of the common law. He noted that after a 1615 sermon at Windsor, Sir Edward Coke sought him out as one his 'owne coat'. When questioned on his reluctance to dine at the royal court, Coke replied 'that whilest he stood by the king at dynner, he [King James] wolde be ever asking of him questions of that nature as he had as life be out of the roome'. Whitelocke reflected that 'I gesse it was concerning matters of the prerogative, which the king wolde take ill if he wear not answered in them as he wolde have it'. Whitelocke was himself to find, over the course of a long career, that an intellectual reflex to invoke the force of customary law was not always well received in wider political circles.[31]

While the precise intellectual context of James Whitelocke's public speeches is difficult to define, it seems significant that his disagreement with the Crown over impositions in 1610 and 1614 flowed naturally from his preoccupation with the regulation of property rights. Respect of legal authority was inherent in his approach: in Whitelocke's own words 'Permutation is a thing... much misliked in the common law'. Here the example of the inns of court and the courtroom itself had taught Whitelocke that deviation from, or alteration of 'customary' principle would result in contradictions or ambiguities likely to undermine the foundations of the law.[32]

In a legal system which laid strong claim to rationality, it was presumed that differences could be resolved by argument and discussion, and that the method adopted to solve disputes was in principle capable of producing, in general, a just solution. Whitelocke's parliamentary speeches on impositions attempted to impose

31 *Liber Famelicus*, p. 48.

32 Lincoln's Inn MS, fol. 44; A.F. Kinney, 'Sir Phillip Sydney and Uses of History' in *The Historical Renaissance: New Essays on Tudor and Stuart Literature and Culture*, ed. Heather Dubrow & Richard Strier (Chicago 1988), pp. 304-5; Hirst, 'Place of Principle', pp. 83, 88; Simpson, 'The Common Law and Legal Theory', p. 380.

'rational' constraints upon Crown actions by demonstrating the ways in which custom regulated property rights in general. The constitutional context for such a position was readily found in Sir John Fortescue's notion of 'dominium politicum et regale', which emphasised a measure of political participation in government by parliament, and stressed that the kingdom was a piece of real property held in trust by the king.[33]

If one considers the intellectual inheritance of English law it becomes obvious (as Pocock noted long ago) that there was a common-law case for the Crown as well as against it. Yet the common law inheritance provided a viable language of political dissent and over three decades it was employed to articulate some broad philosophical differences between parliament and the king that would result, in the end, in political opposition and war. In 1609, Whitelocke argued that his removal from the Earl Marshal's Court did 'much concern our whole order and other gentlemen of England, that naturallie desire to submitt all their fortunes to the rule of homeborn law'. Alan Cromartie has suggested that in 1642, parliamentarians found that a discourse which asserted the place of an 'unapologetically provincial' common law over Continental traditions, and was particularly appropriate to their cause. In chapter 4, it will be argued that the parliamentary language of Jacobean barristers such as James Whitelocke helped to define the character of resistance employed by a new generation of parliamentarians as England stumbled towards political breakdown between 1640 and 1642.[34]

---

33 J.S. Roskell, *Parliaments and Politics*, 3 vols (London 1981), vol. 1, p. 12. Cf Brooks, 'The Place of Magna Carta', p. 58; Sommerville, *Politics & Ideology*, pp. 86-111.

34 Pocock, *Ancient Constitution*, pp. 31, 55; Prest, *Rise of the Barristers*, p. 257; Bodl. MS Smith, fol. 59; Cromartie, *Sir Matthew Hale*, pp. 11-12.

Chapter 3

The Society of Antiquaries

Along with the universities and the inns of court, the Society of Antiquaries represented one of the prominent intellectual forums in Jacobean society. Schoeck has concluded that the Society's 'influence upon English intellectual life, scholarship and literature was considerable', while Peck has argued that the Society displayed 'the several voices of English antiquarianism, its centrality to seventeenth-century political discourse and James' own wariness towards historical investigation'. Acknowledging its importance, historians have struggled to place antiquarian writings – characterised by Sharpe as the 'study of the culture, institutions, custom, and topography of their native realm, principally through research into English sources' – into a clear social or political perspective. This chapter situates the stunted history of the Society within a broader framework of Jacobean legal argument and political dissent.[1]

James Whitelocke's antiquarian endeavours offer, on one level, evidence of the dilettantish predilections of antiquarianism, as he engaged with Continental and English sources in order to define and reinforce an Anglocentric outlook typical of the English common lawyer. On another level, complex lines of entanglement between his Society membership and those legal and political controversies into

---

1 R.J. Schoeck, 'The Elizabethan Society of Antiquaries and Men of Law', *Notes and Queries* 199 (1954), p. 421; Sharpe, *Sir Robert Cotton*, p. 18, 23; Peck, 'Kingship, counsel and law', p. 95. For the importance of antiquarianism cf. A.B. Ferguson, *Clio Unbound: Perception of the Social and Cultural Past in Renaissance England* (Durham N.C. 1979), pp. 1-82, esp. pp. 63, 80; L.L. Peck, 'Court Patronage and Government Policy: The Jacobean Dilemma' in *Patronage in the Renaissance*, ed. G.F. Lytle & Stephen Orgel (Princeton 1981), p. 35; Morrill, *Nature of the English Revolution*, p. 299.

which he was drawn reflect the hazards associated with Jacobean scribal circles, and the centripetal forces at work on a consensual polity. Whitelocke's intriguing involvement in the chequered history of the Society rounds off discussion of the educational influences at work upon the 'common law mind'. His example suggests that while everyone may have spoken 'the same language' in Jacobean England, such language was threatened by differences of emphasis that could force scribal circles, and individuals, into silence.[2]

I

William Camden founded the Society of Antiquaries in the 1580s with his antiquarian protégés Robert Cotton, James Ley and Henry Spelman. Meeting at regular intervals, the Society provided a forum for the discussion of papers generated by antiquarian research. By the turn of the century, the Society conducted its meetings at the private apartment of Sir William Dethicke, Garter King of Arms, at intervals that aimed to coincide with the legal terms when lawyers were resident in the capital. Whitelocke's involvement with the Society is first recorded in a note he made to investigate 'the antiquity, services and dutyes appertayning to a knights fee' for a Society meeting in Hilary term 1599, along with 'Lee' (James Ley), 'Thin' (Francis Thynne), 'Doderidge' (Sir John Dodderidge), 'Tate' (Francis Tate), 'Agar' (Arthur Agarde), 'Holland' (Joseph Holland) and 'Paten' (William Patten).[3]

---

2 J.P. Kenyon, The *Stuart Constitution* (Cambridge 1966), p. 10. The most important work on scribal publishing is Harold Love, *Scribal Publication in Seventeenth-Century England* (Oxford 1993), *passim.*

3 Sharpe, *Sir Robert Cotton*, p. 17; *Archaeologia: or, Miscellaneous Tracts, Relating to Antiquity* (London 1770) vol. 1, pp. v-vi; *Discourses*, vol. 1, p. cxx; CUL MS Dd. 8. 48, fol. 139. For the history of the Society see also Joan Evans, *A History of the Society of Antiquaries* (London 1956); chs 1 & 2.

Whitelocke's mention of fellow Middle Templars such as Dodderidge and Tate suggests that legal colleagues may have introduced him to the Society, underlining strong associations between the inns of court and antiquarianism. Apart from Tate and Dodderidge, members also drawn from the Middle Temple included John Davies, John Savile, Robert Weston, William Bowyer, Richard Carew and William Fleetwood. While the *Liber Famelicus* makes no comment upon the matter, it is likely that the opportunity to reinforce professional contacts motivated Whitelocke to attend Society meetings in the infancy of his career.[4]

The speeches prepared by Whitelocke for discussion at the Society of Antiquaries show an overriding preoccupation with custom. Papers dated 22 May and 28 November 1601 concern, respectively, the 'Antiquity, Use and Ceremony of Lawful Combats in England' and the 'Antiquity and Office of Heralds in England'. An undated address on the 'Antiquity, Use, and Privilege of Places for Students and Professors of the common laws of England' demonstrated Whitelocke's knowledge of his own professional traditions, while another undated manuscript, preserved in draft form along with two autograph copies, discussed the 'Antiquity, Variety and Reason of Motts with Arms of Noblemen and Gentlemen in England'. Whitelocke prepared a paper on 'Our certaine and defininte Topographical Dimensions in England, compared with those of the Greeks and Latins, set down in Order, as they arise in Quantity'. A rough draft on 'The antiquity of terms for administration of justice and their returnes, for al thinges properly belonging thereunto' is also preserved among his papers.[5]

---

4 Schoeck, 'The Elizabethan Society of Antiquaries', pp. 417-21. The discussion on membership in the text is based upon Schoeck's findings, checked against Sharpe and the *Dictionary of National Biography*.

5 'Lawful combats' is treated in *Discourses*, vol. 2, pp. 190-4, BL Additional MS 25247, fols 93-5, BL Stowe MS 596 fols 35-9, BL Harley MS 4176 fols 16-8, Bodl. MS Ashmolean 856 fols 149-53, Bodl. MS Tanner 278 fols 141-2v, Bodl. MS Tanner 85 fols 16-38. Two more manuscripts on this topic I have not inspected are Edinburgh University MS Laing. II. 645/1 fols 34-8, and College of

The survival of twelve manuscript copies of Whitelocke's antiquarian papers underlines the vitality of scribal circles, but the papers evidence little that could be considered as controversial. His discussion of mottoes and coats of arms, for example, begins with an appraisal of the thirty-odd authorities who, in his 'computation', mentioned the subject, suggesting that only Jeronimus Ruscellius, 'in a treatise set out together with Paulus Jovius', pertained directly to his investigation. His brief speech on heralds is hardly more dramatic, tracing the word back to an Anglo-Saxon derivation meaning 'old soldier', comparing the Greek and Roman equivalent, and citing Dionysius of Halicarnassus as a principal source of information on heraldic duties, along with Livy and Aulus Gellius.[6]

As concerted attempts were being made to stamp out the chivalric tradition of the private duel in the reign of James I, Whitelocke's paper on lawful combat, which drew a distinction between unlawful combat, 'fought by private men upon private quarrells', and those 'tolerated in the common wealth for triall of causes which cannot be discussed by evidence on either part', may have held a more contro-

---

Arms MS Vincent 43 fols 26-42; 'heralds' is in *Discourses*, vol. 1, pp. 55-6. 'Students and professors' is in *Discourses*, vol. 1, pp. 78-82, BL Cottonian MS Faustina E.v., fols 51-2 (autograph); 'arms of nobleman' is printed as 'anonymous' in *Discourses*, vol. 1, pp. 268-72, but cf. CUL MS Oo.6.114, fols 106-14 (draft and two autograph copies). 'Terms for the administration of justice' is in Longleat Papers, vol. 24, fols 269-70. 'Topographical Dimensions' is in the 1775 edition of Hearne's *Discourses*, vol. 2, pp. 382-5 [hereafter cited as *Discourses* (1775)].

6 *Discourses*, vol. 1, p. 268; vol. 1, p. 55. Whitelocke's reference to 'Paulus Jovius' refers to *The worthy tract of Paulus Jouius* (trans. S. Daniel, London 1585); his reference to Livy may well have been T. Livy, *The Romane Historie* (trans. P. Holland, London 1598), while it is likely that Whitelocke used Latin texts of Dionysius's *de Urbe Roma* and Aulus Gellius's *Noctes Atticae*, which were not translated into English until the seventeenth century; see R.R. Bolgar, *The Classical Heritage and its Beneficiaries* (Cambridge 1954), pp. 512, 547. For the circulation of manuscripts cf. Morrill, Nature of the English Revolution, pp. 279-81; M.J. Ezell, *The Patriarch's Wife: Literary Evidence and the History of the Family* (Chapel Hill and London 1987), pp. 62-100.

versial edge. Yet as in his other speeches, this discussion drew upon law reports (in particular the *Earl of Northumberland's Case*) that were well known to his legal associates and were reported more or less verbatim. Indeed, far from taking a controversial stance it appears that where Whitelocke felt any risk of discord he deliberately limited his discussion, leaving heraldic customs in England 'to the disclosing of... those that are of the profession', and freely encouraging others, in his speech on mottoes to explore related matters 'to the perfecting of this discourse'.[7]

Whitelocke's speeches are candid about their limitations as an intellectual exercise. In his speech on lawful combat, for instance, Whitelocke suggested that the origin of this tradition in England was something he could 'but gesse at', leaving the issue 'to them that have better instruction of it'. In his speech on the origins of the inns of court and chancery Whitelocke admitted that 'I do not find any evidence for the antiquity of our society of common lawyers in the Temple before Edward the 3's time', guessing that 'the conveniency of the place caused some of that profession to hire and take lodgings there of the knights of the order of St. John of Jerusalem'.[8]

Personal opinion was freely expressed by Whitelocke during his speeches (which may, of course, have also been supplemented by improvisation and interjections from the floor) and an occasional joke emphasised the dilettantish aspect of his speeches. Whitelocke concluded his speech on mottoes by noting that the motto of 'Paul Baglione the Italian', 'thoughe yt be a whole hexamiter' was 'good enough, had yt not been made subject to a bitter jest of an Italian gentleman, for a worse respect then the length of yt'. He went on to recount that Baglione's griffin crest could not save him from the 'treachery' of the Pope, leading friends to jest 'that he might have done himself more good with a pair of winges to have flowen out of

7 *Discourses*, vol. 1, pp. 56, 272; vol. 2, pp. 190-3. For the Earl of Northumberland's Case see *Tilliol v. Percy 1 Henry VI*, in *Year Books of Henry VI: 1 Henry VI*, ed. C.H. Williams, Selden Society 50 (1933), pp. 954-8.

8 *Discourses*, vol. 1, p. 78; vol. 2, p. 194.

the snare, then by defending himself with his beake and talons, to be thus taken prisoner'.[9]

II

It would be misleading to depict Whitelocke's antiquarian endeavours as anything more than a pastime, and attempts to paint the Society of Antiquaries as a hotbed of radicalism show little regard for the sources. John Selden, a cut above Whitelocke in understanding sources, could remark that 'too studious affectation of base and sterile antiquitie' was 'nothing els but to be exceedingly busie about nothing'; another commentator disparaged antiquarianism as nothing more than an ability to 'turn over so many musty Rolls, so many dry, bloodless Chronicles and so many dull and heavy paced Histories' in search of relevant scraps of information. In fact, it appears that some historians may have made rather too much of antiquarian discourse.[10]

Whitelocke's little speeches suggests that the intellectual links between humanist techniques and antiquarian concern towards English institutions, which Ferguson has seen the society as the harbinger of a new mode of historical thought, flowed naturally from a university education and were not peculiar to Society discourse. In consulting his sources Whitelocke worked to amass as many examples as possible from which to build a discussion. Stacked one on top of the other with little attempt at extrapolation or synthesis, his deployment of evidence can hardly be said to represent a new mode of thought. Rather, it

---

9 *Discourses*, vol. 1, p. 272.

10 John Selden, *Historie of Tithes* (London 1618), sig. a2r-a2v; E. Bolton, *Hypercritica, or A Rule of Judgment, for Writing or Reading our Histories* (1618) in *Critical Essays of the Seventeenth Century*, ed. J.E. Spingarn, 2 vols (Oxford 1908), vol. 1, p. 97. It should be noted that some contemporaries such as Simonds D'Ewes felt more sympathy for the antiquarians, perceiving Selden as 'a man exceedingly puffed up with the apprehension of his own abilities'; *Autobiography of Sir Simonds D'Ewes*, ed. J.O. Halliwell, 2 vols (London 1845), vol. 1, p. 256.

suggests an intellectual reflex to cite 'worthy' authorities that was common to all educated Englishmen of Whitelocke's generation.[11]

Along with his duality as both civil and common lawyer, Whitelocke's antiquarian deployment of English and Continental sources offers perspective to an historical brouhaha touching the insularity of English lawyers and English law in the sixteenth and seventeenth centuries. The insularity, or otherwise, of English lawyers is crucial to our understanding of the nexus between law and national identity – did the common lawyers form their bias against continental codes in relative ignorance, or was it an informed understanding of the differences that led them to eulogize their own legal machines?[12]

No one would reasonably contest the presence or absence of European jurists from English bookshelves – knowledge of continental authors is well attested among the more sophisticated advocates of English law, as a survey of the books donated by lawyers to the Gray's Inn library during the 1630s has demonstrated. Such awareness does not, however, presuppose any dependence upon or ambivalence towards civil law in itself. The mental horizons encouraged by such works remain open to question, and more difficult to define, but Whitelocke's example suggests that, for many common lawyers, an abstract appreciation of continental jurisprudence was held in tension with a fundamental ambiguity towards 'foreign' laws as a powerful symbol of national political and religious difference.[13]

---

11 Ferguson, *Clio Unbound*, esp. pp. 1-82, esp. pp. 63, 80.

12 *Discourses* (1775 edition). For arguments on the insularity of antiquarian thought cf. for example, D.R. Kelley, 'History, English Law and the Renaissance', *Past & Present* 65 (1974), pp. 24-51; Sharpe, *Politics and Ideas*, p. 177; *idem*, *Sir Robert Cotton*, p. 23; Prest, *Rise of the Barristers*, pp. 234-82; *idem*, 'Politics and Profession in Early Stuart England: the Diary of Sir Richard Hutton', *Parergon*, New Series no. 6 (1988), p. 177; Ibbetson, 'Common Lawyers and the Law', p. 152; Burgess, *Politics of the Ancient Constitution*, pp. 12-15, 79-82, 87, 104-5.

13 W.R. Prest, 'Law, learning and religion: gifts to Gray's Inn library in the 1630s' in *Protestants, Property, Puritans: Godly People Revisited*, ed. S.M. Jack & B.A. Masters (*Parergon*, n.s. vol. 14 no. 1 (1996), pp. 205-22.

Whitelocke's antiquarian speeches evidence a biased perception of the value and accuracy of English legal texts in which continental sources served to complement a highly Anglocentric world view. Although Whitelocke was quite prepared to acknowledge that English customs arose 'as... have most of our civil actions, by imitation from other nations', he was careful to distinguish English law from continental traditions. Quick to criticise classical authors of 'noe smale creadit', Whitelocke accepted the complete impartiality and historical accuracy of Fortescue's *De Laudibus Legum Angliae* and Dyer's report of trial by combat. Thus Whitelocke's discussion 'Of the Antiquity, Use, and Privilege of Places for Students and Professors of the Common Laws' readily accepted Fortescue's dubious argument that the degenerate form of French used by common lawyers in Whitelocke's day was in Fortescue's time 'far finer than commonly spoken in France'. He accepted, at face value, Fortescue's equally dubious explanation that the universities omitted common law because it employed French, rather than Latin, and was content to leave off his discussion where 'so grave a judge and so expert as Fortescue' did.[14]

According to C.M. Gray, the common lawyers of Whitelocke's generation were mythmakers and practical men, antiquaries stronger on ancestor worship and patriotism than on realistic perspective, polemical and political users of the legal history they discovered or invented. For all of his breadth of learning, James Whitelocke was tied, by virtue of his professional formation in the common law, to a eulogistic view of English law that served as much a psychological as

---

14 *Discourses*, vol. 1, pp. 80-1, 268, 272; *The Order of Serjeants at Law: A chronicle of creations, with related texts and an historical introduction*, ed. J.H. Baker, Selden Society Supplementary Series 5 (1984), pp. 68-87; Baker, *Legal Profession*, p. 435 and cf. W.J. Bouwsma, 'Lawyers and Early Modern Culture', *American Historical Review* 78 (1973), p. 327; Prest, *Rise of the Barristers*, pp. 188-9; Brooks, 'The Place of Magna Carta', pp. 58-9, 84-8. Whitelocke cites Fortescue as *The commendation of the laws of England*, which is the title of the translation provided by Richard Mulcaster in 1567.

an historical need. His deployment of English and Continental sources throughout his antiquarian speeches reflects, perhaps, one aspect of a bipolar feelings of confidence and anxiety about the destiny and relative strength of little England against the larger and wealthier European states which practised civil law.[15]

III

In 1607, to use Sharpe's carefully chosen words, the Society of Antiquaries 'was dissolved, or fell apart... in puzzling circumstances'. Sharpe has speculated that the collapse of the Society may have resulted from external pressure felt by members, as the Crown became concerned about its topics of discussion, and there is evidence that in 1614 attempts to reform the Society were quashed for this reason. An examination of Whitelocke's own involvement suggest, however, that on the first occasion the Society was voluntarily disbanded in response to tensions that were surfacing not from beyond, but from within. In particular, papers on the rights and limitations of the Herald's Court, whose legitimacy was challenged by the common law courts throughout the Jacobean era, acquired a controversial edge.[16]

The Herald's Court (known alternatively as the Court of Constable, Court Military, and Earl Marshal's Court) was governed without the presence of a permanent high constable since the mid-fifteenth century. In the Jacobean period the Earl Marshal presided over the court as president of a commission composed of privy

15 Sir Matthew Hale, *The History of the Common Law of England*, ed. C.M. Gray, Chicago & London, 1971, p. xii; *Discourses*, vol. 2, p. 191. A summary of the lengthy historiography built around the 'reception' or otherwise of Roman law in England is found in Seipp, 'Reception of Canon Law', pp. 389-390.

16 Sharpe, *Sir Robert Cotton*, pp. 28-32. The first historians of the Society were similarly convinced, writing that members abandoned meetings 'for fear of being prosecuted as a treasonable cabal'; *Archaeologia*, vol. 1, pp. xiv-xv.

councillors, although common lawyers had disputed the vaguely-defined jurisdiction of the court increasingly from the last decades of Elizabeth's reign. Until James I resolved the matter with new letters patent to the Earl Marshal in 1622, this jurisdiction was challenged by a legal fiction arguing that the vacancy of the constableship had ended the legitimate jurisdiction of the court.[17]

From its inception the Society of Antiquaries held strong connections with the profession of heralds. It is not surprising, then, to find that heraldic institutions were on the agenda for discussion; besides Whitelocke's paper, others on the Herald's Court and the offices of High Steward, Constable and Earl Marshal survive in their dozens. While the brevity of most papers suggests that the most interesting aspect of Society gatherings was the one entirely invisible in the historical record – the discussions prompted by the speeches themselves – comments such as one preserved in an anonymous paper on 'The Antiquity and Office of the Constable of England' hint at the tensions that surfaced throughout such discussion:

> And if any will complayne, that any plea be commenced before the constable and marshal, that might be tryed by the law of the land, the same complainant shall have a privie seal to the king, without difficulty, directed to the said constable and marshal, to surcease in that plea till it be discussed by the king's councell... otherwise to be tryed by the common law of the realme of England.

Given the presence of lawyers drawn from across the legal spectrum, it may have become increasingly difficult to stop academic endeavour in which, in the words of Francis Thynne, 'there can nothing be over-passed, what civil or common law, or historicall or record matter may afford', from spilling over into legal argument.[18]

---

17 G.D. Squibb, *The High Court of Chivalry* (Oxford 1959), pp. 1-40; P.M. Ashman, 'Heraldry and the Law of Arms in England', *Journal of Legal History* 9 (1988), pp. 69-70.

18 *Discourses*, vol. 2, p. 113. As in a topic proposed for Easter term of 1605 on 'the antiquity and authority of the civill lawe in England', BL Cottonian MS Cleopatra E I, fol. 242 cited in Sharpe, *Sir Robert Cotton*, p. 30.

If academic papers did prompt controversy, such controversy is well demonstrated in Whitelocke's case following the demise of Society meetings. In 1613, Ralph Brooke, a former Society member, employed him as legal counsel in a case against Richard St. George, another former Society man (who along with Spelman, Cotton, Ley, Sir John Davies and William Hakewill, initiated the push for renewed Society meetings a year later). Brooke was already involved in a long and complicated legal dispute with Sir William Dethicke. Whitelocke moved to have Brooke's case redirected from the Earl Marshal's Court, in which Dethicke might have strong influence, to the Court of Chancery, employing the legal fiction of a vacant constableship. His argument met with an unsympathetic response from Chancellor Ellesmere – and Whitelocke, sarcastically declared to be 'omniscious, and [to] know all things', quickly found himself defending his actions before the Privy Council.[19]

In a paper appended to Hearne's *Collection of Curious Discourses* (which suggests that it may at one time have been held among the papers of a Society member), Robert Plott cited this incident in support of his defence of the Earl Marshal's jurisdiction. He remarked that the Chancellor had directed the cause to 'the lords commissioners for the office of earl marshal, as a matter most proper to be decided in their court'. The Chancery then refuted Whitelocke's allegation 'that there was no such court as the earl marshal's court, but the court of the constable and marshal, which could only be held at such a time as there was a constable or commissioners for that office' by means of a public declaration in the Chancery decree and order books.[20]

19 Sharpe, *Sir Robert Cotton*, p. 36; *Liber Famelicus*, p. 36; Squibb, *High Court of Chivalry*, pp. 43-4. Brooke's suit against St George may have been encouraged by the actions of William Penson, Lancaster Herald, who filed a similar suit against colleagues in the Court of Chancery in 1612; A. Wagner, *Heralds of England: A History of the Office and College of Arms* (London 1967), pp. 199-221, 225, 227-30, 232, 235, 384.

20 Squibb, *High Court of Chivalry*, p. 30; Ashman, 'Heraldry and the Law of Arms', p. 70; Robert Plott, 'A defence of the jurisdiction of the Earl Marshal's Court in

An intriguing letter from Whitelocke to his Society associate Sir Robert Cotton provides further clues about undercurrents in antiquarian circles. Of uncertain provenance, this letter has been interpreted by Sharpe as regarding Whitelocke's right to practice before the Privy Council. A closer examination of the context suggests that it relates back to debate on the Earl Marshal's Court. In the letter, Whitelocke reminded Cotton of his presence in the Council Chamber at Whitehall 'when my Lord of Northampton took exception to my practising there before the Lord Commissioners as being unusual and improper to a Professor of the Law of England'. Squibb has shown that in the Jacobean period common lawyers frequently represented parties before the Court of Earl Marshal, although in theory the jurisdiction remained with civilians. Whitelocke went on to tell Cotton of his surprise at Northampton's objection, and his recourse to his qualifications in civil law as an immediate defence. From there, he turned to associates (it is uncertain whether they were from the antiquarian's ranks) to establish beyond doubt in his own mind that common lawyers were entirely within their legal rights to practise in this court. Whitelocke closed the letter by asking Cotton to check the records produced in support of their argument, and then to 'mediate between my Lord of Northampton and our whole profession'. Whitelocke's enlistment of Cotton's support makes sense, as Cotton had been acting as Northampton's chief legal adviser for many years. While Cotton's response to Whitelocke's letter is unknown, this correspondence underlines the complex entanglement between antiquarianism and judicial debate.[21]

---

the vacancy of a Constable, and of his disowning prohibitions sent thither from other courts' in *Discourses*, vol. 2, pp. 259-60; PRO C33/126, fols 122v-23.

21 The BL copy of Whitelocke's letter is dated '1609?' in the left hand margin. Sharpe, *Sir Robert Cotton*, pp. 40-2, 147; Bodl. MS Smith 71, fol. 59; BL Cottonian MS Julius C. III, fol. 89; Squibb, *High Court of Chivalry*, pp. 42-3; Peck, 'Court Patronage and Government Policy', pp. 35-7. A paper prepared by Cotton for the Society of Antiquaries on the Earl Marshal and Constable's jurisdiction is preserved in College of Arms Vincent MS, fols 17-25.

IV

After seven years of silence, attempts were made to revive the Society of Antiquaries in 1614. Whitelocke's incomplete drafts on the terms for the administration of justice, one of two topics proposed for the first meeting, survive as reminders of a speech he never completed or delivered, as plans to renew the Society were abandoned.[22]

Looking back on events, Sir Henry Spelman concluded that royal disapproval of such a revival had been the critical impediment:

> we had notice that his Majesty took a little mislike of our Society, not being inform'd, that we were resolv'd to decline all matters of state. Yet hereupon we forbade to meet again, and so all our labours lost.

Given his sensitivity to legal debate, is not hard to understand the king's reluctance to patronise antiquarian endeavours, as opponents of impositions enlisted antiquarian support to help build a case against the Crown position in the parliaments of 1610 and again in 1614. It is likely that Whitelocke's own leading role in parliamentary debates was due, in part, to his initial familiarity, through antiquarian researches, with the records that he needed to build a case, as he assisted in the exploitation of private and public records for parliamentary ends.[23]

---

22 Longleat Papers, vol. 24, fols 269-70.

23 *Reliquiae Spelmanniae The Posthumous Works*, ed. E. Gibson (1727), pp. 69-70; Sharpe, *Sir Robert Cotton*, pp. 40-2, 147, 154-64. In 1614, Francis Bacon noted that Whitelocke was 'learned and diligent, and conversant in reports and records'; BL Cottonian Titus F IV, fol. 12; BL Lansdowne MS 486, fols 15-16. A later 1617 petition for an antiquarian academy cited, among 'persons fit to keep up and celebrate' antiquarianism, Sir Edward Coke, whom King James dismissed from the King's Bench in 1616 for obstructing the prerogative, Dr Richard Cosin, whom Coke had declared would 'obtrude upon the world' with his claims for the jurisdiction of the courts spiritual, and Dr John Cowell, whose Interpreter caused such a furore in the 1610 session of parliament that James had to suppress its publication. Reference to this contentious trio was hardly likely to create a sense of comfort in the king's mind, and suggested a likely corollary of granting the petition – renewed political argument touching the king's authority; Coke, *Twelfth Report*,

While the 'addled' parliament of 1614 provided a disastrous context for attempts to re-form the Society, political discord may have deepened the fissures within antiquarian ranks anyway. One Society member warned his associates that parliament was 'no place for particular men to utter their private conceits... by spending the time with long studied and eloquent orations: for the reverence of God, their king and their country being well settled in their hearts, will make them ashamed of such toyes'. As an outspoken critic of impositions, James Whitelocke may have felt more comfortable with Francis Tate's reflection that parliament aimed 'to do something to God's glory, the king's good, and the benefit of the whole land'. It was, Tate added, not merely the right, but the duty of members of the lower House to request the redress of grievances, 'being most in number, and such as live in all parts and places of the land... and being weak in power, and most subject to feel inconveniences, as greatness may lay upon them'.[24]

Given the range of viewpoints expressed among members, attempts to paint the activities of the Society of Antiquaries as a kind of 'think-tank' for a radical brand of constitutional thinking have proved unrewarding. Like any other institution promoting learning in the early Stuart state, it accommodated a variety of opinions. Ultimately, however, Whitelocke's involvement with the Society of Antiquaries suggests that legal and political tensions in Jacobean society were pushed beneath the surface, and that they threatened to crack the facade of

---

'Premunire'; Sir Jocelyn Simon, 'Dr. Cowell', *Cambridge Law Journal* 26 (1968), pp. 260-72.

24 *Discourses*, vol. 1, pp. 299-300; 309. In 1617, an anonymous pamphleteer cited the death of several prominent members, together with the lack of royal patronage, as the reason for the Society's demise; see 'A Motion for errecting an Academy Royal, or College of King James, written in 1617', in *Archaeologia*, vol. 1, pp. xvi-xvii, probably written by Henry Ferrars.

public harmony if allowed a public voice. The collapse of the Society suggests the limitations of the consensual ideal promoted in the Jacobean polity. Its addled history provides an appropriate background to James Whitelocke's controversial parliamentary career.

Part II
Parliaments and Politics

Chapter 4

Parliamentary politics

In recent times revisionism has jettisoned 'constitutional' conflict as a meaningful paradigm for early Stuart society, leading some historians to emphasise the specific and limited impact of legal debate upon the political crisis of 1642. Jacobean history is certainly no longer conceivable as the first stage in a parliamentary 'winning of the initiative', and historians have been right to down play a teleological 'high road' to civil war. Finding a clear context, in such an altered landscape, for the coterie of 'wrangling lawyers' drawn into argument with the policies of James I has not proved easy.[1]

In particular, Whitelocke's famous declaration of parliamentary rights during the 1610 debate on impositions been subject to divergent interpretation. In his revised 1989 edition of *The English Civil War,* Robert Ashton reflected that:

> A brilliant parliamentary lawyer such as James Whitelock [sic] might argue in the great debate on impositions in the House of Commons in 1610 that 'the power of

1 Cf. Conrad Russell, 'Parliamentary History in Perspective 1604-1629', *History* 61 (1976), pp. 1-27; *idem*, 'The Nature of a Parliament in Early Stuart England' in *Before the English Civil War: Essays on Early Stuart Politics and Government*, ed. Howard Tomlinson (London 1984), pp. 123-50; Sharpe, *Politics and Ideas*, p. 75; Derek Hirst, 'Court, Country, and Politics before 1629' in Faction and Parliament, pp. 105-6; Wallace Notestein, 'The winning of the initiative by the House of Commons', *Proceedings of the British Academy* 11 (1924-5), pp. 125-75; G.R. Elton, 'A High Road to Civil War?' in his *Studies in Tudor and Stuart Politics and Government*, 3 vols (Cambridge 1974-83), vol. 2, pp. 164-82; Kevin Sharpe, 'Parliamentary History 1603-1629: In or out of Perspective?' in *Faction and Parliament: Essays on early Stuart history*, ed. Kevin Sharpe (Oxford 1978), pp. 37-42; Conal Condren, *The Language of Politics in Seventeenth-Century England* (London 1994), pp. 120-1; Sommerville, *Politics & Ideology*, pp. 71-2, 120, 123-4.

> the King in Parliament is greater than his power out of Parliament, and doth rule and control it', but four years earlier Chief Baron Fleming had handed down a judgement in Bate's Case on the same matter of impositions; although like Whitelock's it distinguished between two forms of royal power, it came to radically different conclusions on their relative priority.

Ashton's appraisal is hardly different from the interpretation of constitutional historians such as J.R. Tanner who wrote at the height of Whig orthodoxy. While Burgess has seen an essential agreement between Whitelocke's 1610 speech on impositions and 'royalist' notions of government, Richard Cust has employed the same speech to trace 'the roots of hostility' toward later 'unparliamentary' forms of taxation. This chapter argues that Whitelocke's speeches, which petitioned the Crown to moderate unpopular and 'unparliamentary' fiscal activities in a search for constitutional consensus, unwittingly contributed to a new language of political opposition that would emerge after Whitelocke's death in 1632.[2]

I

James Whitelocke's parliamentary career began with his selection as one of two MPs for Woodstock on 6 December 1609, when he was returned 'in the place of Sir Richard Lea' who died in office on 22 December 1608, thus forcing a by-election for the borough in which he, as recorder of Woodstock, was the incumbent. Whitelocke's training, both in civil and common law, earmarked him for an active role in parliamentary affairs, and nomination to a range of committees was achieved with the support of fellow parliamentarians who knew him through a range of associations: members of the merchant guilds, lawyers from the inns of court and the courts of law, associates from the Society of Antiquaries, and 'country' associates such as Sir John

---

2 Ashton, *English Civil War*, p. 12; *Constitutional Documents of the Reign of James I*, pp. 245-6; Burgess, *Politics of the Ancient Constitution*, pp. 143-4; Cust, *Forced Loan*, p. 152. Compare especially Tanner's treatment of Fleming's judgement on Bate's case and of Whitelocke's speech.

Croke, who had served as speaker for the House in the first session of 1604. It is clear that members of the Commons saw Whitelocke's potential to contribute. In the fourth session, he would be named to no less than twenty-four parliamentary committees.[3]

Whitelocke's thorough knowledge of local property law, gained through work as steward of St John's and recorder of Woodstock, promoted him immediately as a candidate for several committees, including a committee for resolving the estate boundaries of a Berkshire gentleman and a committee against forcible entry. Knowledge of the principles of common and civil law (and perhaps also a rhetorical ability noted by legal and antiquarian associates) primed Whitelocke for a vigorous role in the more passionately debated issues of the parliament. He helped to prepare for two conferences with the House of Lords during the Commons' vigorous attack on John Cowell's *Interpreter,* and later assisted in the preparation for a conference on the Great Contract, where he suggested that 'this matter of support [by way of a fixed parliamentary subsidy to the Crown] was a thing strange and never heard of in Parliament but once'.[4]

It was the issue of impositions on which Whitelocke took his most visible public role in 1610. Meeting in 1606 under some political pressure from Robert Cecil, the barons of the Exchequer had ruled against John Bate's legal challenge of the king's impositions on currants. Baron Clark, stressing the ambiguity of precedent, declared that matters of royal revenue 'shall not be according to the rules of Common Law, but according to the precedents of this Court wherein these matters are disputable and determinable'. Chief Baron Fleming ruled that the office of the king involved an 'ordinary' and 'absolute'

3 *Liber Famelicus*, pp. 16, 19; W.R. Williams, *Parliamentary history of the county of Oxford, 1213-1899* (Brecknock 1899), pp. 196-8. For Whitelocke's committee work see *Commons' Journal*, pp. 394b, 398b, 399b, 400b, 407a, 418a, 418b, 419a, 419b, 423a, 432a (2), 443b, 444b, 445a (2), 445b, 446b, 447b, 449b, 450a.

4 *Commons' Journal*, pp. 399b, 400b, 407a, 418a, 418b (2), 449b; and see the forthcoming History of Parliament Trust biography of Whitelocke, hereafter cited as History of Parliament Trust.

prerogative. According 'to the wisdom of the King for the common good', he suggested, this loosely defined 'absolute' prerogative was subordinate only to the dictates of statecraft:

> And whereas it is said that if the King may impose, he may impose any quantity what he pleases, true it is that this is to be referred to the wisdom of the King, who guideth all under God by his wisdom, and that this is not to be disputed by a subject; and many things are left to his wisdom for the ordering of his power, rather than his power shall be restrained.

The political import of this ruling was not lost on Cecil, now earl of Salisbury and newly appointed lord treasurer, who used it as the precedent to introduce a new Book of Rates in the Spring of 1608 which extended duties widely, in the face of a royal debt approaching a million pounds.[5]

Reflecting on the outcome of *Bate's Case* in the *Liber Famelicus*, Whitelocke noted that 'the creadit of the judgment given in the Eschequer in the case of currants... did not satisfye me' though 'I only opposed my self at the first to the receiting of it, and so toke hold a little'. Like many other barristers who opposed impositions forcefully in the parliament, Whitelocke's interest in 'the point of right' had been stimulated considerably by the subsequent extension of duties to numerous other types of merchandise – although he provides no evidence of any overt association with a merchant's lobby. Subsequently, the *Liber Famelicus* tells its readers, Whitelocke 'took better hold', directing us to the record 'amplye related by the clerk of the parliament', as well as his treatise 'wherein is expressed the most alledged for the righte of the subject'.[6]

---

5 *State Trials*, vol. 2, col. 382, col. 391; Pauline Croft, 'Fresh Light on Bate's Case', *Historical Journal* 30 (1987), pp. 535-6; Lockyer, *Early Stuarts*, p. 77-8. For a discussion of the arguments employed during Bate's Case cf. Burgess, *Politics of the Ancient Constitution*, pp. 139-44.

6 *Liber Famelicus*, pp. 24, 64; cf. Kenyon, *Stuart Constitution*, 2nd ed., p. 47. In his speech of July 2 Whitelocke noted that impositions 'do extend to the number of many hundreds, as appeareth by that printed book of rates, and are set in

In 1610, disagreement over impositions began with parliamentary attempts to verify the precedent for this type of royal levy. On 1 May 1610, along with Robert Cotton, Roger Owen, Francis Tate, Heneage Finch, Nicholas Fuller and Anthony Dyott, Whitelocke was nominated as member of a sub-committee 'to make search of all such records and precedents as may give light on furtherance of that business'. Pressure from the king to disband the larger committee on impositions, which monitored the activity of this sub-committee, led the Commons to lodge a petition protesting their right to continue this investigation on 24 May. On 16 June, as the Commons moved to frame a petition on the basis of relevant precedents, Whitelocke was asked to bring twenty records from the Tower to the House for presentation to the full committee. On 10 July he was nominated to help gather the arguments assembled for the case of impositions, reduce them into writing, and a 'case to be made thereof'. Although there is evidence that this project never reached fruition, it was from the assembled lists of records on impositions, and joint discussion of them, that a case was created from which members would debate impositions.[7]

The private and public record of Whitelocke's parliamentary involvement suggest emerging mechanisms of parliamentary organisation, and it appears that throughout the session committee members were in close contact with one another and other members of the House. Surviving in Whitelocke's papers is an order for the lawyers of the House of Commons to assemble at the Middle Temple on 12 June to assess copies of records assembled from the Tower and the Exchequer on impositions and report back to the Commons upon their bearing on the Crown's position. On 17 June Whitelocke wrote to

---

charge upon the whole kingdom as an inheritance to continue to the king, his heires and successors for ever...'; *State Trials*, vol. 2, p. 481.

7 *Proceedings in Parliament 1610*, vol. 2, p. 74, 149; *Commons' Journals*, p. 440; Longleat Papers, vol. 1, fols 90: 'Remonstrance on his Majesty's commandment of restraint from debating his right of imposing upon goods exported or imported'.

Robert Bowyer, clerk of the House, urging speed in the dispatch of copied records from the Tower. Their interaction continued as Whitelocke inspected parliamentary rolls dating from the reigns of Edward I and began to prepare a case. The range of individual statutes which Whitelocke cited from the reigns of Edward I to Elizabeth I reflected a thorough search of the available records within the terms assigned to him for the debate.[8]

Whitelocke's early comments to the House of Commons on the matter of impositions were made in response to King James's speech to both Houses on the issue on 21 May 1610. Although the king tried to dampen controversy on the subject before attention was diverted away from his own political agenda, his speech would have done little to inspire confidence in a royal commitment to the rights of parliament. Chiding those who challenged his prerogative on this issue, James warned that it was 'an ill consequent... to say that because kings have done so they have no power to do otherwise... You cannot clip the wings of greatness'. In an assembly acutely conscious of their individual and collective rights as members of parliament, and defensive in the extreme about their political heritage, King James's conclusion that 'Many things I may do without parliament, which I

8 Longleat Papers, vol. 1, fol. 92; H.L.R.O. Main Papers, H.L., 17 June 1610; cited in *Proceedings in Parliament 1610*, vol. 2, p. 149; H.M.C. *Third Report*, p. 13. Many of the notes and records examined by Whitelocke during the preparation of a case on impositions in 1610 (discussed below) survive in Inner Temple Petyt MS 537, vol. 14, fols 187-213v. Of 31 records, four are noted as having been examined by Whitelocke and seven are certified by Robert Bowyer. For his medieval precedents Whitelocke relied mainly upon the statute books, citing 1 Richard III, cap. 2; 5 Edward II, cap. 14; 2 Edward III, cap. 7, 9 Edward III, cap. 1, 21 Edward III, cap. 16, 21 Edward III, cap. 1, 34 Edward III, cap. 1; 1 Henry VII, cap. 19. For the later period he employed a range of legal commentators including Bracton (ch. 8), Fortescue (*De Laudibus Legum Angliae*, ch. 9), Phillipe de Comines, *An epitome of all the lives of the kings of France* (book 4, ch. 8), and particularly the reports of Dyer from the reign of Elizabeth I. Other sources included the parliamentary rolls (2 Henry IV, number 109), and an Exchequer judgment drawn from the court rolls in the seventeenth year of Richard II.

will do in parliament, for good kings are helped by parliament not for power but for convenience that the work may seem more glorious' must have sounded not like a conciliatory remark, but a thinly veiled threat.[9]

As the lower House assembled on the following day, Whitelocke was one who responded to the king's speech. His words suggest a measured reaction to the position taken by the king. Whitelocke urged that while insisting upon their right to discuss impositions, 'some course may be taken by us with duty and respect, not with reluctation and contention, to give the King satisfaction and show him that it is fit for us to proceed'. Whitelocke also suggested, however, that to back down on the issue altogether was detrimental to 'the ancient frame of the commonwealth', reminding members of those points he thought uniquely characteristic of the English constitutional arrangement:

> One is that we are masters of our own and can have nothing taken from us without our consents; another that laws cannot be made without our consents, and the edict of a prince is not a law; the third is that parliament is the storehouse of our liberties. All these are in danger to be lost by this power, for *de modo et de fine non constant nobis.*

His deduction was simple but pointed: 'We know not how this may stretch.'[10]

In the vein suggested by Whitelocke's speech, the House prepared a petition insisting upon their right to debate the matter openly, a copy of which was kept by Whitelocke for future reference. Eager to promote support for the Great Contract, the king wavered and then finally consented to a 'great debate' on impositions, between 23 June and 3 July, in which members could voice their opinions. The fullest

---

9 See *Proceedings in Parliament 1610*, vol. 2, pp. 102-5. Chamberlain wrote to Carleton that James' speeches in 1610 'bred generally much discomfort to see our monarchical power and royal prerogative stretched so high and made so transcendent every way'; *The Letters of John Chamberlain*, ed. N.E. McClure, 2 vols. (Philadelphia 1939), vol. 1, p. 301 [hereafter cited as *Letters of John Chamberlain*].

10 *Proceedings in Parliament 1610*, vol. 2, p. 109.

surviving record on Whitelocke's thoughts upon the question of impositions survives in a manuscript prepared from his speech to the house on 2 July.[11]

Whitelocke's speech focussed attention upon a number of questions which had not, in his opinion, been fully considered in earlier speeches. It made plain his view that the outcome of this debate had wide-ranging constitutional implications. Beyond narrower issues of royal revenue, he maintained, the case of impositions was one of 'our very essence'. Whitelocke then laid out the central thesis of his argument:

> if there be a right in the king to alter the property of that which is ours without our consent, we are but tenants at his will of that which we have. If it be in the king and parliament, then we have propertie, and are tenants at our own will, for that which is done in parliament is done by all our wills and consents.

His assumption was that the terms of the letters patent by which impositions had been set constituted an innovation, disregarding accepted principles of taxation. By prosecuting those who refused to pay imposed customs not ratified in parliament, the king had either unlawfully assumed possession of the goods, or his letters patent had assumed the force of law. These were the issues, Whitelocke stressed to his listeners, which concerned them – and it was here that the danger of the duties lay, 'for if he [the king] alone out of parliament may impose, he altereth the law of England'.[12]

Declining to discuss those 'great mysteries of policie and government' which had prompted the letters patent, Whitelocke suggested his concern for the 'reference to the rights and practices of forraine princes' which prefaced the book of rates. Employing his knowledge

11 Longleat Papers, vol. 1, fol. 90. The treatise prepared from the speech is reprinted in *State Trials*, vol. 2, cols 479-520. How closely Whitelocke's speech followed the surviving treatise is impossible to say, but to read the entire document aloud takes approximately one and a half hours.

12 *State Trials*, vol. 2, cols 479-84: 'But if you will deny, that the king doth in this case take the goods of the subject without his assent, then you must fall upon mine alternative position, that the king's patent hath in this case the power of a law.'

of civil law to stress the differences between Justinian's code and the legal traditions of his own country, Whitelocke reflected that just as, in civil law, kings 'have an absolute power to make law, they have also a power to impose'. He continued with a blunt but perceptive warning on the possible ramifications of a placid endorsement of the king's claim:

> And if this power of imposing were quietly settled in our kings, considering what is the greatest use they make of assembling of parliaments, which is the supply of money, I do not see any likelihood to hope for often meetings in that kind, because they would provide themselves by that other means.[13]

Turning to legal precedent, Whitelocke admitted the essential ambiguity of evidence already discussed and debated, but suggested the need to seek the constitutional conventions which underlay the practice of kings in former times. An uncomplicated vision of custom propelled an argument that was simultaneously ahistorical and persuasive, placing the issue of impositions in a long sequence of supposed right and obligation. 'Can any man give me a reason' Whitelocke asked members, 'why the king can only in parliament make lawes? No man ever read any law whereby it was so ordained, and yet no man ever read that any king practised the contrary'. Here was direct reply to the philosophy of kingship which underlay Fleming's 1606 Exchequer judgment and the king's speech to the House of 21 May, for the inference was that in matters of statecraft the king was bound to respect conventions which, Whitelocke argued, were immutable and sacrosanct.[14]

Whitelocke acknowledged that 'unparliamentary' impositions existed in the past, but suggested that kings had overstepped the mark in each instance, and had been subsequently forced to seek parliamentary sanction for their actions: 'never any imposition was set on by the king out of parliament, but complaint was made of it in parliament: and not one that ever stood after such complaint was made, but

---

13 *State Trials*, vol. 2, cols 481, 486-7.

14 *State Trials*, vol. 2, col. 483.

remedy was afforded for it'. Whitelocke could raise some clear examples to demonstrate that earlier parliaments had taken strong exception to royal impositions levied without their consent, and that kings had found it politically expedient (if not, as Whitelocke implied, imperative) to remove these impositions. He chose to ignore, however, the frequently blurred lines between exception, right and obligation that surrounded their dealings. Ignoring the malleability of parliament over its long history, this blinkered reading of custom allowed Whitelocke to argue that the past must dictate the 'natural policy and constitution of our commonwealth'.[15]

In appealing to custom as a reasonable benchmark by which to weigh issues 'requiring certainty in matter of profit between the king and the subject', Whitelocke joined Hakewill, Fuller, Sandys, and the others who spoke against impositions in 1610. By exploring the range of rights guaranteed to the royal prerogative in law, all of these men argued that customary boundaries could be shown to operate on non-parliamentary methods of taxation. No one but Whitelocke went on to define the supposed structure of English political sovereignty itself. Here it would appear that Whitelocke's thoughts were once again encouraged by his understanding of the evidence, which in his eyes stressed a balance of political power, shared by kings and their parliaments, that flowed naturally from their mutual obligations.[16]

Like all Jacobeans, James Whitelocke was forced to reconcile the office of kingship to the person of the king by means of two (loosely corresponding) capacities, the 'ordinary' and 'extraordinary' prerogative. Personal experience as a lawyer would have impressed upon him practical limitations upon the prerogative and underlined the institutional mechanisms through which royal power was exercised. The respect that Whitelocke afforded parliament reflected, in part, its central role in the construction of law, as well as its importance as the place of final legal recourse. Whitelocke noted that when 'a judge-

15 *State Trials*, vol. 2, cols 503, 514.

16 *Constitutional Documents*, p. 250.

ment be given in the King's-bench, by the king himselfe, as may be, and by the law is intended, a writ of error, to reverse the judgement, may be sued before the king in parliament'.[17]

In his brief but often quoted consideration of sovereignty, Whitelocke stressed two forms of royal power more or less corresponding to the 'ordinary' and 'extraordinary' prerogative. 'The soveraigne power', he told members, 'is agreed to be in the king: but in the king is a two-fold power; the one in parliament, as he is assisted with the consent of the whole state; the other out of parliament, as he is sole, and singular, guided merely by his own will.' He argued that the 'subordinata' or personal prerogative was always responsive to the 'suprema potestas', or public prerogative achieved with parliamentary sanction. 'It will then be easily proved', he claimed 'that the power of the king in parliament is greater than his power out of parliament, and doth rule and control it'.[18]

It does not appear that Whitelocke intended this simple and perhaps daring conclusion to be inflammatory. Indeed, lawyers such as James Whitelocke did not consciously set out to question the nature of the constitution in the parliament of 1610; rather, the King's legal authority was forced into question under the specific pressure of events. As Whitelocke told members, while the inconvenience of the impositions to merchants 'needs no debate', establishing 'the point of right' was vital to those more 'desirous that the truth may be knowne, and right be done, than that the opinion of myself or any other prevail'. Defined and debated in the House, an ambiguous theoretical framework of obligation and right summed up in Bracton's tautology that the 'King can doe nothing upon earth (seeing he is the servant and lieutenant of God) but that which he may lawfully doe', was

17 *State Trials*, vol. 2, col. 482. The ordinary and extraordinary prerogative of the king had been considered at length in Calvin's case (1608); *State Trials*, vol. 2, cols 611-58.

18 *State Trials*, vol. 2, col. 482; *Liber Famelicus*, pp. 32-3.

shown to be an arrangement broad enough in its maxims to accommodate important, perhaps critical differences of emphasis.[19]

Heneage Finch underlined the tensions in this situation when he raised the pointed question of prerogative rights as the debate on impositions was getting under way:

> I hear sometimes of indisputable prerogatives and I agree there are such, namely those that are prerogatives so clearly to be yielded that they are without dispute.... Other sense of this word I am yet to learn... for it hath been already disputed both here and in the Exchequer and we are not yet agreed. I will not deny the distinction of two powers in the king, a limited power and an absolute... but what absolute power is, is all the question.

It was a question that the Commons now attempted to clarify as they sought to gain the king's acceptance of a petition 'not to put the question of right to condemn... the judgement of the Exchequer in the mater of currents', but to acknowledge the general necessity of parliamentary consent to new taxation.[20]

Whitelocke was appointed to help draft this petition on 3 July, and over the following week he continued to be at the forefront of attempts to 'digest the dispute on both sides'. It must have been with some satisfaction that Whitelocke viewed the fifth section of the final draft, presented to James on 7 July, treating 'Impositions upon merchandise', which distilled the substance of his own thoughts on the issue. 'The policy and constitution of this your Majesty's kingdom', it reminded James, 'appropriates unto the kings of this realm, with the assent of parliament, as well the sovereign power of making laws, as that of taxing or imposing upon the subjects' goods or merchandises, wherein they justly have such a propriety, as may not without their consent be altered or changed'. The assumption mirrored Whitelocke's own: that the king was obliged to act in

---

19 *Bracton De Legibus*, vol. 2, p. 305; *State Trials*, vol. 2, col. 480.

20 *Proceedings in Parliament 1610*, vol. 2, p. 234; *The Court and Times of James the First; Illustrated by Authentic and Confidential Letters, From Various Public and Private Collections*, ed. Thomas Birch, 2 vols (London 1849), vol. 1, p. 122. 'Dudley Carleton to Sir Thomas Edmondes, 13 July 1610'.

accordance with an historically demonstrable convention, 'in imitation likewise of your noble progenitors'.[21]

By their petition of grievances, the Commons attempted to steer a middle path, allowing the king to retain existing customs duties while stressing their right to regulate all subsequent duties. As an attempt at compromise, it met with little success. On 10 July Salisbury replied to the petition on behalf of the king. Standing on the legal ruling in *Bate's Case*, he refused to yield to the Commons' claims on the point of right. 'The King hath the law to justify him and precedents to speak for him. I know not what he should have more' was his unequivocal reply. The weak response of the Commons to this message says more about the transient nature of parliaments than the feelings of MPs towards the treasurer's response. On 19 July, Sir Edwin Sandys reported to Salisbury that the 'lawyers [have] gone to their circuits and out of the town and our bodies [are] much wasted'. James Whitelocke and others in the House would have a second chance to voice their concerns in the parliament of 1614.[22]

II

For Whitelocke and many others summoned for James I's second parliament in February 1614, such occasion provided a second opportunity to voice concern over issues which had been dismissed, rather than resolved, by the dissolution of parliament four years earlier. From the outset, the question of impositions threatened to sour proceedings. By 19 April, John Chamberlain observed that the Commons 'is now altogether occupied in crying down impositions, and searching

21 *Commons' Journals*, pp. 445a, 445b, 446b, 447b, 450a; *Proceedings in Parliament 1610*, vol. 1, pp. 129-134. It is notable that the petition is presented as a preface to his arguments in the manuscript that records his speech.

22 *Proceedings in Parliament 1610*, vol. 1, p. 154; *Debates in 1610; edited from a member of the House of Commons*, ed. S.R. Gardiner, Camden Society Old Series 81 (1862), pp. 155-8.

records for that purpose'. From the notes that survive, Whitelocke's attitude seems to have hardened against impositions between 1610 and 1614, in the face of an increase from two or three items liable to duties at James's accession to more than 1,000 commodities. In a brief and often disorderly session in which neither bills nor supply were passed, Whitelocke's experience was recognised as he again took a leading role in voicing opposition to the Crown's continued exaction of extra-parliamentary duties.[23]

As more volatile tempers flared throughout the 1614 parliament, Whitelocke stressed the need for consensus but maintained his opposition to impositions. From the outset he was one of the more prominent members of the lower House; named to nine committees, he is recorded as making ten speeches over parliament's short duration. Appointed to a committee on 11 April to examine the precedents for admitting Attorney-General Bacon, he took the moderate line that Bacon should be admitted, but that henceforth the attorney be barred from parliament in the traditional manner. On 12 April, he supported Secretary Winwood's motion for immediate supply 'that it may be disposed to the end for which given', the 'desire of justice for grievances'. On 20 April, Whitelocke supported the merchants of Exeter and Bristol in their condemnation of the London-based French Company's patent, noting speeches 'cast abroad that, sitting the parliament, we may dissolve what monopolies we will; after the parliament they shall all up again'.[24]

---

23 *Letters of John Chamberlain*, vol. 1, p. 531; Clayton Roberts & Owen Duncan, 'The Parliamentary Undertaking of 1614', *English Historical Review* 93 (1978), pp. 481-98; *Proceedings in Parliament 1614*, pp. xix-xxii, 95.

24 *Commons' Journals*, pp. 456b, 458a, 460a, 463a, 465a, 467a, 468b, 470a, 472b, 473a, 474a, 489a, 494b, 495b, 498a; *Proceedings in Parliament 1614*, pp. 37, 55-56, 67, 95, 114, 148, 157, 161-2, 213, 245. Although dated, the standard narrative of events is still T.L. Moir, *The Addled Parliament of 1614* (Oxford 1958); cf. the introduction to *Proceedings in Parliament 1614 (House of Commons)*, ed. Maija Jansson, American Philosophical Society 172 (1988), pp. xiii-xxxvi, and Roberts & Duncan, 'Parliamentary Undertaking of 1614'.

Pressing for a revision of the Crown's policy on impositions on 5 May, Whitelocke held that the king could be persuaded to change his views by reconsidering the lesson shown by custom. Recalling an example from the reign of Edward III, Whitelocke argued that by 'joining with the Lords in this great business', a 'petition to the King by both houses' could persuade King James 'whereby he is misinformed'. Restating many of the more pertinent arguments he had used four years earlier, Whitelocke was confident that through such a conference parliament could show that impositions were 'no flower of the crown', quipping 'if a flower, a long winter, not budding in 160 year[s]'. His concluding remarks urged the House 'not to proceed as with a duel with the King', but to 'proceed in our own business with true hearts; in the King's with loyal and loving affections, and so to make it a parliament of love'.[25]

In 1614, the reliance on sub-committees for the handling of business which had gained momentum in the parliament of 1610 was maintained and refined. On 12 May, anticipating a conference with the Lords after the Easter break, members of the lower House landed Whitelocke and a number of colleagues, who had distinguished themselves in 1610, with the task of preparing a new case against impositions. For those nominated to the task, this exercise involved refining rather than constructing a case. Of the group Sir Edwin Sandys, Sir Roger Owen, Thomas Crew, Nicholas Hyde, Thomas Wentworth, John Hoskins and William Hakewill had all worked with Whitelocke in 1610. Two other barristers – Charles Chibborne and Dudley Digges – were new faces.[26]

Judging by Whitelocke's notes in the *Liber Famelicus*, they quickly organised a comprehensive argument to present to the Lords. The level of cooperation achieved among them is suggested by his account

---

25 *Proceedings in Parliament 1614*, pp. 148-9.

26 *Proceedings in Parliament 1614*, pp. xiii-xxxvi; 'Parliamentary Diary for 1614' in *Commons Debates in 1621*, ed. W. Notestein, F.H. Relf and H. Simpson, 7 vols (New Haven 1935), vol. 7, p. 638 [hereafter cited as *Commons Debates in 1621*].

> Sir Edwyn Sandes was to shew that the king's imposing without assent of parliament was contrarye to the naturall fram and constitution of the policye of our kingdom, as that it was a righte of majestye and soveraigne power whiche the kings of England could not exercise but in parliament, as that of law making, naturalising, *ultima provocatio*, and the like.
>
> Mr. Thomas Crew was to shew the reason and judgement of the common law of the land, that whiche is *jus privatum* or *contentiosum* to be the same.
>
> I was appoynted to begin to shew the practise of the state in the verye poynt, as being the best evidence to shew whether it wear a soveraignty belonging to the king in parliament or out of parliament, and to me was assigned the raignes of Edward I., Edward II., and Edward III., the heat of all the busenesse.

Following Whitelocke, Wentworth and Hoskyns were to continue his argument from the fiftieth year of Edward III's reign until the third and fourth years of Phillip and Mary, Nicholas Hyde was to follow it from this time into the present, while Jones, Chibborne and Hakewill answered objections raised by the House. Owen, Digges and Sandys would conclude with a general consideration of the English political system, and of impositions' 'inconvenience to the common profit of the kingdom'.[27]

As April turned to May, and a somewhat factious upper House debated the Commons' request for a meeting on impositions, all appearance of political harmony began to disintegrate. In what must have been a difficult situation for Whitelocke, the comments of his friend and supporter Bishop Richard Neile's against 'seditious' speeches in the lower House were met with outrage. Whitelocke is not mentioned as making any comments during his service to the committee which considered prosecuting Neile, but in the increasingly heated environment there was no longer any question of a moderate line holding sway. With no prospect of supply being granted without another politically damaging debate on impositions, James I brought this 'addled' parliament to a rapid and unsatisfactory conclusion. It ended two months after it had begun, having achieved nothing other

27 *Liber Famelicus*, p. 42; cf. *Proceedings in Parliament 1614*, pp. 213-14.

than to reopen political sores that had festered in the years since 1610.[28]

The *Liber Famelicus* leaves a strong impression of Whitelocke's feelings on the outcome of events:

> On Tuesday the 7 of June, 1614, the parliament was dissolved, in that manner that all good people wear verye sorye for it; I think it not fit to play the part of a historiographer about it, but I pray God we never see the like.

Unfortunately, it is impossible to assess the quality of Whitelocke's case on impositions in 1614 or that of his associates. The controversial character of the document in which he prepared his argument, which ran to twenty-four hand-written sides, is suggested by its physical history. Whitelocke noted that all those who had been assigned a role in the conference on impositions were summoned to the Council Chamber at Whitehall on 8 June, where they 'wear all commanded to burn our notes, arguments, and collections we had made for the preparing of ourselves to the conference'. Whitelocke watched his own notes burned before the Council as the king spied secretively from behind a hanging in the clerk's chamber.[29]

In a nervous account which repeats itself on several matters, the *Liber Famelicus* noted that four 'parliament men' – Sir Walter Shute, Christopher Neville, Thomas Wentworth, and John Hoskins – were then sent to the Tower. Sir John Savill, Sir Edward Giles, Sir Edwyn Sandys, and Sir Roger Owen were among 'divers others' who were questioned by the Council and released upon bonds of assurance, while Owen, Savill, Sir Edward Phellips, Nicholas Hyde and 'divers other' MPs were struck off the commissions of the peace. Whitelocke noted that over the following days others were also sent to the Tower for their part in a conference with Hoskins.[30]

Obviously Whitelocke must have felt himself lucky to avoid a spell in prison, leaving his readers to guess his opinion upon matters

28 *Proceedings in Parliament 1614*, pp. xxxi-xxxii; 346.

29 *Liber Famelicus*, pp. 41-2; cf. Moir, *Addled Parliament*, p. 146.

30 *Liber Famelicus*, pp. 42-3.

he 'wold not meddle witheall'. He was probably saved from harsher treatment in 1614 by the conciliatory tone of his speeches, which left him free to reflect from a distance on the price of political dissent. Here it seems that a degree of pragmatism accompanied disappointment. Assessing the rumour that his friend Sir Edward Phellips had died through an illness exacerbated by the king's displeasure with his son's parliamentary activities, he wrote 'I cannot think a man can be sutche a mope.' It seems that with a resilient disposition to accompany his strong views, Whitelocke returned his attention to the business of the bar. By the time of the next parliamentary session, seven years on, Whitelocke's legal advancement would hinder his involvement.[31]

III

In December 1620, as King James summoned his third parliament in strained domestic and foreign circumstances, James Whitelocke was elected to represent Woodstock for the final time. Although Whitelocke's position as chief justice of Chester did not preclude him from sitting in parliament, the *Liber Famelicus* suggests that routine judicial business at Ludlow between January and March, and then circuit work in Chester beginning in April, kept him away from parliament until early in May. On 5 May he relegated his continuing legal duties at Bewdley to his puisne, Sir Henry Townshend, as he 'went up and sat in Parliament'. It may be that Whitelocke, who stayed for just one day, knew that pressure was being mounted in the Commons to declare his election null and void; on 22 March it was asked in the House: 'whither Whitlocke, Justice of Chester, not coming… a new choise shalbe made.'[32]

---

31 *Liber Famelicus*, p. 43.

32 *Liber Famelicus*, pp. 84; 88-9; History of Parliament Trust; *Commons Debates in 1621*, vol. 6, p. 81.Williams, *Parliamentary History of Oxford*, p. 199. For a discussion of the parliament of 1621 cf. Russell, *Parliaments and English Politics*

It is certain that Whitelocke was in the House between 16 and 29 May, during which time he was named to two committees to consider legal bills and one for a bill on Lichfield parish, and was ordered to assist Sir Julius Caesar in reporting the adjournment conference of 29 May. On 4 June the House of Commons ordered that two bailiffs who had violated parliamentary privilege by arresting one of Whitelocke's servants 'shall aske forgivenes at the barr upon ther knees of the howse and Sir James Whitlock', but of Whitelocke himself, who was keeping term at Bewdley again by 18 June, we hear nothing more.[33]

Whitelocke cannot be fairly be criticised for failing to appear in parliament while important duties (discussed in chapter 6) awaited in Chester and Wales. His changing station in life may also have made a prolonged stay in the Commons politically uncomfortable as the administration of the border shires became, for yet another of James's parliaments, a contentious issue. Notes in Whitelocke's possession analyse the strengths and weaknesses of a petition 'cited by the House of Commons as desiring a redresse of a Grievance concerning four Counties', arguing that any 'alteration from the government' of the Marches was 'a noveltie and therefore dangerous'. Writing to Whitelocke on the last day of February 1621, the earl of Northampton informed him of a 'general desire' to repeal a clause in the 1543 act, which gave the king exclusive power to appoint judges to the Court of Great Sessions by commission. Whitelocke replied on 8 March that he had been present during earlier parliamentary debates on the matter, suggesting that if the clause was repealed 'there must be special saving and provision for the full upholding and maintaining of the King's power of altering, adding, and administering the Instructions for this Court'. Yet the issue of impositions was the one on which Whitelocke had risen to prominence in the Commons, and

1621-1629 (Oxford 1979); Robert Zaller, *The Parliament of 1621: A Study in Constitutional Conflict* (London 1971).

33 *Commons' Journals*, pp. 569aa, 629b, 631a, 638a, *Liber Famelicus*, p. 89; *Commons Debates in 1621*, vol. 5, p. 197; cf. vol. 3, p. 335, vol. 2, p. 426.

with its retreat from parliamentary consciousness, his impact on events also diminished.[34]

IV

It is not surprising that historians have found it difficult to situate James Whitelocke's parliamentary 'opposition' to impositions within the 'consensual' revisionist framework of early Stuart politics. His example makes the point that while no coherent group of 'rivals' can be said to have existed in opposition to the Crown in 1610, committees were rapidly formed which served as a nucleus for opposition to particular Crown policies. Dominated, as they were, by lawyers and antiquarians, these committees formed a 'particular public' and promoted a particular constitutional perspective.[35]

The Crown's reception of such issue-dominated 'opposition' indicates the hazards of political dissent. In light of Ellesmere's brief to the Privy Council against those that 'quarrel and impeach his Majesty's prerogative... touching his right and power of impositions and rates of merchandises', it needs emphasising that seven of the eleven members of the parliamentary committee on impositions were formally censured for opposing the interests of the Crown between 1603 and 1621. Most lost municipal or provincial office, and five

---

34 Longleat Papers vol. 24, fols 81-4; HMC *13th Report* IV, pp. 260-1 (Dovaston MS fols 104v). Jacobean debate over the legal implications of this act (34 & 35 Henry VIII, c. 26, reprinted in *Statutes of the Realm*, vol. 3 pp. 926-37) has been extensively discussed in P. Roberts, 'Wales and England after the Tudor 'union': Crown, principality and parliament, 1543-1624' in *Law and government under the Tudors* ed. C. Cross, D. Loades & J.J. Scarisbrick (Cambridge, 1988), pp. 111-138, and cf. D.X. Powell, 'Sir James Whitelocke, Chief Justice of Chester 1620-1624', *Transactions of the Historic Society of Lancashire and Cheshire* (1993), pp. 18-21.

35 For the nature of parliamentary political 'opposition' of otherwise cf. in particular Mark Kishlansky, 'The Emergence of Adversary Politics in the Long Parliament', *Journal of Modern History* 49 (1977), pp. 617-40.

served terms in prison. King James saved his fiercest invective for those 'wrangling lawyers' that would have his prerogative 'tossed like tennis balls in the House', but the Crown's response to political opposition was hardly rhetorical.[36]

Whitelocke's own example stresses that political dissent held a somewhat precarious place in the confined world of Jacobean law and politics. His close friend Humphrey May, who as groom of the Privy Chamber could be expected to know the king's mind, told Whitelocke after the session had ended 'that the king had taken offence at my actions in parliament, in maynteyning the cause of impositions so stifly', warning him that in political terms he 'had doon good no way by it, but had hurt myself very mutche'. Whitelocke's parliamentary conduct may well have cast a pall over his subsequent career. In 1613, he was imprisoned for criticism of government policy. In 1618, both Whitelocke and Thomas Crew were named by the king as men whom he would not permit to hold the office of recorder of London, leading Whitelocke to surmise that his parliamentary conduct had jeopardised his chances of election to office.[37]

Placing James Whitelocke's speech on impositions into a constitutional context is not easy. While most would agree that Whitelocke stepped out onto new ground in 1610, exactly where he went, or indeed where he had come from, is open to question. Many commentators have treated his argument for the supreme power of king-in-

---

36 Thomas Egerton, 'Special Observations Touching all the Sesssions of the Last Parliament' (1611); Ellesmere MS 2599, reprinted in *Proceedings in Parliament 1610*, vol. 1, Appendix II, pp. 279-80 [and cf. *Law and Politics*, pp. 254-62]; PRO SP 14/8/93 'James to the Council, 7 December 1610'. The censured MPs were James Whitelocke, Thomas Wentworth, Nicholas Fuller, John Hoskins, Sir Roger Owen, Sir Edwyn Sandys, and Sir Robert Cotton.

37 *Liber Famelicus*, pp. 32-3. It is interesting, that May 'did continually inculcate' this warning to Whitelocke long after parliament had ended, until, Whitelocke noted, he did run into trouble with the Crown. The forthcoming History of Parliament Trust biography suggests that a single comment, made by Whitelocke during the fifth session against the thirty members closeted by the King, led to James's displeasure. I would place far greater emphasis upon May's exact words.

parliament as a progression from contemporary views, marking a shift in constitutional thinking that would eventually find fuller development in parliamentary arguments levelled against Charles I. Derek Hirst, echoing the view of Kenyon twenty years ago, has argued that in 1610 Whitelocke was 'alone' in finding a clear view of the balance between king and parliament, while 'the rest remained in the morass'. Hirst does not make it explicit whether Whitelocke stumbled or strode towards this higher intellectual ground. Weston and Greenberg, and more recently Burgess, have attempted to relocate Whitelocke's views by arguing that his concept of a king-in-parliament would find fruition in royalist, and not parliamentary arguments during the civil war. Arguing for the essentially conservative character of the concept of the 'king-in-parliament', Conrad Russell has suggested the need to look back to the speeches of Lord Burghley for an Elizabethan parallel to Whitelocke's arguments.[38]

This range of interpretations suggests that before one can place Whitelocke's arguments within a firm constitutional context, such

---

38 Rabb & Hirst, 'Revisionism Revised', p. 88; Burgess, *Politics of the Ancient Constitution*, pp. 143-4, and cf. C.C. Weston & J.R. Greenberg, *Subjects & Sovereigns: The Grand Controversy over Legal Sovereignty in Stuart England* (Cambridge 1981), p. 19; J.W. Gough, *Fundamental Law in English Constitutional History* (Oxford 1955), pp. 58-60. Kenyon originally noted that Whitelocke was the only man able to rise above the 'incorrigible antiquarianism of the Commons'; *Stuart Constitution*, 1st ed., p. 56). Russell's comparison with Burghley was made to me during private conversation in March 1992, but see Conrad Russell, 'English Parliaments 1593-1606: One Epoch or Two?' in *The Parliaments of Elizabethan England*, ed. D.M. Dean and N.L. Jones (London 1990), pp. 191-213, and cf. G.R. Elton, *England under the Tudors* (London 1955), p. 14; J.S. Roskell, *Parliaments and Politics in Late Medieval England*, 3 vols (London 1981), p. 464. For 'constitutional' views on Whitelocke see *Constitutional Documents*, p. 245; *Divine Right and Democracy: An Anthology of Political Writing in Stuart England*, ed. David Wootton, (London 1986), p. 34; Sommerville, *Politics & Ideology*, p. 179; the Earl of Birkenhead went so far as to suggest that the logical fruition of Whitelocke's arguments were found in the Settlement of 1688; *Diary and Correspondence of John Evelyn, F.R.S.*, 4 vols (London 1862), vol. 1, p. 27.

context must be defined. Yet as Oakely and Levack have observed, constitutional theory at the turn of the seventeenth century was, to say the least, vague. Roskell has noted that what 'really mattered in medieval political life was that the king should govern responsibly, not who should be responsible for government', and this sentiment was maintained in the political language of Jacobean England. Whitelocke's 1610 speech emphasises that early Stuart political thought was more heterodox in outlook and influences than has sometimes been assumed and that it was characterised by competing notions of the nature of the contract between the king and his subjects. Perhaps unwittingly, Whitelocke's argument recast 'customary' precedents in such a way as to shift emphasis away from a particular political issue to broader constitutional definitions of sovereignty. By proposing a definition of sovereignty in 1610 which advocated a clear measure of parliamentary control over royal policy, Whitelocke was undoubtedly right to note in his diary that he had 'expressed the most alledged for the righte of the subject'.[39]

And what of the ideological force of his argument? Russell's *Causes of the English Civil War* has stressed the inconsistent, and, in Russell's eyes, incoherent nature of early Stuart parliamentary speeches touching the contract between king and parliament. Pointing to the basic similarities between James I's view of his obligations and that of his parliamentarians, Russell plays down the force of pre-civil war ideology as a catalyst for conflict. In part, he has rightly done so: in 1610, James Whitelocke (and no other member of the Commons) would have dared openly to question the king's personal actions or accountability. The trial of Charles I in 1649, by judging the king

39 Francis Oakely, 'Jacobean Political Theology: The Absolute and Ordinary Powers of the King', *Journal of the History of Ideas* 19 (1968), pp. 339-40; B. P. Levack, 'Law and Ideology: The Civil Law and Theories of Absolutism in Elizabethan and Jacobean England' in *Historical Renaissance*, p. 226; Roskell, *Parliaments and Politics*, p. 13; Daly, 'Cosmic Harmony and Political Thinking in Early Stuart Society', *Transactions of the American Philosophical Society* 69 no. 7 (1979), p. 18; Condren, *Language of Politics*, p. 6; *Liber Famelicus*, p. 24.

unfit to rule over a system in which he was sovereign, represented not only a political breakdown but the collapse of a mental culture. How then, do Whitelocke's views hold relevance to later events?[40]

In his desire to balance the teleological histories of the past, Russell may have overlooked the way in which ideas, and particularly publicly-recorded ideas preserved in manuscript or printed form, built bridges in people's consciousness during the reigns of James and Charles I. By making particular conceptions of reality seem predictable and logical, previously expressed theories of political sovereignty were the stepping stones which provided people with the confidence to move into uncharted waters. In this sense, what went before 1642 was entirely significant, because it was something to grasp, something to re-read and reinterpret in light of present troubles. In this context, the impact of James Whitelocke's speech on impositions, touching several hundred men at best, was far less significant than the impact of the manuscript treatise prepared from it.

The Crown's vigilance in monitoring constitutional manuscripts is fairly demonstrated in Whitelocke's case, which also suggests, in the final instance, the source of such anxiety. In 1613 Whitelocke was made to recant opinions expressed in a 1609 tract on the naval commission, which was apparently destroyed. In 1614 the speech he had refined for a renewed parliamentary attack upon impositions was burned by royal order. His 1610 speech captured historical attention because it survived. Presented together with the Commons' petition to the king, this treatise was widely circulated in manuscript form after the session ended, and further copied from prepared manuscript versions, as by Sir John Davies in his notes on the debate. In 1641, the speech made its way from the printing press as *A learned and necessary argument to Prove that each Subject hath a Propriety in his*

40 Russell, Causes of the *English Civil War*, p. 160, and cf. Sharpe, *Politics and Ideas*, pp. 64-5.

Goods in the opening shots of a propaganda war with the king that would reach its climax in 1649.[41]

Once preserved, Whitelocke's arguments on impositions were always open to reinterpretation in a shifting political context, a context with which Whitelocke himself would have been, by the end, entirely unfamiliar. Looking back on events in 1640, his own son argued that his father had been a 'stout assertor of the rights and liberties of the free-born subjects of the Kingdom' and had suffered 'particularly by a straight and close imprisonment for what he did as a member of this house in a former parliament'. As Whitelocke's parliamentary voice reflected and fuelled broader political discourses in 1610 and 1614, it marked him as an articulate and, for some, a troublesome figure who must be brought into line.[42]

41 A brief search of the major English manuscript repositories for Whitelocke's 1610 speech revealed four copies: BL Additional MS 36,082, fols 105-76v; BL Stowe MS 298, fols 89-140v; CUL MS Dd. 2.25; Lincoln's Inn MS Maynard 52 (4). For Davies' notes see CUL MS Ff .3.17, fols 73-113.

42 Whitelock, *Memorials* (1732), p. 38 and see Blair Worden, 'The '*Diary*' of Bulstrode Whitelocke', *English Historical Review* 153 (1993), pp. 122-134.

Chapter 5

Politics out of parliament

William Shakespeare, whose fame was already considerable by the time James Whitelocke began his long association with the royal courts of law, had Tranio urge his listeners in *The Taming of the Shrew* to

> do as adversaries do in law
> Strive mightily, but eat and drink as friends.

Tranio's admonition raises questions about consensus and conflict in the legal arena of early Stuart England which historians continue to debate. At the heart of these issues is the impact of legal argument upon broader political debate, at a time when the day-to-day business of central government was carried out at the royal court amid factional rivalry and tangled webs of political intrigue.[1]

The role of patronage marks a point of collision between Whig and revisionist thinking on the independence and 'initiative', or otherwise, of members of the House of Commons in the early decades of the seventeenth century. While Whig historians have been drawn to public documents such as parliamentary and legal speeches as evidence of the constitutional tensions at work in early Stuart England, revisionists have pointed to the less highly-visible hand of patronage as a source of political faction and intrigue. Clearly, there is a case for both. James Whitelocke's experience bridged a watershed in the history of court politics, brought about by the king's unprecedented concentration of favour into the hands of George Villiers, duke of

1 'The Taming of the Shrew', I, ii, 276-7 in *The Complete Works of William Shakespeare*, ed. J.P. Wilson (London 1980), p. 276.

Buckingham. His controversial career offers perspective on the relationships at work between public argument and professional advancement in the reign of James I.[2]

I

In a recent study of political patronage under the early Stuarts, Peck has emphasised the importance of corruption in fuelling the language of political dissent. As Henry earl of Northampton began a campaign of reform against corruption Whitelocke was drawn into unhappy involvement with court politics as legal advocate for Sir Robert Mansell, Sir Henry Neville and a number of other courtiers. In 1608, at Northampton's instigation, King James established a royal commission of enquiry into naval corruption, attacking Admiral Sir Charles Howard and his deputy Sir Robert Mansell. Replying to a report which argued that 'two of the chief officers' of the navy 'have conveyed all or most of the chiefest offices of trust and profit either by possession or reversion to the hands of their own followers', Whitelocke prepared a legal defence, now lost, in order to challenge the inquiry. In the short term, Whitelocke's legal defence of the Department of the Navy was of less significance than the king's reluctance to pursue to naval reform, which turned Northampton's recommendations into a 'fruitless' exercise.[3]

---

2 Cf., for example, Russell, 'Parliamentary History in Perspective'; Sharpe, *Politics and Ideas*, pp. 78-87; *Faction and Parliament*, pp. 1-42; Rabb & Hirst, 'Revisionism Revised', pp. 55-99; David Underdown, *A Freeborn People: Politics and the Nation in Seventeenth-Century England* (Oxford, 1996) pp. 1-7.

3 Peck, *Court Patronage and Corruption*, *passim*; Peck, 'Court Patronage and Government Policy', pp. 34; 36-7; L.L. Peck, 'Corruption at the Court of James I: The Undermining of Legitimacy' in *After the Reformation: essays in honour of J.H. Hexter*, ed. B.C. Malament (Manchester 1980), p. 89; Lockyer, *Early Stuarts*, p. 88; *The Jacobean Commissions of Enquiry, 1608 and 1616*, ed. A.P. McGowan, Navy Record Society 116 (1971); Sir Ralph Winwood, *Memorials of affairs of state*, 3 vols (London 1725), vol. 3, p. 462.

Whitelocke's willingness to challenge the naval commission of enquiry, and a reputation in constitutional argument enhanced by his parliamentary activities, marked him out as a controversial legal figure of some ability. Linking his obstructions to Crown directives in an out of parliament, Peck has suggested that Whitelocke was motivated by a desire to set limits on the royal prerogative. It seems more likely that his public voice flowed from a dogmatic view of common-law rights, rather than from any conscious desire to contest the issue of legislative sovereignty. In 1613, Whitelocke would be forced to weigh the cost of such outspokenness.[4]

Whitelocke's troubles with the Crown escalated in 1613 with a controversial legal challenge to the Court of Earl Marshal, discussed in chapter 3. The essence of Whitelocke's legal argument was the jurisdiction of the Earl Marshal's Court, whose commissioners maintained in a formal quasi-judicial manner a domestic jurisdiction over the College of Arms and the heralds, lapsed in the absence of a High Constable. By his actions in this case, Whitelocke again set himself on a collision course with the powerful Howard family, as Henry earl of Northampton, and his cousin Thomas, earl of Suffolk, were the principal commissioners of the Earl Marshal's Court.[5]

Whitelocke was particularly unfortunate that he was forced to present his case against the Earl Marshal's jurisdiction to Lord Ellesmere in Chancery. In this late stage in his career, Ellesmere appears to have assumed an antagonistic stance towards the courts of common law and their practitioners, and it is likely that he had already been aggravated by Whitelocke's vocal opposition to Crown policies in 1610. In Whitelocke's account of events, Ellesmere's desire to 'give him an item for olde desertes' had intensified in a previous cause

4 Peck, *Court Patronage and Corruption*, p. 113; Peck, 'Court Patronage and Government Policy', pp. 34; 36-7; Peck, 'Corruption at the Court of James I', p. 89.

5 Squibb, *High Court of Chivalry*, p. 39; Plott, 'A defence of the jurisdiction of the Earl Marshal's Court', p. 260. Whitelocke obviously appraised the king's commission to the officers of the Court of Earl Marshal, which is preserved in the Longleat Papers, vol. 1, fol. 42.

before Chancery, in which Whitelocke had prepared a defence for the College of Westminster (of which he was steward) against the bishop of London. The *Liber Famelicus* implies that Ellesmere had done everything in his power to favour the bishop in this case, redirecting the cause three times and leaving the legal counsel for Westminster almost no time to prepare their argument.[6]

As Whitelocke cited legal precedents to refute the authority of the Court of Earl Marshal, a characteristically acerbic Ellesmere

> began openly and sharply to invey against those lawyers that studyed prerogative, and by name condemned Mr. Whitelocke for one of them, and taxed him in this case that he had denyed the king's power to give authority to the commissioners to keep a court.

Realising at this point that he was in trouble, he attempted to turn their disagreement back to legal technicalities, but Ellesmere declared that he would 'appeal to the king in this particular, and would acquaint him with this great affront made to his regal power'. Unfortunately for the embattled Whitelocke, his legal work for Sir Robert Mansell was known to Ellesmere, who now used it to convince the king of Whitelocke's repeated intransigence towards royal authority, requesting his censure. Swayed by Ellesmere and the Howards, the king agreed for Whitelocke to be summoned before the Privy Council. Brought before them for questioning on Tuesday 18 May 1613, he testified and was sentenced on the same day to imprisonment at his majesty's pleasure.[7]

Whitelocke's troubles may be viewed, on one hand, as the natural consequence of his involvement in faction and intrigue. As Northampton moved against his opponents, armed with Whitelocke's 1609 naval argument, Sir Robert Mansell was also imprisoned and others at court were quick to distance themselves from events. In a

---

6 *Liber Famelicus*, pp. 33-5; Prest, *Rise of the Barristers*, p. 303; Baker, *Legal Profession*, pp. 205-29.

7 *Liber Famelicus*, pp. 31-2; 36; *Acts of the Privy Council 1613/14*, pp. 28, 41; *Calendar of State Papers Domestic: James I 1611-1618*, p. 186 (13 June, 1613).

letter from Sir Henry Neville to Sir Ralph Winwood of 18 June 1613, Neville noted that he had been cleared of an allegation 'that I had some hand in the matter wherewith Sir Robert Mansell and Mr. Whitlock were charged'. Mansel also attempted to divorce himself from the views of Whitelocke as much as he could, writing to Sir John Holles from the Fleet prison that he 'would have gained their lordships better opinion of me and my cause then they or the heavens could guess at considering the way I gave to extenuate Mr. Whitlock's offence'.[8]

The other evidence that attests to Whitelocke's alliances at court is equally cryptic. Upon Neville's death in July 1615, Whitelocke reflected that he

> was a most faytheful frend unto me, *tam in adversis quam secundis*, and I dealt as well withe him, for at the time I was committed to the Fleet, he was hunted after by the erl of Northampton, as the author of the opposition against that irregular commission... but, althoughe he was an actor in it withe far greater men, yet his good lordship could never finde it out, notwithstanding he cawsed me to be kept close prisoner and examined by the lords of the counsell; the truthe is, he durst not name him playnly, althoughe he aymed at him, and I had reason enoughe to conceal him.

Such concealment led Whitelocke to prepare a separate and detailed account of events which he intended to insert in the *Liber Famelicus* 'as those do fail who I know will be readye to take advantages against me'; it may well have perished with the dispersal and partial destruction of his papers during the Civil Wars. No copy of his 1609 naval argument appears to have survived, although brief notes among the family papers may have been used in its preparation. White-

8 Winwood, *Memorials*, vol. 3, p. 462; HMC *Portland* IX, p. 40. Cf. HMC *Downshire* IV, p. 133 (Downshire Misc. MS V, fol. 83); William Norton to William Trumbull, London, 10 June 1613: 'Sir Robert Mansfield has been three weeks in Marshalsea. His cause is heard today before his Majesty and the Privy Council, together with a Mr. Whitelocke, a counsellor of his, now prisoner in the Fleet. The cause of his imprisonment is not certainly known.' See also Kevin Sharpe, 'The Earl of Arundel, His Circle, and Opposition to the Duke of Buckingham, 1618-1628' in *Faction and Parliament*, pp. 215-18.

locke's epitaph to Neville highlights his compliance in faction-driven obstruction to Northampton's reforms.[9]

II

Although historians have emphasised the factional nature of patronage relationships in Jacobean politics, consideration of the relationship between legal patronage and political ideology remains somewhat neglected. In his study of civil lawyers in early Stuart England, Brian Levack distinguished the kind of argument that civilians employed in defence of the so-called 'prerogative' courts from those employed by their common-law associates. Civilians articulated, he suggested, 'constitutional theories which exaggerated the power of the Crown and minimised that of Parliament and of the common law judges', asserting

> that since the King was the fountain of justice who had delegated his personal jurisdiction to the judges of his various courts, he was empowered to continue to regulate that distribution of legal authority. If a dispute should arise as to where the exact boundary between two jurisdictions lay, the monarch alone was entitled to solve the problem.

Conversely, as Whitelocke justified his opposition to the policies of the Crown in parliament or in the courts of law, he fell back upon a particular line of argument placing emphasis on certain elements of the widely venerated (but imperfectly defined) English constitution. To get to the heart of the ideological differences which set Whitelocke and other common lawyers at odds with Crown officials such as Chancellor Ellesmere during the reign of James I, one has to explore

---

9 *Liber Famelicus*, pp. 39, 46-7; Longleat Papers, vol. 1, fol. 52. For details of the destruction of Whitelocke's papers see Bulstrode Whitelocke, *Memorials of English Affairs, or, An Historical Account of what passed from the Beginning of the Reign of King Charles the First, to King Charles the Second his happy Restauration* (London 1725), p. 65; *Contemporaries of Bulstrode Whitelocke*, ed. Ruth Spalding (Oxford 1990), p. 428.

the lines of argument by which their views on the constitution were substantiated.[10]

What knowledge there is of Whitelocke's legal challenge to the 1608 commission of inquiry comes from the record of its inspection by the Privy Council in 1613. It reports that as he questioned the jurisdictional propriety of this commission, he termed it 'irregular', 'without president', 'of a new mould', and 'such as he hoped should never have place in this Commonwealth'. The charges laid against Whitelocke also stated that 'emboldened by that which ought reallie to have refrayned him (which was his science and profession in the lawe)' he had presumed 'in a very strange and unfit manner to make an excursion into a general censure and defining [of] his Majesty's power and prerogative'. This argument was apparently derived from the 'customary' principles that had also given force to his speeches in 1610.[11]

In his second 'contempt', Whitelocke maintained that the king could 'neither by comission nor in his owne person, medle with the bodyes, goods, or landes of his subjects' except 'by legal procedinge in his ordinarie courts of justice'. The Council attacked this 'presumption' on several grounds. Whitelocke's pedantic insistence on point of law, they argued, challenged the government's right to act in affairs of state which could not be corrected by 'the remedies of justice'. Such a position was 'not onlie grossely erroneous... but daungerous, and tending to the dissolving of governmente'. In the instance before them, they argued, the naval commission was acting

---

10 Levack, *Civil Lawyers*, pp. 82-3. The relationship between Whitelocke's actions and political ideology receives fuller discussion in D.X. Powell, 'Why did James Whitelocke go to jail in 1613? "Principle" and political dissent in Jacobean England', *Australian Journal of Law & Society* 11 (1995), pp. 169-90, and cf. Sommerville, *Politics & Ideology*, *passim*; Burgess, *Politics of the Ancient Constitution*, pp. 121-9.

11 BL *Lansdowne* MS 160, fol. 83, printed as an appendix to Bruce's edition of the *Liber Famelicus*, pp. 114-18; BL Additional MS 4149, fol. 173, printed in *Works*, vol. 11, pp. 348-53; *Acts of the Privy Council 1613/14*, pp. 211-17.

for the king in a matter touching the defence of the realm, and inquiring into a government department in which

> the shippes and vessells, with all their furniture and the materials thereof, are the kings owne, and the persons whom the said commission did concerne are his officers and servants... so that his Majestie... hath a power of examinacione and correctione, not onlie as a kinge, but as a master and owner.

The Council prosecutors argued that by a misconstruction of general legal principles, Whitelocke threatened to undermine the whole system by which sovereignty was maintained.[12]

The arguments used by the Council against Whitelocke in 1613, linking a specific challenge to jurisdictional rights with a broad assault on the foundations of government, had been well rehearsed over the first decade of James's rule. Attorney-General Bacon, who later assisted Whitelocke in obtaining his pardon and release, employed almost identical arguments in the 1613 hearing as he had during a debate on the jurisdiction of the Council of the Marches in Wales seven years earlier, in which he warned that if

> the King's prerogative, the ancient and main foundation upon which this jurisdiction was built, be questioned and shaken, then of necessity the Council of York must fall... and the Court of Requests must follow... and what further may be opened to Parliament or lawyers to dispute more liberties, may rather be feared than discovered...

In incomplete notes prepared for Whitelocke's 1613 censure which survive in the Lambeth Palace Library, Bacon used a similar line of reasoning to challenge Whitelocke's 'presumptuous and licentious censure and defying of his majesty's prerogative' and 'slander and traducement of one act or emanation thereof' (the naval commission). Elaborating in characteristically florid style, Bacon found Whitelocke's offence against the king in three degrees:

> First, that he presumed to censure the king's prerogative at all. Secondly, that he runneth into the generality of it more than was pertinent to the present question.

12 *Liber Famelicus*, p. 113-14; 116.

> And lastly, that he hath erroneously and falsely, and dangerously given opinion in derogation of it.[13]

On 10 June 1613 John Chamberlain noted in a letter to Sir Ralph Winwood that 'Whitlock the lawyer is in the Fleet for two causes; first, for speaking too boldly against the authority of the Earl Marshall's Court, and then for giving his opinion that this commission was not according to law'. In the Privy Council's charge against Whitelocke and Sir Robert Mansell, the treasurer of the Navy was condemned as 'the meanes to divulge those daungerous positions tending so much to the diminution of his Majesties royal power'. These allegations emphasise that beyond their expression of factional or legal rivalry, Jacobean arguments for and against competing judicial bodies articulated competing notions of good government which acquired a controversial dimension.[14]

If Whitelocke's constitutional opinions were at the heart of affairs in 1613, it might be asked what the consequences of this kind of political dissent could be. As the Crown took steps to establish the legitimacy of the Earl Marshal's judicial powers, Chancellor Ellesmere publicly refuted Whitelocke's assertions against the Earl Marshal's Court in the Chancery decree and order books, further recording his retraction of his arguments against the naval commission in the acts of the Privy Council. Whitelocke was imprisoned in the Fleet prison from 18 May to 13 June, and there was probably a hint of truth in his mannered confession that 'hee hath most worthily drawne your Majestie's heavie displeasure upon him, and thereby is more afflicted in his own soule and conscience then hee can be by anie other calamitie of this worlde'.[15]

---

13 'A View of the Differences in Question betwixt the King's Bench and the Council in the Marches', reprinted in *Works*, vol. 10, pp. 368-80; Lambeth Palace Library, Gibson MS 936, no. 249 (2 fols), reprinted in *State Trials*, vol. 2, cols 766-8; *Works*, vol. 11, pp. 353-6.

14 Winwood, *Memorials*, vol. 3, p. 466; *Liber Famelicus*, p. 117.

15 PRO C33/126, fols 122v-123, reinforced in letters patent issued to the Earl Marshal's Court by James I in 1622; College of Arms MS SML 3, fol. 228

Whitelocke gained pardon and release by appealing to the king's 'naturall goodness, clemencie, and princely disposicion'. Professing by way of petition to King James that his 'rash and unadvised... opinion' against the naval commission was 'a matter too high and wayghtie... to intermeddle withall', Whitelocke was informed by Chancellor Ellesmere that the king was pleased with his employment of a florid sentence from Tacitus stressing the 'glory of obedience' which had been suggested by Bacon as a suitable balm for the king's angered nerves. Whitelocke concluded his briefer, surviving account of the affair in the *Liber Famelicus* with his personal motto, *nec beneficio, nec metu* (the old legal adage 'without favour or fear') and as he was at the head of a second challenge to impositions during the 1614 parliament, he seems to have taken this motto seriously.[16]

After 1613 Whitelocke was forced to side-step Ellesmere and Northampton as he pursued his career at the bar. We have seen that Whitelocke sought Robert Cotton's help to gain audience in the Earl Marshal's Court, but in the end he was probably saved from further trouble by the death of his 'ill affected frend the erl of Northampton' on 15 June 1614. Given his relations with Chancellor Ellesmere, one might reasonably conclude that Whitelocke's chances of gaining an audience in the Court of Chancery after 1613 were non-existent. However, as the Chancellor's deputy, the Master of the Rolls, was commissioned 'to hear and determine all causes in Chancery, whether the Lord Chancellor was present or not', and as the 'Lord Chancellor's political duties did not permit him to spend much time

---

reprinted in Ashman, 'Heraldry and the Law of Arms', pp. 70-1; *Acts of the Privy Council 1613/14*, pp. 41; 218-19. The warrants for Whitelocke's imprisonment and release are preserved in the Longleat Papers, vol. 1, fols 46, 47, and were copied by Whitelocke into the *Liber Famelicus*, pp. 39-40.

16 *Liber Famelicus*, p. 40; *Acts of the Privy Council 1613/14*, pp. 41, 218. Quoted as Tibi summum rerum imperium Dii dederunt, nobis obedientiae gloria relicta est by Whitelocke, the passage from Tacitus reads 'tibi summum rerum iudicium di dedere, nobis obsequii gloria relicta est'; *Annals*, vol. 4, ch. 8, line 7, or in translation: 'The gods have given the greatest command to you, for us the glory of obedience has been bequeathed'.

in Chancery', Whitelocke sought to gain the favour of successive Masters of the Rolls, apparently with some success. Three presents he gave at Christmas 1614 which can reasonably interpret as seeking to enlist patronage went to Sir Edward Coke, newly appointed chief justice of the King's Bench, Sir John Croke, Whitelocke's uncle and another judge of that court, and Sir Julius Caesar, newly appointed Master of the Rolls in the Court of Chancery, who as a member of the Privy Council had taken notes at Whitelocke's 1613 hearing. Caesar gained the Chancery appointment following the death of Whitelocke's 'verye good frend' Sir Edward Phellips in September 1614. It thus seems reasonable to conjecture that Ellesmere's animosity did not entirely shut off Whitelocke's options in the Court of Chancery, and that support from the Master of the Rolls may explain his continued presence in the records of that court after 1613.[17]

An unhappy chapter in Whitelocke's life ended with the passing of Chancellor Ellesmere on 15 March 1617. Whitelocke wasted no sentiment on a man who had in recent years caused him considerable personal and professional grief, concluding:

> It had been good for this commonwealth if he had been out of the world 20 years before, for he was the greatest enemy to the common law that did ever bear office

---

17 Prest, *Rise of the Barristers*, p. 27; Sharpe, *Sir Robert Cotton*, pp. 41-2; Peck, 'Corruption at the Court of James I', pp. 34-5; Bodleian MS Smith 71, fol. 59; BL Cottonian MS Julius C. III, fol. 89; *Liber Famelicus*, pp. 27, 30, 39, 43, 45, 76-7; John Haywarde, *Les Reportes del Cases in Camera Stellata*, pp. 338-41; Bodl. MS Smith 71, fol. 59; BL MS Cott. Jul. C.3, fol. 54; CUL MS Gg. 2.23, fol. 90. BL Lansdowne MS 160, fol. 83; *Liber Famelicus*, p. 45; L.M. Hill, *Bench and Bureaucracy: The Public Career of Sir Julius Caesar, 1580-1636* (Stanford 1988), pp. 195-7; 200-3; Mervyn James, *Society, Politics & Culture: Studies in early modern England* (Cambridge 1986), pp. 330-1. Tracing Whitelocke's business through the voluminous decree and order books, Clendenin has suggested that he was heard in at least five causes each term in either King's Bench, Chancery, Exchequer or Requests in the years between 1600 and 1612; T. Clendenin, 'The Common Lawyers in Parliament and Society: A Social and Political Study of the Common Lawyers in the First Jacobean Parliament' (1975 University of North Carolina Ph.D), p. 47.

of state in this kingdom; he was thereupon termed viscount Breaklaw for viscount Brakely.

His thoughts were, in this instance, kept private. By opening up grounds for political controversy between 1609 and 1614, Whitelocke's parliamentary and legal actions educated him about the price of political dissent. By the time he began to censor his own comments in the *Liber Famelicus* in 1613, Whitelocke may have seen that his arguments were condemned as much for their theoretical challenge to the Crown's exercise of sovereignty as anything else. In the aftermath of the 1614 parliament he was quieter in public about the constitutional rights of the subject.[18]

By 1615, Whitelocke had come to appreciate that a dogmatic insistence upon the constraining force of the common-law, such as that pursued by Sir Edward Coke, placed common lawyers in an invidious situation. In 1616, Whitelocke noted Ellesmere's 'bitter invective' during his famous legal battle with Coke with concern, rating the sacked chief justice 'the most just, honest, and incorrupt judge that ever sate on benche'. The price of his own legal dissent was, from this time, carefully weighed. In a peculiar document among Whitelocke's private papers, he wrote under numbered headings that 'The absolute prerogative of the crowne is no subject for the tongue of a lawyer', 'It is presumption and treason in a subject to dispute what a king may doe', 'Presume not to meddle with kings against the king's prerogative or power' and so on, in a list of the king's favourite aphorisms about 'wrangling' lawyers. Most of these sayings seem to be taken from the king's remarks in the *Case of Commendams* (1616) and may have served for Whitelocke as a reminder to avoid contesting, or even defining, the nature of political sovereignty.[19]

---

18 *Liber Famelicus*, p. 39.

19 *Liber Famelicus*, pp. 48, 51, 53; Baker, *Legal Profession*, p. 225; Longleat Papers, vol. 24, fols 393-4.

III

By 1616, James Whitelocke had outflanked and outlived his enemies at court, as the surviving generation of Elizabethan courtiers disappeared from the political landscape. His rise from barrister to serjeant at law and chief justice of Chester in 1620 shadows the emergence of the duke of Buckingham as an increasingly powerful patron of royal office. Concern about Buckingham's manipulation of patronage in judicial appointments provided a focus for opposition to the inordinate influence he wielded in the second decade of the seventeenth century, and from 1614 observations in the *Liber Famelicus* suggest a growing sense of distress over Buckingham's power over judicial appointments and Crown manipulation of the bench.[20]

In 1614 Whitelocke condemned a request by the Crown for £600 in return for acceptance of the position of serjeant-at-law, many candidates for which 'were not worthe the money, and sum never likely to see it halfe againe in their practise'. It was a payment, he noted, that his friend and relative George Croke refused to make on matter of principle, 'bycaus he sayd he thought it was not for the king'. In 1616, Whitelocke noted the fortunes of three of his long-time associates from the Oxford circuit, John Walter, Thomas Coventry and Sir Henry Yelverton, with concern. It was widely suspected that Coventry's rise to power was gained through Buckingham's patronage, and Whitelocke inferred that something was amiss in his assessment of the situation:

> Mr. Thomas Coventree... a green reader, being newly chosen recorder of London, came to be sollicitor and knighted... how and *quibus gradibus ascendit ad hæc culmina, quære.* Mr. John Walter, the prince's attorney, the fittest man in England

20 Peck, *Court Patronage and Corruption*, p. 66 and *passim*; Hirst, 'Court, Country and Politics', p. 111; cf. Wilfrid Prest, 'Judicial Corruption in Early Modern England', *Past & Present* 133 (1991), pp. 80-1. For the rise of Buckingham cf. Hill, *Bench and Bureaucracy*, p. 196; Lockyer, *Buckingham*, pp. 53-88.

for it, and ancient to Mr. Coventree a dozen years or more, was omitted, whome all the world had destinated to the place.[21]

Whitelocke's concern with Buckingham's influence was also clear in his discussion of Sir Henry Yelverton's contested promotion to the rank of attorney-general. Recounting at length a conversation with Yelverton, the *Liber Famelicus* recalled how, after King James had advised the Privy Council of his determination to have Yelverton advance to that office, some of its members were made aware that Buckingham had extended his patronage elsewhere. After a string of courtiers had failed to convince Yelverton to give up the office, Buckingham sought tacit acknowledgment that the appointment depended upon Buckingham's favour, which he was happy to provide 'notwithstanding Sir James Lea had offered 10,000l. to have the place'. Yelverton professed to Whitelocke 'that he nether gave to the erl nor to any other subject in the kingdom on farthing to cum into the place, nor contracted anything, nor promised anything', although he 'freely... of his dutye' gave the king £4000, but Whitelocke could hardly fail to see the pyrrhic nature of Yelverton's victory.[22]

In a series of notes set down 'for posteritye to know the course of things in our profession' Whitelocke made it clear that Buckingham's increasing dominance over legal patronage threatened not just the integrity but the competence of the judiciary. In 1616 Anthony Ben, at that time a bencher of the Middle Temple, was made recorder of London, an office that Whitelocke noted had been 'procured by a great on about him, to wit, the erl of Buckingham'. In Whitelocke's estimation Ben was 'well enough spoken', but Walter Pye, also a Middle Templar but in this case only an utter-barrister, was promoted to a Welsh circuit from which Sir George Snigg had been displaced 'by the meanes of the erl of Buckingham'. Even more troubling was the appointment of Sir Robert Naunton as Surveyor of the Court of Wards through the patronage of Lady Compton (Buckingham's

21 *Liber Famelicus*, pp. 44, 53-4; Lockyer, *Buckingham*, p. 40.
22 *Liber Famelicus*, p. 55-7.

mother); Whitelocke noted with concern that in this instance an appointment 'ever held by men lerned in the law' had gone to 'a scholler, but meer stranger to the law'.[23]

Whitelocke saved his harshest criticism for Sir Lionel Cranfield, whose spectacular rise to power became a major criticism in parliamentary proceedings against Buckingham in 1626. Whitelocke belittled Cranfield as an apprentice boy 'thrust into the acquayntance of great men' and a man poorly qualified to hold the position of Master of Requests, to which he ascended in 1616 'by the erl of Buckingham's meanes'. The Mastership, Whitelocke lamented in light of Cranfield's appointment, was 'a place requiring a man lerned, ether in the civill or common lawes, and so they have allwayes been'.[24]

Buckingham's inordinate power over court affairs was personally demonstrated during a flurry of interest in the lucrative clerkship of enrolments in King's Bench, so long in the hands of the Roper family that it had become known as 'Roper's Office'. In July 1612 Whitelocke was promoted by Sir John Harrington as an agent to hold a joint patent to the clerkship in return for eight percent of the proceeds. Harrington aligned himself with the earl of Somerset who put in Robert Heath as the other agent, but following Harrington's death Somerset moved to gain control of Whitelocke's patent, and Whitelocke was forced to forgo an active role in the management of the clerkship in return for a one-off payment of £800.[25]

With Somerset's fall from royal favour in 1616, Whitelocke may have hoped to gain some advantage from his nominal role as patentee, but he quickly found out that Buckingham was, if anything, more capable than Carr in asserting his authority over the sinecure, and

---

23 *Liber Famelicus*, pp. 54-5.

24 Prest, *Rise of the Barristers*, p. 141; *Liber Famelicus*, pp. 54-5.

25 Baker, *Legal Profession*, pp. 83-4; Stone, *The Crisis of the Aristocracy 1558-1641* (Oxford 1965), p. 444; G.E. Aylmer, *The King's Servants: The Civil Service of Charles I 1625-1642*, 2nd ed. (London 1974), p. 214; *Liber Famelicus*, pp. 27, 46.

Whitelocke was 'blowen out of the office of the Kinges Benche' in November 1616. While Sir John Roper, who was technically still in control of the patent, appears to have backed Whitelocke to keep his place as a joint-patentee in the office, Buckingham was keen to see Robert Shute gain control of the rights. Whitelocke condemned Shute in private as Buckingham's 'hangby and petifogger', but there was little he could do to stop him from taking his place short of begging the duke to accept his own allegiance.[26]

On 18 November 1616 Whitelocke was ordered to relinquish control of the patent into the hands of Chief Justice Montagu, who had replaced Sir Edward Coke as the supreme legal functionary after Coke's recent dismissal. Whitelocke claimed that Montagu was paid £500 for his compliance in this matter, undermining the supposed impartiality of the chief justice in but one of many areas in which technically came under his control. In refusing to seek Buckingham's favour, Whitelocke noted that Heath had managed to retain his position of patentee, remarking that 'Heathe dealt suspiciously in this matter, and I doubt he will never have any great katche by it'. In fact, as Buckingham became the sole patron of the office following the death of Sir John Roper in October 1618, Heath retained his patent (and his share of the proceeds). Whitelocke noted privately that the new patentees 'will be but bankers, or cashemen, at the erl of Bukingham's command', but there may have been a whiff of desperation in his conclusion that 'I am a freeman, and hope so to continue'. The price of this freedom was brought home once and for all in his failed attempt, two years later, to gain the office of recorder of London.[27]

---

26 *Liber Famelicus*, p. 58.

27 W.J. Jones, *The Elizabethan Court of Chancery* (Oxford 1967), p. 22; Kopperman, *Sir Robert Heath*, p. 16; *Liber Famelicus*, pp. 58-9.

IV

In the period 1603-1642 the city of London and the royal court several times vied for influence over civic appointments, and the complex political machinations that ensued at election time are nowhere better evidenced than in the 1618 election. In November 1618, Richard Martin, who claimed the office of recorder of London less than two months earlier from Anthony Ben, died of smallpox. Whitelocke claimed that Martin had gained office through 'the sollicitation' of Sir Lionel Cranfield, and even suggested that Martin's illness was exacerbated by his inability to meet Cranfield's demand for £1500 in gratitude for the appointment. Cranfield sought this money to repay Sir Edward Zouche, and Martin's death on 7 November left him £1500 out of pocket, and eager to gain some advantage from his trouble. He sent for Whitelocke the morning after, who was 'advised to cum in as a peeser up' of the 'bracke' between Zouche and Cranfield.[28]

As Whitelocke accepted Cranfield's offer, one can see the shifting sands upon which his own political fortunes were henceforth constructed. Having criticised Cranfield as 'an apprentice boy... thrust into the acquaintance of great men' in 1616, Whitelocke reinvented him three years later as the 'sun of a citizen...free of the mercers [who]... came into the notice of the king by shewing diligence and circumspection in the case of his profit'. By 1618, Cranfield's prominence at court was an established fact, and Whitelocke, canvassing support for his nomination to the recordership among the aldermen

28 Valerie Pearl, *London and the Outbreak of the Puritan Revolution: City Government and National Politics, 1625-1643* (Oxford 1961), *passim*; *Liber Famelicus*, pp. 63-4; Guildhall Corporation Record Office, Report of the Court of Aldermen 33, fol. 403; *Calendar of State Papers Domestic James I 1611-1618*, p. 591: November 7, 'John Pory to Carleton', 'John Chamberlain to Carleton'. For the rewards and responsibilities of the recordership cf. Kopperman, *Sir Robert Heath*, p. 20; G. Cumberlege, *The Corporation of London: Its Origin, Constitution, Powers and Duties* (London 1950), pp. 58-60; F.F. Foster, 'Merchants and Bureaucrats in Elizabethan London', *Guildhall Miscellany* 4 (1972), pp. 152-3.

and common council, was reluctant to turn down his patronage. Unfortunately for Whitelocke, Buckingham now moved to reassert his former influence over the office of recorder by promoting Robert Shute as his own candidate.[29]

As Whitelocke had seen Shute replace him in the clerkship of enrolments he was hardly free of bias, but his comments suggest that Buckingham's interest in the recordership led Crown officials to a tasteless attempt at solicitation. Written endorsements of Shute were presented to the aldermen by Sir Francis Bacon, Chief Justice Montagu and the king himself 'so soone as Mr. Martin's breathe was out of his bodye', while Montagu solicited the support of aldermen 'withe mutche gesture and importunitye' at a church service on the very day of Martin's death. Whitelocke's response was to canvass his own support with the backing of prominent aldermen including Sir William Cockayne and Sir Thomas Bennet.[30]

As Mark Kishlansky has shown, contested elections were often at great cost to social harmony. As the 1618 election for the recordership of London pitted the ambitions of two powerful courtiers against one another, it drew the Crown and the City of London into an unwanted dispute about electoral freedoms, and the *Liber Famelicus* emphasised the antagonistic nature of proceedings. On All Souls' Day 1618 Shute appeared at the Guildhall 'withe manye of his frends accompanying him' presenting himself as a candidate 'in great braverye'. Whitelocke's supporters retorted to public protests that the king, in pressing them to elect Shute, had broken an earlier promise not to interfere in the election process. They also argued that Shute had been outlawed for bankruptcy, and moved to block his nomination as 'a man knowen to be unworthye and unfit for the place'. As the 'altercation grew warm' between Shute's men and

29 Lockyer, *Early Stuarts*, pp. 87-93; *Liber Famelicus*, pp. 54, 63-4, 77.
30 *Liber Famelicus*, p. 64.

Whitelocke's supporters, the election disintegrated into a rowdy shouting match, and was abandoned by both parties.[31]

As the election broke up, the Crown and the alderman both moved to assert their influence over the election. Bacon summoned aldermen for questioning, while a delegation from the Corporation met with Buckingham and the king to request that 'they mighte, according to their charters, have a free election, without being pressed by letters'. Shute, they argued, was not eligible to stand as a candidate anyway, forcing Buckingham to press another of his clients, Robert Heath, upon the aldermen. Whitelocke showed contempt for Heath after his apparent duplicity in the dealings over Roper's Office, describing him in acid prose as 'the marqueses creature... well acquaynted with the Scotts in the bedchamber... and a great agent in new suites and projects for greedy courteours', and the aldermen found little to choose between Shute and Heath. Whitelocke noted that it 'was perceaved that the king's commendation wold not prevail', but he underestimated Buckingham's stranglehold on influence at the royal court. On the day of the election it was Whitelocke's original patron, Sir Lionel Cranfield, that arrived at the Guildhall to announce that if Heath was not to be elected 'they shold forbear to proceed until they had given his majestie reasons for their refusall'. As in the earlier aborted attempt, the election broke up at this point.[32]

As the aldermen and the Crown now settled into another round of negotiations, Whitelocke was presented to the king as one of four prominent lawyers acceptable to the aldermen (along with John

31 *Liber Famelicus*, pp. 64-5; cf. 'Chamberlain to Carleton, 7 November 1618' in *Court and Times of James the First*, vol. 2, p. 104; *Letters of John Chamberlain*, vol. 2, p. 180. Four candidates were nominated to observe correct procedure, but only Whitelocke and Shute were genuine contenders.

32 *Liber Famelicus*, p. 66; *Court and Times of James the First*, vol. 2, p. 105; Chamberlain recounted that 'the Aldermen took great exception to him as well of yeares, gravitie, learning in the law and that he had ben divers times out-lawed upon record, and ben bound to the goode behaviour, so that he was altogether uncapable and insufficient for such an office'.

Walter, Thomas Crew and William Jones). Ignoring their suggestions, the king asked them 'how they could like of one Heath', which met with silence. This impasse led the king to denounce Crew as a man 'he wold bar from the place', and to object 'in particuler against Master Whitlocke by name' when he was proposed as a suitable candidate. Not surprisingly, Whitelocke felt that the king's insistence upon Heath reflected upon his own parliamentary conduct, noting that King James had precluded him from the election 'as if ther had been a remembrance of my not pleasing the king in parliament', and concluding that:

> I was barred from that by highe hand whiche by the libertye of a subject was lawfull for me to ask, and I was sure by a fair course to have obteyned, and this as a revenge for doing my duty in parliament...[33]

In fact, while the king may have used the parliamentary reputation of Whitelocke and Crew to justify his opposition to their election, his firm support for Heath probably reflected, more fundamentally, an increasingly irrational desire on his part to support Buckingham. More than anything, the unhappy course of the election reflected the difficulties that Buckingham's inordinate political influence were beginning to create for political harmony. Whitelocke was now placed under direct pressure to resign from the contest, as 'false brethren' among the aldermen moved to placate the king, and he grudgingly advised Sir William Cockayne, his principal sponsor, of his intention to withdraw. At this point, his 'frendes' showed the kind of political obstinacy, born as much of social pride as any political ambition, that made contested elections such a volatile business for all concerned. They quickly hatched a new plot to thwart Heath's election, moving to nominate Whitelocke's old friend and associate Sir John Walter, whom Whitelocke considered 'so famous and worthye that the voyces wear likely to go for him, if it mighte appear

33 *Liber Famelicus*, p. 67, 69; 'Chamberlain to Carleton, 14 November 1618' in *Letters of John Chamberlain*, vol. 2, p. 182; *Court and Times of James the First*, vol. 2, pp. 105, 107.

he wold accept of it'. Whitelocke assured his city friends that if nominated Walter would stand.[34]

'This plot being layd', the final stage of this long and complicated affair began on 14 November 1618, 'in full court of the lord maior and twenty-four aldermen'. Confusion quickly followed as Whitelocke (to everyone's surprise including his own) was nominated as the first candidate, by a member unaware of his new position. As supporters expected to endorse him remained silent, Cockayne informed those present that, while 'verye mutche beholding to them for thear loves', Whitelocke had now decided not to contest the position. With his usual candour, Whitelocke went on to assure future readers of his journal that 'Mutche was spoken on my behalf, and more muttered of the course taken against me, and so an end of my businesse'.[35]

The outcome of the election, which had seen such intense manoeuvring on the part of both parties, was a tight result. Of the two real candidates (Whitelocke suggests that Sir Thomas Ireland and Thomas Hedley of Gray's Inn were both 'cyphers'), eleven of the twenty-five 'voyces' went for Walter, and one (Sir John Garrett) abstained from voting, declaring that in the normal course of events he would happily have voted for Whitelocke. This left Heath with a majority of one, in Whitelocke's eyes an empty victory. While Whitelocke (possibly inaccurately) noted that the new recorder was now required to pay £1500 for the office in a continuation of the complicated financial dealings started between Sir Lionel Cranfield and Richard Martin, he was consoled by friends, among them several of the Westminster Hall judges, who jokingly told him that he was '*Reminiscor* though not recorder, and that Mr. Thomas Crew was *Memini*'.[36]

---

34 *Liber Famelicus*, p. 68.

35 *Liber Famelicus*, p. 68.

36 *Liber Famelicus*, pp. 68-9; Guildhall CRO, Report of the Court of Aldermen 34, fol. 4v; *Court and Times of James the First*, vol. 2, p. 107; cf. Kopperman, *Sir*

V

As James Whitelocke's professional ambitions were checked in the electoral fiasco of 1618, he was forced to see that after the demise of Somerset, all factional alliances in the court flowed back, in one way or another, to the duke of Buckingham. While his unceremonious dumping from Roper's office may have shaken him, Cranfield's *volte-face* during his attempts to gain election as recorder of London must have brought this point home once and for all. Buckingham's known catholicity in his dispensation of patronage was essential to Whitelocke's professional advancement after this time. With Ellesmere's passing, Buckingham had gained the office of Lord Lieutenant of Buckinghamshire, and Whitelocke was appointed to commissions of the peace in Buckinghamshire in November 1617, and then Oxfordshire in May 1618. While the strong position of Whitelocke in these counties undoubtedly pressed his claim to office, it is notable that Buckingham requested Whitelocke's appointment to a special commission for the city of Westminster, established at the duke's instigation in December 1618.[37]

Given his earlier scorn towards Buckingham's 'creatures', Whitelocke was hardly likely to stress his dependence upon Buckingham in later years, and what clues he does furnish about the duke's importance in his promotions after 1618 are oblique. David Lemmings has commented upon the 'galaxy of grandees' who assembled for Whitelocke's reader's feast in 1619, and suggests a strong political motivation behind his lavish display of hospitality. In fact, the reciprocal nature of this hospitality should be stressed, as guests provided gifts for the feast to the value of around £130, more than a third of Whitelocke's total expense of around £370. Yet Lemmings is right to stress a political motivation behind Whitelocke's guest list, which included

---

Robert Heath, p. 19. Chamberlain noted that Heath disclaimed 'all such contracts wherfore he [Cranfield] must find some other way to be restored'.

37 Peck, *Court Patronage and Corruption*, p. 83; *Liber Famelicus*, pp. 60, 62, 69-70.

influential courtiers such as Sir Lionel Cranfield, Sir John Davies, and Sir Robert Heath – all proteges of Buckingham, and the latter two poorly regarded by Whitelocke in private.[38]

Whitelocke's dependence on Buckingham is further suggested by his nomination of the duke as one of two 'demandants' who initiated his formal admission to the rank of serjeant, along with William earl of Northampton who was to serve as Whitelocke's nominal superior in Chester. Whether this tacit admission of the realities of power at the royal court equates with any form of political subservience is questionable as, for obvious reasons, evidence of this nature is unlikely to be found in Whitelocke's account of events. The *Liber Famelicus* noted only the official correspondence that informed him of his promotion as serjeant-at-law on 18 June 1620, as well as a second warrant received on the same day in which Buckingham instructed him that he was to be promoted to chief justice of Chester.[39]

Whitelocke's list of expenses arising from his appointment to serjeant mention only customary requirements of office – his need for new apparel, the cost of a feast, and small fees given to the officers executing the ceremony – no 'gift' is recorded in his total outlay of £207 6s. 11d. Beyond the customary rings he had made up for the occasion at a cost of £45 14s. 8d., he offered a gift of plate valued at £19 3s. 5d. given to Sir Francis Bacon (lending some support to Spedding's claim that Bacon's patronage ensured Whitelocke's promotion). A title added to the total cost of his promotion in October 1620, with 'fees for knighthood' coming to £44. 17s, a sum which

38 Lemmings, 'Ritual and the Law', p. 7; *Liber Famelicus*, pp. 70-5 and cf. Prest, *Inns of Court*, pp. 226-7. Note Whitelocke's comments on Heath and Davis, and his initial comments on Cranfield, *Liber Famelicus*, pp. 54-5, 59, 105. Whitelocke's list, which Prest has suggested is 'the most complete surviving guest list for any reader's feast before the Civil War', shows that invited guests also included friends such as Sir Henry Yelverton and Bishop Buckeridge, and patrons such as Sir Julius Caesar.

39 *Liber Famelicus*, p. 78; Lincoln's Inn MS Misc. 586 (3), unfoliated, in *Order of Serjeants*, p. 437. For the role of the demandant see *Order of Serjeants*, pp. 91-2.

was hardly comparable to the £4000 given to James I by Yelverton for the solicitor-general's place or the £600 demanded of the serjeants in 1614.[40]

Whitelocke's path to promotion provides a telling reflection on Buckingham's stranglehold on royal offices, and in advancing he was implicated in the diminishing legal standards he had himself criticised. Writing to Sir Dudley Carleton on 9 November 1620, John Chamberlain remarked

> Sir James Whitelocke is gone to be judge of Wales and Chester, which place came not to him gratis, though perhaps his knightship was cast into the bargain.

In the 1626 parliament a committee moving to indict Buckingham for corruption searched to find out 'what Sir James Whitelocke gave for his place of Chester to the Lord Duke', but found that while a payment 'was infered at the committee... there was no color or ground of proof for it'. Ironically, while dissatisfaction with Buckingham's influence over the judiciary failed to tarnish Whitelocke in 1626, the king's actions threatened to destroy his judicial reputation on the eve of the civil war.[41]

---

40 *Liber Famelicus*, p. 84; *Works*, vol. 14, pp. 100-2.

41 *Court and Times of James the First*, vol. 2, p. 105; The speech against Buckingham is taken from John Glanville's report from the committee as quoted in History of Parliament Trust.

Chapter 6

Politics and the bench

In 1640, as the political nation stumbled towards internal paralysis, members of the Long Parliament moved to impeach James Whitelocke posthumously for judicial misconduct. Whitelocke's slide into obloquy, fully seven years after his death, mirrored general bitterness about a 'collapse' in judicial standards, and historians since Judson have underlined the impact of judicial misconduct upon the eventual outbreak of political opposition to the Crown. This chapter argues that Charles I's manipulation of the judiciary challenged parliamentarians and the judges themselves with new and unwanted concepts of government. It suggests, through a study of Whitelocke's difficult years as a royal judge, that a constitutional crisis emerged during the 1620s that could not be redressed within the framework of consensual politics, because it could not be articulated within the prevailing taxonomies of constitutional discourse.[1]

I

Until recently, James Whitelocke's career as chief justice of Chester has been almost entirely overlooked by historians. The County Palatine of Chester, lying on the north-eastern boundary of the Kingdom of Wales, had served since the Conquest as a base for the projection of English power across the border. By virtue of his appointment to the office on 29 October 1620, Whitelocke was to administer justice in Crown and common pleas throughout the County Palatine of Chester, and to administer justice 'in all causes concerning

---

1 Jones, *Politics and the Bench*, pp. 13-24; Reeve, *Charles I*, p. 137; Judson, *Crisis of the Constitution*, *passim*; Prest, *Rise of the Barristers*, p. 268.

his Majesties subjects' within the Welsh counties of Denbigh, Flint, Montgomery, and the four English border counties contentiously attached to the Council in the Marches of Wales. Whitelocke's 'complementary' role within Chester and the Council in the Marches gave him a unique position among common-law judges, and to him fell the delicate task of 'balancing out the needs and requirements of both provincial society and the royal government'. Appointed to act in quorum with the president and vice-president, Whitelocke was in reality the chief working member among the legal staff of the Council in the Marches.[2]

Upon his appointment to Chester, Whitelocke was advised, in a speech by Lord Keeper Bacon, to 'keep good quarters with Westminster Halle', to 'look to suppresse the powr of sutche gentlemen in the countrye that seek to oppresse and suppresse ther poor neighboures', and to 'keep a good correspondencye with the lord president, under whome, in a manner, yow serve'. By his own admission a 'stranger to the mysteries of government', Whitelocke found the maintenance of good relations with the central government, the county community, and Spencer Compton, second earl of Northampton and president of the Council, a delicate juggling act. Whitelocke's need to show respect for the Crown's wishes was complicated by his obligation to satisfy Compton and his reliance, in the absence of any prior contact with the region, upon the information of well-entrenched local administrators. It appears that Whitelocke achieved a measure of success in carrying out his judicial duties, but failed to adapt well to the warp and woof of palatine politics.[3]

---

2 *Liber Famelicus*, pp. 80-1.

3 Keith Wrightson, 'Two concepts of order: justices, constables and jurymen in seventeenth-century England' in *An Ungovernable People: The English and their law in the seventeenth and eighteenth centuries*, ed. John Brewer and John Styles (London 1980), p. 26; T. Rymer, *Foedera Conventiones, Literae et cujuscunque generis Act Publica, inter Reges Angliae*, 10 vols. (London 1745), vol. 7, p. 30. For a detailed study of Whitelocke's achievements as Chief Justice of Chester see D.X. Powell, 'Sir James Whitelocke, Chief Justice of Chester 1620-1624',

From the 1580s the chief justice of Chester had tended to assume control of the Council in the Marches in the absence of the president, and while royal correspondence went so far as to refer to Whitelocke as 'Chief Justice of the Marches of Wales', such recognition did not always sit well with council members more accustomed to ranking by social pedigree. Bacon's 1620 charge to Whitelocke included a warning to 'make no clashes of renewing old sores' between the chief justice and the lord president, but upon his arrival in Bewdley in Trinity term 1621, Whitelocke was immediately challenged for precedence by Lord Compton – 'and all the reason he gave', the *Liber Famelicus* noted indignantly, was 'bycause my predecessor gave it to him'. Reflecting upon the unhappy relations that had existed between former chief justices and presidents, Whitelocke quickly set about ratifying his 'place and precdence... next to the Lord President'. Although he won the battle, the smooth functioning of the Council in the Marches was obviously hampered by their poor relations and on 13 October 1624 he received instructions from Lord Keeper Williams that, 'upon unkindnesses between your chief and yow' and with the 'high favour and good opinion' of the king assured, he was to be appointed to the Court of King's Bench. Considering himself 'verye wearye of the life I led at the counsell', he consulted with Williams on 15 October, and assented to his own removal from Chester.[4]

II

James Whitelocke was made a puisne judge of the Court of King's Bench on 18 October 1624. In an affirmation of his commitment to the 'true dutye of a judge... whiche dutye by God's grace, I will ever endeavour to observe', Whitelocke reminded his audience of Tacitus,

---

Transactions of the Historic Society of Lancashire and Cheshire 143 (1993), pp. 1-34.

4 *Works*, vol. 14, p. 103; Longleat Papers, vol. 2, fols 44, 172; *Liber Famelicus*, pp. 80, 91-2, 96-7.

to instruct them 'that to do well was not always safe, to do ill did most times escape blame, but to do little was least dangerous, bycaus it was lest subject to accoumpt'. Recalling his four years of service in Chester, Whitelocke reflected that, while he 'was not willing to put a hazard upon myself in leaving knowen paths to runn into unknowen', he was 'no stranger to the forms and procedures of the King's Bench', having worked in the court as a lawyer 'for the space of twenty-three years and above'. Despite his familiarity with the central courts, Whitelocke faced an entirely unknown path after the death of James I on 27 March 1625.[5]

The accession of Charles I ushered in a new relationship between the Crown and the judges, at a time when significant changes were occurring to the English political landscape. As parliament became deeply ambivalent about the broad schema of royal policy between 1625 and 1629, Charles's commitment to war, and the reluctance of many subjects to support his expensive and spectacularly unsuccessful forays into Europe, turned a number of unpopular fiscal exigencies into constitutional test cases. By repeatedly cajoling, ordering, threatening and ultimately dismissing the authority of his judges thereafter, Charles made a mockery of his pledge to assist them 'in all honest endeavours in doing justice to the law and the commonwealth', and Whitelocke and his fellow judges found themselves (in the words of Bill Jones) serving as both 'participants and ammunition' in an ongoing political controversy.[6]

Events in the 1625 parliament outlined the issues around which the prestige of the judiciary would dissolve during the Caroline era, and it is particularly unfortunate that a review of 'passages in term and

---

5 PRO C 66/2324; *Liber Famelicus*, pp. 97-9.

6 *Liber Famelicus*, p. 103; *Diary of Sir Richard Hutton*, pp. 56-7; Jones, *Politics and the Bench*, p. 30; cf. Barry Coward, 'Was there an English Revolution in the Middle of the Seventeenth Century' in *Politics and People in Revolutionary England*, ed. Colin Jones, Malyn Newitt & Stephen Roberts (Oxford 1986), pp. 20-1, Morrill, *Nature of the English Revolution*, pp. 9, 289-92; Cust, *Forced Loan*, p. 13-39.

parliament', which Whitelocke evidently compiled in a separate book from the *Liber Famelicus*, has since been lost. We have seen that in earlier times Whitelocke was himself deeply troubled by Buckingham's influence in judicial appointments, but now, as John Pym questioned how justice could be done when high officials 'use their favour about the King to procure places of judicature for money' during the push to impeach Buckingham, Whitelocke's sat uncomfortably on the other side of the bench. While allegations of corruption surrounding his own appointment were not sustained, the reputation of King's Bench was hardly enhanced by John Glanville's charge that its former chief justice, Sir James Ley, had procured the office of treasurer through a bribe of £2000 for the duke's 'owne use'. The *Liber Famelicus* itself endorsed rumours that George Vernon had been made a serjeant-at-law and then a Baron of the Exchequer in 1627 'for money'.[7]

Crown attempts to enlist the judges as parliamentary political allies in 1625 further corroded the credibility of the King's Bench as an impartial constitutional arbitrator. After the king's request that the *Earl of Bristol's case* 'proceed by way of indictment in the Kings Bench' met with polite disapproval in the Lords, some of Buckingham's 'partisans' requested that the clerk of King's Bench be allowed to sit in on hearings, in order to ensure that the case could be continued in King's Bench if parliament was dissolved. This request was refused, but the king now intervened to prevent any response, on the part of the judges, to a question sent by the Lords on the admissibility of the king as a witness in the case. Not for the last time, the king's personal intervention had placed Whitelocke and his colleagues in a politically sensitive position.[8]

7 *Liber Famelicus*, pp. 104, 108; John Rushworth, *Historical Collections of private passages of state*, 8 vols (London 1659-1701), vol. 1, pp. 334-8; History of Parliament Trust; Prest, 'Judicial Corruption', pp. 80-1.

8 Russell, *Parliaments and English Politics*, pp. 309-17; Rushworth, *Historical Collections*, vol. 1, pp. 267-9.

As parliamentary attempts to enforce ministerial responsibility strained relations with the new king in 1626, a lukewarm response to the financial requirements of war in Europe led the Crown to raise a Forced Loan without parliamentary consent. Cust employs Whitelocke's earlier thoughts on 'unparliamentary' forms of taxation in 1610 to trace 'the roots of hostility aroused by the Loan'. In 1614, Whitelocke considered it a 'great pitye' that the government was resorting to an extra-parliamentary 'benevolence' to increase its solvency, responding with a characteristic blend of principle and pragmatism:

> For the benevelences I was left out in the countrey, for when my name was proposed before the justices, they bad let me alone... so I was altogeather omitted, yet in Michaelmas term I got the rolle into my hands and put myself 40s., whiche I did to avoyd the danger of giving more singlye.[9]

Twelve years later, as the king professed his readiness to 'sweep all their benches', Whitelocke agreed (in collaboration with the other judges) to subscribe to the Forced Loan with a proviso that this was 'not to set an example to the people'. It was the first of a series of unhappy compromises he was to make as a judge. Whitelocke offered no personal comment, but his eulogy of Sir John Davies, who had written *Jus imponendi Vestigalia* supporting the king's right to levy

---

9 *Liber Famelicus*, p. 45; Cust, *Forced Loan*, pp. 152, 185; *idem*, 'Charles I, the Privy Council and the Forced Loan' pp. 208-9; cf. Lockyer, *Early Stuarts*, p. 223; Reeve, *Charles I*, pp. 13-15. For historiographical debate on the Loan see Cust, *Forced Loan*, pp. 6, 150. For Russell the Loan 'threatened a co-operation between the King and county gentry for which no substitute existed, and for which no substitute was desired.' In his view this co-operation was strained, but ultimately held intact through a desire for political harmony; Russell, *Parliaments and English Politics*, p. 334. For Cust, the extent to which this financial innovation created political tension has been underestimated by Russell who, by taking an absence of overt opposition as evidence of consensus, has downplayed the need for self-censorship in a charged political environment; Cust, *Forced Loan*, pp. 184-5, 328, and see also Russell's reply in Conrad Russell, *Unrevolutionary England, 1603-1642* (London 1990), pp. xxvi-xxx.

the Loan and was regarded as the likely candidate to replace Randle Crew, sacked as chief justice for his recalcitrance in endorsing the Loan, offers perspective:

> He was in communication to have been made chief justice of the King's Benche, in the place of Sir Randle Crew. But God prevented so inconvenient an intention to the common wealthe. [10]

The judges' refusal to ratify the legality of the Forced Loan threatened to have a major impact upon its reception at all levels of society after 1626, fuelling hopes that the courts would allow organised resistance to this and other arbitrary actions of the Crown. In October 1627 a formal legal challenge to the Privy Council was initiated on behalf of the 'five knights' held in London as 'refusers' to the Loan (Sir Thomas Darnel, Sir John Corbet, Sir Walter Erle, Sir John Heveningham and Sir Edmund Hampden), with the request 'that counsel might be assigned them to plead for their relief out of prison'. The case of *Rex v. Darnel* (the five knights' case) would turn upon two actions by the Crown that served to stifle opposition: the issuing of a warrant of detainment 'by his majesty's special commandment', without specific grounds for imprisonment, and an archival subterfuge attempting to prove the issue of discretionary imprisonment had been adjudged for the Crown. Such actions turned legal proceedings into a highly publicised, highly controversial constitutional test case, with Whitelocke and the other judges standing squarely in the middle.[11]

---

10 *Liber Famelicus*, p. 105; *Court and Times of Charles the First; Illustrated By Authentic and Confidential Letters, From Various Public and Private Collections*, ed. Thomas Birch, 2 vols (London 1848), vol. 1, pp. 172, 174, 181; *Diary of Sir Richard Hutton*, pp. 66-9; Gardiner, *History of England*, vol. 6, p. 14, vol. 7, p. 149; D'Ewes, *Autobiography*, vol. 1, p. 49; Rushworth, *Historical Collections*, vol. 3, p. 240; Whitelocke, *Memorials* (Oxford 1853), vol. 1, p. 47.

11 Cf. Gardiner, *History of England*, vol. 6, pp. 149-50; *Court and Times of Charles the First*, vol. 1, pp. 176, 280; Cust, *Forced Loan*, pp. 3, 61, 112; *idem*, '*Charles I*, the Privy Council and the Forced Loan', pp. 224-8; *Diary of Sir Richard Hutton*, p. 72. The writ for Heveningham to appear in court, dated 15 November

Whitelocke's public opinion upon the five knights' case survives in a speech he made in the House of Lords on 14 April 1628, after dubious dealings by Sir Robert Heath led parliament to question the legality of the court's ruling. Whitelocke opened his speech by raising what he saw as the basic issue at hand. 'My Lords,' he declared,

> we are by your appointment here ready to clear any aspersion of the House of Commons in their late presentment upon the *Kings-bench*, that the subject was wounded in this judgement there lately given... I say there was no judgement given whereby either the prerogative might be inlarged, or the right of the subject entrenched upon.

Whitelocke proceeded to outline the details of the case: how the judges had awarded legal counsel at the knights' request, how the case had then been allowed to proceed, and the Crown's warrant of detainment had been returned 'by his majesty's special commandment'.[12]

Whitelocke was careful to emphasise that due legal process had determined the actions of the King's Bench, arguing that 'if the King did not shew cause, wherein we should have judged the King had done wrong, and this is beyond our knowledge, for he might have committed them for other matters then we could have imagined.' To ignore the principles of legal knowledge and 'take notice otherwise' was to break the rules of admissible evidence in a way generally 'hurtful to the subject' – even if prejudicial to the detained in this particular instance.

1627, along with Whitelocke's notes of the precedents used in the case, survive in the Longleat Papers, vol. 3, fol. 152v.

12 The following is taken from copies of the speech preserved in *Proceedings in Parliament 1628*, ed. M.R. Keeler, M.J. Cole and W.B. Bidwell, 5 vols (New Haven 1977-83), vol. 5, pp. 219-20 [hereafter cited *as Proceedings in Parliament 1628*], a second version reprinted in *The Soveraigns Prerogatiue and the Subjects Privilege, comprised in several Speeches, Cases, and Arguments of Law* (London 1658), pp. 147-8, which has been reprinted in *State Trials*, vol. 3, cols 161-2. The arguments made against the judge's ruling in the 1628 parliament are reprinted in *State Trials*, vol. 3, cols 59-160.

Whitelocke went straight to the point in rebutting criticisms that the judges might have bailed the prisoners at their own discretion: such an action, he argued, would have 'given a blow to the King's act, for then it would have bred a doubt whether the King had done wrong.' And while

> they might say thus, they might have been kept in Prison all their dayes, I answer no, but we did remit them, that we might better advise of the matter, and they the next day might have had a new Writ, if they had pleased, but they say, we ought not to have denied bayl, I answer, if we had done so, it must needs have reflected upon the King that he had unjustly imprisoned them.

Reminding the Lords that a 'sovereign power rests in all commonwealths', he asked rhetorically: 'Is there not a trust to be reposed in the sovereign to restrain a prisoner for some convenient time?'

It was a question bound to draw silence, but, as Whitelocke went on to assure the House, if no cause was forthcoming, then the court had not denied the right of those detained to seek legal redress. Answering John Selden's charge that the return of the court roll (which had the decision noted as *remittitur* rather than *remittitur quosque*) attempted to overlook the right of the defendants to seek bail, Whitelocke remarked

> whereas they will have a difference betwixt *remittitur* and *remittitur quosque*... I confess I can find none, but these are new inventions to trouble old Records. And herein my Lords we have dealt with my knowledge and understanding, for had we given a Judgement, the party must have thereupon rested, every Judgment must come to an issue, in matter, in fact, or demur in point of Law, here is neither, therefore no Judgement.

Whitelocke knew that from this point on, he was treading on very delicate ground. John Guy has shown that *remittitur quosque* was the 'standard entry used when defendants were returned to gaol *without formal resolution of the question of bail*'. Endorsing Whitelocke's own views, he has suggested that 'if the terms *remittitur* and *remittitur quosque, etc.*, were interchangeable, it was impossible for the Crown ever to prove in the aftermath of a rule of court that a prisoner's application for bail had been refused' – unless the final entry on the court controlment roll could be changed to show 'that the substantive issue of discretionary imprisonment had been adjudged in its favour'. And this, Guy has demonstrated, was exactly the 'archival perversion' attempted by Whitelocke's old nemesis Sir Robert Heath, who had been appointed attorney-general in 1625 with Buckingham's patronage. Heath's blatant coercion was resisted by the clerk, John Keeling, who sought the judges' advice. In a parliamentary hearing, Keeling testified that despite the judges' refusal to allow the change, Heath had placed constant pressure on him throughout Hilary term, and finally secured the altered entry from him a week before parliament sat.[13]

Fully aware that he stood squarely between an agitated parliament and a volatile monarch, Whitelocke now offered his side of the story. Although the judges had been 'touched' that they 'intended to enter a judgment, and a judgment draw', Whitelocke assured the Lords that 'the chief justice only spoke as it might be but a rule and no judgment'. Heath's subsequent activities, 'pressed... for his Master's service', were treated with caution. Whitelocke suggested that Heath had done 'the office of a good servant' for the king, but pointed out that the judges commanded Keeling not to remove the original entry, 'we being sworn to do right betwixt the King and his subjects'. Claiming ignorance of Heath's continued pressure, the judges had never, he stressed, seen the tampered entry before it was read in parliament.

The essentials of Whitelocke's line of testimony were repeated by the other judges over this and the following day. They made it clear that the King's Bench had not expressly supported Charles's right of discretionary imprisonment, nor did the court assent to any modification of the existing ruling that would make this possible. The Lords appeared satisfied by this argument, printing a formal declaration in their Journal that the judges 'have given no judgment at all, for it was

---

13 Guy, 'Origins of the Petition of Right', pp. 295-297; Kopperman, *Sir Robert Heath*, pp. 38, 50.

but a rule', since 'the next day, or the next term, a new *habeas corpus* might have been demanded by the parties, and they must have done justice'. Endorsing the claims by which the judges defended their actions, Guy has pronounced the judges 'vindicated' from any allegations of wrong-doing on the strength of their reply.[14]

Notes dispersed among James Whitelocke's personal papers both add to and detract from Guy's verdict. In a draft speech prepared for his speech to the Lords, Whitelocke noted in it that upon the return of writs of *habeas corpus*, the judges heard legal counsel for the five knights and the Crown, 'whence being done they found this cause to be of exceeding consequence as on the one side concerning the power of the king and on the other side the liberty of the subject'. The judges provided no 'definitive judgement', remanding the prisoners 'that they mighte be further advised, & left it to the clerk to enter the rule in like manner as had ben used in like cases by ther predecesors'. According the Whitelocke, the first he or the other judges knew of Heath's subterfuge was after the legal term, when Keeling indicated that he had 'received direction to draw a formal judgement in an extraordinary manner'. In Whitelocke's account, Keeling 'was forbidden by everye of them to make any other entry than was usuall at his perill'.[15]

This account endorses Guy's point that the judges had not, in remanding the prisoners into custody, handed down a binding judgement. It suggests also that they opposed Heath's subterfuge. Undated notes among Whitelocke's papers also suggest, however, that the Crown had ascertained its right to imprison the five knights *in advance of the trial*, shifting the arguments on to the stronger ground of Charles's prerogative. Two questions, almost certainly directed to him by Heath before the case was heard in court, asked whether 'there

14 *Lords Journals* [15 April], p. 740; Guy, 'Origins of the Petition of Right', pp. 292-6, 301; cf. Russell, *Parliaments and English Politics*, p. 364.

15 Longleat Papers, vol. 24, fols 231, 232. For a fuller treatment see D.X. Powell, 'Sir James Whitelocke's extra-judicial advice to the Crown in 1627', *Historical Journal* 39 (1996), pp. 737-41.

be any law that in expresse words takes away the Councell's power to imprison upon reason of state without declaring the cause', and whether the words '*per legem*' in Magna Carta 'be only understood to mean the common law presented in Westminster Halle', or extended to the 'law of State' exercised under the royal prerogative.[16]

In reply to the first question, Whitelocke replied that he and the other judges could find no law 'that in expresse word either taketh away the kings or Counsells power to imprison upon reasons of state without declaring the causes or that mentions *in expresse words* any power of the king or Counsell to imprison upon reason of State'. Whitelocke further instructed the Crown that '*for the law of state we neither know what is intended thereby nor the extent or latitude thereof it being a matter not falling properly in our cognizance*'. These questions and answers throw critical light on the five knights' case, which contested the king's right to imprison 'by his majesty's special commandment' without further cause. Clearly, no matter how skilfully the defence counsel argued that such cause of detainment subverted the 'infallible maxims' of legal reason, the Crown, forewarned of the judges' position, could merely insist that 'they on the other side cannot cite one Book, Statute, or any other thing, to prove, that they who have been committed *per speciale mandatum domini regis*, are bailable'. In handing down its ruling, the King's Bench declared in public that which Whitelocke had almost certainly already told the Crown in private, that 'if no cause of the committment be expressed, it is presumed to be for matters of state, which we cannot take notice of'.[17]

Whitelocke was undoubtedly speaking in all honesty as he told members of the upper House that as he had spent 'all my studies in the King's Bench... upon my soul he never saw nor knew any thing which did contrary to what we have done' in the case of the five

16 Guy, 'Origins of the Petition of Right', p. 291; Longleat Papers, vol. 24, fol. 232.

17 *State Trials*, vol. 3, cols 27, 42, 57. Brief notes taken by Whitelocke on *habeas corpus* survive in the Longleat Papers, vol. 3, fols 155v and 176v.

knights. Before 1626, only Sir Edward Coke was prepared to question in what instances the king's right to legal advice from his judges compromised the rights of his subjects to seek recourse in a royal court of law, and even Coke's stentorian voice faltered on the issue of pre-judicial opinion. Bulstrode Whitelocke later argued that his 'Father did often and highly complain against this way, of sending to the Judges for their private opinions (before the case had gone to trial)'. He did not add that these were personal opinions that James Whitelocke would not make public. Bulstrode could not admit that furnishing the Crown with such counsel made a farce of his father's arguments about the technicalities of due legal process.[59]

Sharpe has suggested that 'the common law in early Stuart England was expected to resolve problems, not to support positions'. Perhaps the most troubling aspect of the judges' conduct in the five knights' case was that by insisting upon the legal technicalities that upheld their actions, the judges allowed the law to do neither one nor the other. This judicial shortcoming was a critical concern in the Petition of Right which 'cast invention out of necessity' as Commons, Lords and Crown searched for some kind of agreement over issues highlighted by the five knights' case in the 1628 parliament. John Reeve has demonstrated that the Petition was conceived as a legal document that defined those limits on the royal prerogative that had been tested, without satisfaction, in the king's courts. As Sir Dudley Digges warned parliament: 'We are now upon this question whether the king may be above the law, or the law above the king. It is our unhappiness, but it is put upon us.'[60]

---

59 *Proceedings in Parliament 1628*, vol. 5, p. 220; Whitelock, *Memorials* (1732), p. 13; Lockyer, *Early Stuarts*, pp. 56-7.

60 Sharpe, 'Parliamentary History', p. 31; Guy, 'Origins of the Petition of Right', p. 302; L.J. Reeve, 'The Legal Status of the Petition of Right', *Historical Journal* 29 (1986), pp. 257-77; *Proceedings in Parliament 1628*, vol. 2, p. 325; see also F.H. Relf, *The Petition of Right* (Minneapolis 1917); J.S. Flemion, '"A savings to satisfy all": the House of Lords and the Petition of Right', *Parliamentary History* 10 (1991), pp. 27-44.

The judges' response to the Petition of Right is evidenced in advice that they provided to Charles in advance of his Janus-faced answer to the Petition. Weighing up the implications of the Petition for discretionary Crown imprisonment, the judges instructed Charles that 'some cases may require such secrecy that the King may commit a subject without showing the cause, for a convenient time'. Although 'the party ought by the general rule of law to be delivered... the Court in discretion may forbear to deliver the prisoner for a convenient time, to the end that the Court may be advertised of the truth thereof'. By emphasising their rights to discern each case on its merits, the judges also left doubts in the king's mind about his chances of persuading them to continue in the same manner as they had in the five knights' case. They cannot be commended for this outcome.[20]

IV

If the King's Bench ruling in the five knights' case fuelled the creation of the Petition of Right, then the Petition, indirectly, led the judges into *Eliot's Case*, the second great constitutional test case in the reign of Charles I. Through Whitelocke, one can see how the judges were drawn yet again into an adjudicating role in the trial of John Eliot and his co-conspirators in the House of Commons which tested their basic political loyalties. Much of the legal debate that engaged the attention of Whitelocke in the hearings centred upon the words used to commit Eliot and his colleagues, and the term 'sedition' in particular, 'probably the most unspecific, non-capital offence with such treasonable undertones that could be devised by the government'. Counsel for the Crown sought to assert the king's right to punish those who openly inculcated dissent toward government policy, and to extricate this prerogative from attempts to constrain it under the

20 BL Hargrave MS 27, fol. 97; BL Stowe MS 561, fol. 24; SP 16/105/94; PRO SP 16/105/93 cited in Gardiner, *History of England*, vol. 6, p. 294; Reeve, *Charles I*, pp. 118-71; Reeve, 'Legal Status of the Petition of Right', pp. 259-60.

provisions of the Petition of Right. Counsel for the defence sought bail and demanded a legal restraint upon the king's right of arbitrary imprisonment. To this end, the insufficiencies of the cause shown in the writ of detainment, rather than the circumstances of detainment itself, were emphasised and tied back to the requirements of the Petition of Right.[21]

As in the five knights' case, the Crown manipulation of the right to counsel from the judges placed Whitelocke and his colleagues in a difficult position, but met with greater resistance. In April 1629 the king sought opinion from the judges on a series of questions, obviously referring to the circumstances of the 1628 parliament, and deliberately constructed to condemn the actions of the detained as a conspiracy. Lying well beyond the realm of technical advice, these questions sought to incriminate the detained MPs in advance of the case, soliciting the support of the judges by underlining the attack upon their own position in the events of the last session. Despite Charles's insistence that he 'must know what the nature of this offence is being fully proved', the judges stonewalled the king, insisting that the no firm judgement could be given in advance of trial, but only 'as the circumstances shall fall out, upon the truth of the fact'.[22]

---

21 Reeve, *Charles I*, p. 124; *idem*, 'Arguments in King's Bench', pp. 271-81; *State Trials*, vol. 3, cols 244-51.

22 PRO SP 16/141/44; *State Trials*, vol. 3, notes to col. 138; Rushworth, *Historical Collections*, vol. 4, p. 23. See also Chief Justice Finch's comments to the House of Commons on extra-judicial opinion, quoted in Jones, *Politics and the Bench*, p. 193. The range of questions asked by Heath and then the King in 1629 can lead to some confusion; Heath's questions, noted by John Brampton's *Autobiography*, pp. 49-54, are reprinted in *Historical Collections*, vol. 1, pp. 663-4, and *State Trials*, vol. 3, cols 237-9. The King's questions, noted in Gardiner, *History of England*, vol. 7, pp. 89-90, are in calendared in SP 16/141/44, and are reprinted in *State Trials*, vol. 3, in the notes to col. 238. None correspond to the two questions in Whitelocke's hand that I have interpreted above as arising from the five knights' case. Cf. Jones, *Politics and the Bench*, pp. 50-2; Kopperman, *Sir Robert Heath*, pp 178-9.

In legal hearings from early May until June, the judges agreed with the defendants' claim for parliamentary privilege to exempt them from prosecution in Star Chamber, leading the Crown to drop its case in that court. Kopperman has seen this passage of events as a 'notable victory' for the prisoners; it was also a victory of sorts for the judges, but it still left Whitelocke and his fellow judges of the Court of King's Bench to weigh the arguments of both parties, as the question of bail was argued in Easter and Trinity term of 1629.[23]

It is clear that, as lawyers, the Crown officers were no match for John Selden and Edward Littleton as the case of *habeas corpus* was debated in the Court of King's Bench. Despite Heath's vague assurance that the government was moving to prosecute the prisoners 'in convenient time', and an open appeal to the judges to side with the Crown, the government faced opponents who were quick to press home the legal advantages they had secured through the king's reluctant concessions in parliament during the interim. Convinced by their arguments, the judges now drafted 'an humble and stout letter to the king' advising him that 'by their oaths they were to bail the prisoners'.[24]

S.R. Gardiner declared a century ago that the 'Petition of Right had strengthened the hands of the judges as arbitrators between the King and his subjects'. In fact, this was true only if the king was prepared to act in the spirit of the petition's resolutions – which he now refused to do. Before bail could be granted, Whitelocke was informed that Charles required the judges of King's Bench to meet him at Greenwich. 'Accordingly', Bulstrode Whitelocke recounted, 'the Judges attended the king, who was not pleased with their determination; but commanded them not to deliver any opinion in this case without consulting with the rest of the Judges'. This command implied doubts about the adequacy of the King's Bench ruling which

---

23 Reeve, *Charles I*, p. 122; Kopperman, *Sir Robert Heath*, p. 180.

24 Reeve, *Charles I*, p. 127; *idem*, 'Arguments in King's Bench', pp. 274-8; *State Trials*, vol. 3, cols 253-79; Whitelock, *Memorials* (1732), p. 14.

was not supported by the other judges, who would not offer an opinion on a case they had played no part in, and it pushed the justices of King's Bench to act against the king's will. Having resolved to hand down their ruling, they summoned three of the detained, Hobart, Strode and Long, to appear before the King's Bench on 23 June, before the end of term halted legal process for the summer.[25]

The Crown's response to this show of impartiality has rightly been described by Reeve as a 'despicable and "dirty" trick'. By removing the three prisoners from the custody of the Marshal of the Court and placing them in the Tower, Charles I dismissed not only the legal authority that he had delegated to his common law judges, but also the law itself. If the judges could not be enlisted, then they would be ignored, and there is fair irony in the warrant sent by the king to the judges informing them that Hobart, Strode and Long would remain in the Tower 'until by due course of law they... shall be thence delivered'. Charles now informed the judges of his intention to retain the prisoners in custody 'until we should find their temper and discretions to be such as may deserve [release]'. In short, the king implied, bail was to be equated with pardon, and pardon was negotiable only on submission to the authority of the Crown.[26]

Recognising that the judges would move to bail the prisoners when term resumed, the Crown moved in September 1629 to have them released and removed from 'popular applause', but only upon public demonstration of repentance. Accordingly, the king wrote to the judges, instructing them to offer bail to the prisoners on condition of a bond of good behaviour, and accompanied with a warning that if the king's grace was refused they should 'neither have liberty by his letter or by other means till they had acknowledged their fault'. According to Bulstrode Whitelocke 'chief-justice Hyde, and my father, were sent

25 Reeve, *Charles I*, p. 127; Gardiner, *History of England*, vol. 7, p. 87.

26 Reeve, *Charles I*, p. 127; PRO KB 29/278 membrane 45; King's Bench Controlment Roll, Trinity term 1629; *State Trials*, vol. 3, cols 286-287; *Historical Collections*, vol. 1, pp. 679-84.

for by the king at Hampton Court, who advised with them about the imprisoned Parliament-men; and both these judges did what good offices they could, to bring on the king to heel these breaches'. Unfortunately, the only personal record of this crucial meeting that survives among James Whitelocke's papers is a summons to attend the king 'on the morrow', dated 29 September 1629. A letter from Secretary Dorchester informing Hyde on 30 September noting 'that his Majesty understood your mind and Justice Whitelocke's, who was with you, yet because he would as well be satisfied of the rest before he gave order for the prisoners' release, he hath commanded me to dispatch a messenger', does seem to imply that the judges persuaded Charles to reconsider his approach, albeit briefly.[27]

Whatever the case, the king returned to his original position thereafter, and the judges were forced to offer bail only upon security for good behaviour, and under royal letters patent. Whitelocke must have realised that the Crown could present its actions as an act of clemency under force of the prerogative, and that for the prisoners to abrogate all rights to a legal hearing was, as even the Venetian ambassador could plainly discern, 'to accept liberty at the cost of their conscience'. John Selden later suggested that the judges were indeed conscious that 'he and his fellow prisoners had done nothing that required them to find sureties for their good behaviour', but neither were they prepared to disobey a royal command. On 3 October, just before the legal term opened, the prisoners were brought to Serjeants' Inn by Charles's direction. There they were individually questioned

---

27 PRO State Papers 16/147/74; Reeve, *Charles I*, p. 136, n. 84; p. 138, n. 90; Gardiner, *History of England*, vol. 7, p. 110, n. 1; Whitelock, *Memorials* (1732), p. 14; Longleat Papers, vol. 4, fol. 27; *Calendar of State Papers Domestic Addenda 1625-1649*, p. 351; Cf. Reeve, *Charles I*, p. 128-40. An order of 24 September 1629 from the Privy Council for Whitelocke and Croke to 'be at your lodgings at Serjeant Inn by Twesday next at the farthest' survives in *Acts of the Privy Council 1629/30*, p. 140. Reeve suggests that Charles, in concession to the arguments made by Whitelocke and Hyde on behalf of the court, may have altered his original insistence that the judges make any second offer of bail conditional upon request of pardon for refusing the first.

by the judges about their willingness to accept release upon a bond of good behaviour. Apart from Long, who weakened only to later recant and once again seek detention, they stood fast and waited for the courts to re-open to insist upon a decision on bail.[28]

In Eliot's case, the argument employed by the counsel for the defence centred upon claims that 'Parliament is a transcendent court, and of transcendent jurisdiction', thus exempting the parliamentary conduct of the prisoners from prosecution by the King's Bench. It was somewhat ironic that Whitelocke – who had, of course, felt himself professionally penalised for his parliamentary service – should caution the defence against this line of argument. It was not royalist leanings, but practical experience which led him to ask

> that that which is done in parliament by consent of all the house, shall not be questioned elsewhere: but if any private members *exuunt personas judicem, et induunt malefacientum personas, et sunt seditiosi*, is there a sanctimony in the place, that they may not be questioned for it elsewhere?

He suggested that the case had been 'reduced to a narrow room, for all the Judges are agreed, that an offence committed in parliament against the king or his government, may be punished out of parliament. So now the sole doubt which remains is, whether this court can punish it'.[29]

---

28 *Calendar of State Papers Venetian 1621-1632*, p. 205: 'Soranzo to the Doge and Senate, 2 October 1629'; George Johnson, *Memoirs of John Selden, and notices of the political contest during his time* (London 1835), pp. 187-8; John Selden, *Joannis Seldini Jurisconsulti Opera Omnia tam edita quam inedita*, 3 vols (London 1726), vol. 2, 1429; Hyde to Dorchester, SP 16/149/110; Gardiner, *History of England*, vol. 7, p. 110; *Court and Times of Charles the First*, vol. 2, pp. 30-1.

29 *State Trials*, vol. 3, cols 294-304; Reeve, *Charles I*, pp. 150-1. In 1621 James I had argued that he was 'very free and able to punish any man's misdemeanours in parliament, as well during their sitting as after; which we mean not to spare hereafter, upon any occasion of any man's insolent behaviour there that shall be ministered unto us'; *Select Statutes and other Constitutional Documents illustrative of the reigns of Elizabeth and James I*, ed. G.W. Prothero (Oxford 1894), p. 310.

From this point, counsel for the defence were in an untenable position. Their case argued that the King's Bench lacked the jurisdiction to pass judgement, on the basis of the alleged jurisdictional inferiority, in a ruling to be handed down by the judges of the self-same Court of King's Bench. Eliot's allegation of a conspiracy between the judges and the Crown to 'trample under their feet the liberties of the subjects of this realm, and the liberties of this House' cannot have helped their cause. Small wonder, then, that counsel for the Crown emphasised this attack upon the dignity of the judges, or that the judges of the King's Bench now moved to assert that 'the court, as the case is, shall have sufficient jurisdiction, although these offences were committed in parliament, and that the imprisoned members ought to answer'.[30]

In his summing up of Eliot's case, Whitelocke showed little sympathy towards the prisoners. Speaking for the court, Whitelocke warned Selden that 'the surety of good behaviour is a preventing medicine of the damage that may fall out to the commonwealth; and it is an act of government and jurisdiction, and not of law'. The action of Eliot and his accomplices, Whitelocke assured the court, 'though it be not capital... is criminal, for it is sowing of sedition to the destruction of the commonwealth'. If one could be punished for words in the pulpit which were 'scandalous to the state', so

> in this case, when a burgess of parliament becomes mutinous, he shall not have privilege of parliament. In my opinion, the realm cannot consist without parliaments, but the behaviour of parliament-men ought to be parliamentary. No outrageous speeches were ever used against a great minister of state in parliament which have not been punished.[31]

By constructing the issue as one of individual rather than parliamentary dissent, Whitelocke shifted the emphasis away from parliamentary rights and toward the powers of the Crown. 'The question now', he told the court

---

30 *State Trials*, vol. 3, cols 66, 79.

31 *State Trials*, vol. 3, cols 289, 308.

is not between us that are Judges of this Court, and the parliament, or between the king and parliament, but between some private members of the House of Commons and the king himself: for here the king himself questions them for those offences, as well he may.

'In every commonwealth', he declared, 'there is one super-eminent power, which is not subject to be questioned by any other, and that is the king in this commonwealth'. Accordingly, the judges ruled for the Crown. John Eliot was to be canonised, upon his death in prison two years after the trial, as a martyr for the cause of 'parliamentary liberty'. Like Whitelocke, a parliamentary champion from an earlier time who departed the world a few months after him, he was spared the painful constitutional questions forced upon those who lived on into the turbulent decades to follow.[32]

VI

How does one assess the impact of James Whitelocke's judicial conduct during his time as Justice of King's Bench? Members of the Long Parliament concluded that Hyde, Jones and Whitelocke had failed to uphold the law by refusing to grant bail in Eliot's case without sureties of good behaviour (Croke was excused 'as differing in opinion from the rest'). It was left to Bulstrode Whitelocke to remind the Commons that 'Judge Whitelocke had been a faithful, able and stout asserter of the rights and liberties of the free-born subjects of this Kingdom, for which he had been in many ways a sufferer'. Bulstrode's inspired speech in defence of his deceased father apparently met with respect from John Hampden 'and divers others' in the Commons, who 'expressed themselves with great respect and

32 *Reports of Sir John Croke* in *English Reports* 79, pp. 1121-3; Jones, *Politics and the Bench*, p. 13; *State Trials*, vol. 3, cols 307-8; Reeve, *Charles I*, pp. 153-4. Imprisoned 'at the king's pleasure' for 'conspiracy... to slander the state, and raise sedition and discord between the king, his peers, and people', the defendants faced fines ranging from £2000 for the ringleader Eliot to £500 for Valentine, the least affluent.

honour to the memory of the deceased Judge', and James Whitelocke 'was thereupon reckoned by the House, in the same degree with Judge Crooke, as to their censure, and proceedings.'[33]

In fact, Whitelocke should have been convicted, by both the letter and the spirit of the law. Russell has concluded that in 1630 'Whitelocke, as in 1610, showed signs of having a concept of sovereignty, but seemed less disposed than he had been in 1610 to repose sovereignty in the King in Parliament.' Of course, Whitelocke could never have conceived in 1610 or 1630 that parliament might one day assert its right to rule in the name of the king. In cutting through the political sophistry of the defendants, it was Whitelocke who pointed out that they were in effect 'questioning the supreme authority of the King'. To the end of his life, James Whitelocke refused to accept that it was possible, by upholding this authority, to subvert the rights of the subject.[34]

It is important to remember that in 1610, Whitelocke's stance placed emphasis on the interdependence of royal and parliamentary rights – a far cry from Eliot's 'potentially revolutionary' appeal 'over the King's head to the country at large'. This rapidly shifting context is something that a new generation of parliamentarians struggled to comprehend as they attempted to make sense of their own parliamentary traditions. In 1628, Sir Robert Phelips cited the Exchequer verdict that Whitelocke had countered superbly in 1610 with his King's Bench ruling on the five knights, as rulings 'exceeding one another in prejudice of the subject'. By establishing 'constitutional' comparisons that ignored the separate issues at hand, Phelips suggested the ways by which a new generation of parliamentarians redacted their collective memories of royal appeals to an 'inalienable prerogative', and fuelled a new and more radical political ideology.[35]

---

33 Jones, *Politics and the Bench*, pp. 13-24; Whitelock, *Memorials* (1732), pp. 38-9.

34 Russell, *Parliaments and English Politics*, p. 364; Jones, *Politics and the Bench*, p. 80.

35 Russell, *Parliaments and English Politics*, p. 415; Whitelocke, *Memorials* (1732), p. 39; *Proceedings in Parliament 1628*, vol. 2, p. 63; *State Trials*, vol. 3, col. 66;

A century ago, Gardiner reflected sympathetically on the position of the Kings' Bench judges in the reign of Charles I. 'Events', he said, 'had conspired to thrust forward the judges into a position which it was impossible for them to hold.' Reviewing James Whitelocke's passage through the stormy political waters that greeted him after 1625, it is hard to avoid the conclusion that his own opinions were always secondary to the changes that were occurring around him. Reeve has described these changes as 'an uncharacteristic and in many ways an unwanted' development. 'They were', he suggests, 'the politics of a non-parliamentary England, politics which came about with the breakdown of traditional political and constitutional process'. As a Justice of King's Bench, Whitelocke was drawn into a damaging political debate which threatened to destroy his personal and professional reputation at their apogee.[77]

The suspension of Chief Baron Walter from office for during Eliot's case has been taken to mark the low water mark of judicial independence in the Caroline period. As Charles turned his anger to Walter, there were widespread rumours that James Whitelocke was now to be offered the position of Chief Baron, an office that Whitelocke had shown willingness to accept as 'a good preferment' from his office in Chester. Bulstrode Whitelocke reflected that in the troubled circumstances of 1630 his father

> had no great mind to succeed Walter, because Walter alleged that his patent of that office was *quam diu se bene gesserit*, and that he ought not to be removed but by a *scire facias*.

Cromartie, *Sir Matthew Hale*, p. 31. Sir John Davies notebook moves directly from Whitelocke's 1610 speech to John Eliot's petition to the Crown, leaving one to speculate upon the associations that were later established between the circumstances of these 'constitutional' matters in this and similar documents; CUL Ms Ff. 3.17, fols 113-114.

77 Gardiner, *History of England*, vol. 7, p. 111; Reeve, *Charles I*, p. 2.

As Walter's cry of technical foul prevented his dismissal Whitelocke did not have to decide if he would accept the position, but there is fair irony, given Humphrey May's earlier warning to Whitelocke over his outspoken parliamentary comments in 1610, that King Charles considered him 'a stout, wise, and learned judge, and one who knew what belongs to uphold magistrates and magistracy in their dignity'. Whitelocke's admission to high legal office, which brought him great financial and personal reward in the last years of his life, had also become the source of stresses that mirrored larger problems facing the English nation – problems which, by the time of his death, were beginning to tear at the fabric of political harmony.[78]

78 Reeve, *Charles I*, pp. 146-7, 149; cf. *Diary of Sir Richard Hutton*, pp. 78, 83; Prest *Rise of the Barristers*, p. 268; *Court and Times of Charles the First*, vol. 2, pp. 33, 35; Longleat Papers, vol. 2, fol. 175; Whitelock, *Memorials* (1732), p. 11; Aylmer, *The King's Servants*, p. 112. In his *Memorials* (cf. 1853 ed., vol. 1, p. 31) Bulstrode Whitelocke conflated an earlier comment of the king's, drawn from his father's papers to suggest that he was in good favour with the Crown at this stage. Whitelock, *Memorials* (Oxford 1853), vol. 1, pp. 35-6. The king's recommendation was expressed in a letter from Sir Humphrey May to James Whitelocke on 8 May 1629 which survives in the Longleat Papers, vol. 4, fol. 9.

Part III
Family and Friends

Chapter 7

County connections

Upon his appointment as a judge in 1620, James Whitelocke observed that 'the whole course of life of a professor of the law is devided into three passages' – his 'time of study', his 'time of practise' ('the fruit of his studye'), and

> his time of service to his countrye, and that is the discharge of his civill dutye to the commonwealthe in sutche place as he shall be called unto. So he begins *philosophus* in getting knoledge, goethe on *œconomus* in getting meanes of livelihood, ends *politicus* in serving his countrye.

Whitelocke's notion of service to his 'country' centred upon the counties in which he would establish a lasting presence: Oxfordshire, Buckinghamshire, and Berkshire. Holmes and Heal have argued that gentry lawyers such as Whitelocke, once known to historians almost exclusively by their parliamentary reputations, must be located within 'their own *pays*, in the environment in which they logically exercised authority', so that their political identities might be related back to localist concerns, and to those supra-provincial constructions of identity of which Whitelocke, given his educational and professional contacts with the centre, is almost an archetype. By questioning the place of family and 'friends' in Whitelocke's rise to prominence, this chapter traces his economic and social progress in the county community, to give context to his overall achievement in early Stuart society.[1]

---

1 *Liber Famelicus*, p. 80; Heal & Holmes, *The Gentry*, p. x; Clive Holmes, 'The County Community in Stuart Historiography', *Journal of British Studies* 19 (1980), p. 73. Of course, Whitelocke's use of the term friendship in the *Liber Famelicus* must be thought of, in part, as an active disposition towards professional support; James, *Society, Politics & Culture*, pp. 330-1.

I

Whitelocke began his life in London as a merchant's son. His connections with the region in which he would acquire property, settle his family and leave the greatest monuments to his success were nominal at birth, and developed from his marriage to Elizabeth Bulstrode. Whitelocke's first remarks about Elizabeth Bulstrode dryly note that she 'was born at Hugley Bulstrodes, in the countye of Buckingham, the last of July 1575; so she was 27 year olde, and I within two monethe of 32, when we wear maryed'. Negotiated by their widowed mothers Cecilia Bulstrode and Joan Whitelocke, this marriage was consummated on 9 September 1602, at a stage in life when Whitelocke had established his professional credentials but had little in the way of material resources. The most immediate financial benefit to Whitelocke was £500 and eighteen months of free board in Cecilia Bulstrode's Fleet Street mansion.[2]

The strong bond and mutual respect that developed from the union of James and Elizabeth Whitelocke presaged Whitelocke's professional success. While the demands of assize or term work, coupled with his need to travel and hear causes in the steward's courts, combined to keep Whitelocke away from his family for weeks or even months at a stretch, he was fortunate that in Elizabeth he found (in the words of his son) 'a most fitt and loving companion to her husband' who was 'so expert in business, that whilest her husband was imployed in publique affayres, he wholly trusted her with the management of his private affayres, contracts with tenants[,] receipts

2 Wallace MacCaffrey, 'Place and Patronage in Elizabethan Politics' in *Elizabethan Government and Society: Essays presented to Sir John Neale*, ed. S.T. Bindoff, J. Hurstfield & C.H. Williams (London 1961), p. 107; Prest, *Rise of the Barristers*, ch. 8; *Liber Famelicus*, p. 15; the articles of marriage, slightly damaged, are preserved in the Longleat Papers, vol. 1, fol. 37. The great success of his marriage probably contributed to Whitelocke's scorn towards matches made 'without consent of frendes', such as his sister-in-law Dorothy's marriage to Sir John Eyre; *Liber Famelicus*, pp. 25-26.

and disbursements'. In between running the household in her husband's absence, Elizabeth Whitelocke also took charge of the education of Bulstrode (and presumably his sisters), being 'well furnished with learning' in divinity and history, and expert in French. In her epitaph, James would write movingly of his affection for Elizabeth. The grief that he expressed at her passing suggests the strength of the bond that grew between them over thirty years of married life.[3]

Social historians have suggested that gentry fascination with genealogy extended, in part, from pragmatic interest in the benefits to be accrued through kinship. James Whitelocke was obviously proud of his marriage into old gentry stock, noting that the Bulstrodes were 'born [to] the best and most worshipfull offices in the countye'. Although of declining economic status, they had significant prestige in Buckinghamshire, as one of perhaps forty families who dominated local office holding among 200 or so local gentry families. Bulstrode Whitelocke's claim that 'severall of them were knights, matched into good families and were of esteem in their countrey' was substantially correct, although his proviso that they 'did more affect hospitality and generous living att home then Court preferments or bought titles' smacks of rationalisation, and James Whitelocke searched eagerly for obscure connections with the royal household ranging from his sister-in-law Dorothy, who was a gentlewoman of Queen Anne of Denmark's bedchamber, to distant figures like Cecilia Bowstread, related through the Croke family, who had been maid of honour to Catherine of Aragon.[4]

---

3 *Diary*, p. 44, 63; *Liber Famelicus*, p. 44. Financial records in the family papers testify to her active role in household administration; see Longleat Papers, vol. 3, fol. 180, vol. 4, fol. 137.

4 David Cressy, 'Kinship and Kin Interaction in Early Modern England', *Past & Present* 113 (1986), p. 49; J.T. Cliffe, *The Yorkshire Gentry from the Reformation to the Civil War* (London 1969), p. 10; *Liber Famelicus*, pp. 15, 17, 20; *Diary*, p. 43; A.M. Johnson, 'Buckinghamshire, 1640-1660' (1963 University of Swansea MA thesis), pp. 1-7, quoted in Peck, *Court Patronage and Corruption*, p. 78.

For Whitelocke, establishing kinship with the Crokes (Elizabeth Whitelocke's family on her maternal side) was doubly advantageous as this family, of distinction in Buckinghamshire since the sixteenth century, were prominent in the legal profession. Wilfrid Prest has observed that the 'judge's favourite, often son, brother, nephew, cousin, or relative by marriage, was a familiar figure in the courts of Elizabethan and Stuart England'. Whitelocke's uncle, George Croke, was a successful lawyer with major land holdings in Buckinghamshire and Oxfordshire while Sir John Croke, his other uncle, was speaker of the House of Commons in 1601, and Justice of King's Bench from 1608 until his death in 1619. Whitelocke never admitted to relying upon the professional patronage of Sir John Croke, and an obituary noted that he was 'very kinde and affable to all lawyers that practised before him' – but it can hardly have been disadvantageous to Whitelocke that such an eminent figure of the law was 'my wife's unckle by her mother'.[5]

Mervyn James has pointed to the extended family as 'the circle within which what was most deeply felt in the active life of the time was played out' among the English gentry classes. The *Liber Famelicus* provides a detailed record of family baptisms, marriages and funerals which suggests that a fluid, extended reliance on kinship flowed naturally from the union of Whitelocke and Bulstrode. Given the high rate of infant mortality and the ever present threat of disease, death was for James Whitelocke a ready fact of life, and forms a recurrent theme in the *Liber Famelicus*. During her first decade of marriage, Elizabeth Whitelocke gave birth to seven children, of whom four – Mary, Joan, Dorothy and James – died in infancy, leaving Elizabeth and Cecilia to extend the family line, and Bulstrode to carry the family name.[6]

---

5 Prest, *Rise of the Barristers*, p. 27; A. Croke, *The genealogical history of the Croke family, originally named Le Blount*, 2 vols (Oxford 1823), vol. 2, pp. 409-484; *Liber Famelicus*, p. 76.

6 Mervyn James, *Family, Lineage and Civil Society: A Study of Society, Politics, and Mentality in the Durham Region 1500-1640* (Oxford 1974), p. 19;

The death of his mother and four of his children were obviously occasions of great sadness in the life of James Whitelocke. When his mother Joan, who 'went away even with olde age even as a candle goethe out', departed this world on 21 February 1607, Whitelocke comforted himself that she

> had her senses and her memorye to the last gasp, and was full of spirit and comfort among her children, and she did often remember herself on the deathe bed to my wife and children, whome she loved most deerly.

Between 1608 and 1614, James Whitelocke also grieved the loss of Elizabeth's grandparents, Sir John Croke and Lady Croke, her uncle Henry Croke, her sister Anne Bulstrode and sister-in-law Mary Reed.[7]

Whitelocke family names were drawn from an intimate circle of family and friends and 'celebrated family and friendship connections in the past, present and in the future'. Although it was customary among the merchant classes to adopt the mother's family name as a Christian name for the child, Whitelocke was obviously not impressed by the demand of Edmund Whitelocke to name his godson Bulstrode. When 'asked if he would not give it another name' at the christening, his older brother insisted that the child bear one or the other of his mother's maiden names, leaving James Whitelocke with Elizabeth as his only other choice! In fact, once Bulstrode had added fame to the name, Whitelocke boys would continue to take it over the generations.[8]

Collectanea Topographica and Genealogica, ed. J.G. Nichols, 8 vols (London 1834-1843), vol. 5, p. 369; *Liber Famelicus*, pp. 15, 26. Bulstrode was born at the Fleet Street address on 6 August 1605, Mary in Buckinghamshire on 6 October 1606, Cecilia in London on 10 March 1607, Joan on 6 August 1609 at Hedgely Bulstrode in Buckinghamshire, Dorothy on 15 September 1610 in Fleet Street; *Liber Famelicus*, pp. 16, 17, 18, 19, 20, 25. The family tree is in Spalding, *Improbable Puritan*, pp. 20-1.

7 *Liber Famelicus*, pp. 16, 17, 25, 45.

8 Peck, *Court Patronage and Corruption*, p. 77; *Diary*, p. 43. In the Whitelocke family, there seems to have been little false modesty in such celebrations. The right to name Whitelocke's eldest daughter was reserved by his wife's

The troubled lives and early deaths of two of his brothers led Whitelocke to rely upon his wife's family as a source of guidance and support. Of twenty-three godparents, fifteen were his wife's relatives, ranging from Sir William Bulstrode (her father's uncle) to John Searl, her sister Anne's husband. Six godparents were drawn from outside the family ranks, including John Buckeridge, who was godparent to Mary, and John Harington who was Cecilia's godfather.[9]

Harington's example stresses the nebulous character of kinship ties. He had become acquainted with James Whitelocke through his father, Lord John Harington, whose close friendship

> grew by the consanguinitye between his wife and mine, for the olde ladye Harington was the sole daughter and heir of Robert Keylway... and of Cecilie his wife, daughter of Edward Bulstrode of Hedgely Bulstrode and widow of Sir Alexander Unton of Barkshire, and mother to Elizabeth wife of olde Sir John Croke, my wife's grandfather.

In effect, the younger John Harington was Whitelocke's distant cousin via Elizabeth Unton neé Bulstrode, kinship serving in this instance as an introduction to a lasting family friendship.[10]

The importance of godparents in the family link is suggested by the procedure taken by Whitelocke during the hurried christening of his daughter Dorothy. Whitelocke originally invited Humphrey May, his longstanding friend from St John's and the Middle Temple, and

---

grandmother Elizabeth Croke, who 'gave her her owne name'. It seems likely that Mary was named after Mary Croke who served as Dorothy's godparent; Cecilia also linked the Bulstrodes and the Whitelockes by using the name of Elizabeth's mother. One need not look hard for the inspiration to name Whitelocke's second son James; as godfather to Edward Nevill's son in 1615, Whitelocke similarly called the boy James. In the case of Joan Whitelocke, whose godmothers came from outside the family, James Whitelocke appears to have had the final say. 'I was desirous to have her named Joan, in memorye of my good and kinde mother', he wrote, obviously getting his wish. Showing that he could look beyond family, Whitelocke named Dorothy 'for the respect I had of her godmother the Lady Wrighte'; *Liber Famelicus*, pp. 15, 18, 20, 46.

9 *Liber Famelicus*, pp. 15-26.

10 *Liber Famelicus*, p. 31.

Lady Dorothy Wright to be godparents at a ceremony scheduled for early October 1610. As his daughter succumbed to illness, Whitelocke was forced to employ deputies at a premature christening toward the end of September. While one of his appointed godparents (his sister-in-law Mary Croke) was present, Whitelocke was careful to name May and Lady Wright as godparents at the birth of his next child James, noting in his journal that they had already 'bespoken sutche an office' through the previous arrangement.[11]

In such times of reflection as baptisms and funerals, but also on purely social occasions, kin were a ready source of comfort and provided James Whitelocke with some respite from his driven professional life. Bulstrode Whitelocke recalled his father's 'generous mind in his intertainment of friends, and old English hospitality', and the *Liber Famelicus* records a visit made by James and Elizabeth to their brother Henry Bulstrode's estate at Parlant Park in August 1612, from where they proceeded to Essex to visit their mother Cecilia, returning to Buckinghamshire via Sir John Tyrell's Essex estate. In the summer of 1616, Whitelocke was 'royally enterteyned' at the house of Richard Moore, an associate from the Middle Temple, bound through the kinship of their wives.[12]

As a man of professional expertise and growing social influence, Whitelocke actively supervised the affairs of family members. In 1620 he had his nephew placed at Magdalen College, Oxford on behalf of his brother. Between 1620 and 1623 he negotiated the marriage of his daughter Elizabeth to Sir Thomas Mostyn, settling a marriage portion of £2500 (brought down from £3000 in protracted communications) in return for the guaranteed inheritance of Mostyn's extensive land holdings in Carnarvon, Flint, Denbigh and Chester to the first male heir from their union. Hard bargaining on Whitelocke's part stifled negotiations over a match between Cecilia and Sir Edward

11 *Liber Famelicus*, pp. 20, 26.

12 BL Additional MS 53726, fols 68-9, quoted in *Contemporaries of Bulstrode Whitelocke*, p. 428; *Liber Famelicus*, pp. 29, 49-50.

Tyrrell, while Bulstrode was married to Rebecca Bennet in 1630 only after several speculative matches had fallen through on financial grounds, securing a marriage portion of £3000 for the union.[13]

James Whitelocke's preoccupation with family 'posteritye' rested overwhelming upon the shoulders of his son. There can be little doubt that in places the *Liber Famelicus* was composed as a source of instruction to Bulstrode, as James Whitelocke determined that his son should follow in his footsteps. From the age of seven, Bulstrode boarded at Eton and then lived at his father's Fleet Street address while attending Merchant Taylors' School. He was admitted to the Middle Temple as a fourteen-year-old with his father's assistance, who thereafter enlisted the help of William Laud to ensure that his son was well supervised during his stay at St John's College, Oxford.[14]

After the completion of Bulstrode's education, his father sought to ensure his son's professional success. In 1623, when Whitelocke encouraged Bulstrode to follow the assize circuit, he was (not surprisingly) 'treated with much kindness and civility, by the Judges, Counsellors[,] officers and others, and by the gentlemen in the severall Countyes'. Such encouragement stopped short of personal favours in court, and Bulstrode begrudgingly acknowledged the purity of his father's actions in showing him 'no more countenance or favour then to other practisers [on circuit], to satisfy his own conscience and testefy his impartiality'. In 1625, Whitelocke used his influence to secure his son a parliamentary seat for Stafford, which Bulstrode accepted while politely declining another seat offered by his father's old friend Sir Humphrey May. While Bulstrode Whitelocke transcended any paternal influence to become keeper of the Great Seal, it is obvious that his opportunities for advancement owed

---

13 *Liber Famelicus*, pp. 88, 94; *Diary*, pp. 50, 60-1; University College of North Wales, Mostyn MS 7294; Clwyd Record Office, Mostyn MS D/M/3608.

14 *Diary*, pp. 45-8; Heal & Holmes, *The Gentry*, pp. 134, 249.

much to his father, who sought advantages for his son through his own rise to prominence.[15]

While Whitelocke reinforced and reiterated an ordered, intimate set of social relations which bound friends and kin, a second circle of association in his life further defined the boundaries of his social and professional status. His first clerk, Gaven Champineys, was employed three years before his call to the bar, most likely to assist him in his work for St John's. He employed Anthony Ball as a second clerk in 1602, and took on John Griffin in 1606 to look after the horses required for his peripatetic profession. Richard Oakely was employed as a third clerk from 1609. One can surmise that conditions in Whitelocke's employ were favourable, as Griffin left his master's house briefly at the time of his marriage but returned shortly after.[16]

Whitelocke sought Oakely's admission to the Middle Temple in 1614, and was delighted when he was appointed, through Whitelocke's recommendation, as a secretary to Lord Keeper Williams in 1621. By the end of his life, Whitelocke had a domestic entourage consisting of more than twenty servants, an organist, and a personal chaplain. Organ music was obviously a central feature of family life, and Whitelocke encouraged his servants and his children to join him in song on regular occasions. It is pleasing to note his son's observation that despite a 'grave' concern for his family's progress, James Whitelocke found time to 'sport' with his children, to sing with them, and to love them.[17]

---

15 *Diary*, pp. 51, 53, 60.

16 *Liber Famelicus*, pp. 21, 31; and cf. *Contemporaries of Bulstrode Whitelocke*, pp. 427-8.

17 *Liber Famelicus*, p. 90; *Diary*, pp. 44, 45, 51-2, 65; p. 67, n. 1; *Contemporaries of Bulstrode Whitelocke*, pp. 427-8; *Diary of Sir Richard Hutton*, p. 91; Heal & Holmes, *The Gentry*, p. 295.

As a practising lawyer, Whitelocke belonged to a social and professional coterie whose connections with the state were in many ways distinctive. Prompted by early Stuart eulogies of the great financial benefits of the law, historians have explored the wide-ranging financial possibilities of the profession, during a period of expanding litigation across English society and rapid growth in the size of the English bar. Whitelocke was clear in his own mind that, after his legal training, his social and political position depended upon his 'getting meanes of livelihood'. John Bruce largely omitted the financial records interspersed throughout the *Liber Famelicus* as detrimental to the 'little continuity which is to be found in Sir James's narrative'. Among the fullest surviving accounts for a barrister of this era, they are worthy of consideration as an important indicator of Whitelocke's rise to prosperity.[18]

The *Liber Famelicus* furnishes only partial details of client fees and expenses, but it does list the total amounts received and spent upon legal work, by term, throughout Whitelocke's entire career. In his first five terms at the bar, Whitelocke collected £39. 3s. 7d., while his first full legal year (1603) yielded £82. 14s. 4d. In 1604, his total income over four terms was £188. 6s. 8d., while his expenses ran to £162. 1s. 11d., leaving a surplus of £26. 4s. 9d. In 1607, one of his most profitable years of practice, he raised £452. 15s. 8d. from fees and expended £209. 5s. 10d., leaving a substantial profit of £243. 10s. 2d.

---

18 *Liber Famelicus*, pp. xiii-xiv; Prest, *Rise of the Barristers*, pp. 49-79, 146-55; *idem*, 'Lawyers' in *The Professions in Early Modern England*, ed. W.R. Prest (London 1987), p. 74; *idem*, 'Counsellors' Fees and Earnings in the Age of Sir Edward Coke' in *Legal Records*, pp. 171-4; *idem*, 'Judicial Corruption', p. 77; C.W. Brooks, 'The Common Lawyers in England, c. 1558-1642' in *Lawyers in Early Modern Europe and America*, pp. 56-7; *idem*, 'Litigants and Attorneys in the King's Bench and Common Pleas, 1560-1640' in *Legal Records*, p. 43; Barnes, 'Star Chamber Litigants', p. 8.

Whitelocke's gains between this time and 1616 varied from £41. 15s. 3d. in 1608, to the substantial figure of £180. 1s. 7d. in 1614.[19]

From March 1606 to August 1610, the yearly totals provided in the *Liber Famelicus* are supplemented by an additional lists of fees in Whitelocke's notes of assize work. In 1607, Whitelocke's assize profits of £32 16s. 8d. in Lent Vacation, and £67. 3s. 6d. in Trinity made up slightly less than half of his annual profit of £243. 10s. 2d. In 1609, his total assize fees of £101. 3s. made up about a quarter of his annual income of £401. 17s. 10d., while his expenses on assize, totalling £36. 1s. 11d., contributed only slightly to his total expenditure of £345. 6s. 11d. for the year. The following year, Whitelocke recorded a profit of £57. 13s. 14d. from assize work, which represented more than half of his final profit of £99. 7s. 8d. However his total assize fees of £96. 6s. 6d. represented less than a quarter of his total annual income of £432. 19s. 8d. before expenses.[20]

Comparing the totals from 1608, 1609 and 1610, it appears that Whitelocke's fees from assize work had an upper threshold of about £100, representing a significant proportion of Whitelocke's income in his early years at the bar, but a constantly diminishing proportion thereafter. By 1616, Whitelocke could also expect to gain a total of about £46 per annum from legal retainers from Woodstock, Eton, St John's, Westminster, the dean and canons of Windsor, and a variety of lay and ecclesiastical patrons. It thus becomes apparent that the bulk of his income came from specific payment, by lay clients, for work in the central courts. In this sense, Whitelocke's interest Roper's office, which probably yielded about £300 between July 1612 and

19 BL Additional MS 53725, fols 31, 36, 38, 70. Whitelocke's first term of practice was Michaelmas 1600, which he included in his profits for 1600, thereafter listing his totals from Hilary term of the previous year with those from Easter, Trinity and Michaelmas of the next year.

20 Longleat Papers, miscellaneous parcels box 9, assize book, fols 64, 91, 134, 150, 163, 181 [hereafter cited as assize book]; BL Additional MS 53725, fols 39-40. As the assize book is unfoliated, I have numbered each folio (2 pages) from 1 to 182.

August 1613, was probably less important than the associations he cemented with the judges of King's Bench during his exercise of the patent as clerk of the rolls.[21]

Given Aylmer's estimate of an average annual income of £800 and £4000 for knights and peers respectively in the 1630s, Whitelocke's declared income of around £600 in 1616 is somewhat less than one might have expected for one of the most successful lawyers of the day. It is clear that in his second decade of legal practice, only a policy of financial brinkmanship sustained Whitelocke's determined push to place himself into the ranks of the gentry. By covering the massive expenditure needed to pay for the acquisition of Fawley Court (the Buckinghamshire property he bought from Sir William Alford in 1616), his readership at the Middle Temple in 1619, and the cost of a knighthood in 1620, Whitelocke cemented his professional and social status, but pushed his financial resources to the limit.[22]

Prest has noted that Whitelocke's accumulated expenses amounted to £4,313 between 1616 and 1620, yet his stated income came to only £2,466. Questioning Whitelocke's ability to pay for Fawley Court, he has rightly posited three possible sources of extra income: gains from the sale of wood, money made from loans at interest, and compensation received from the surrender of a reversion to a share in Sir John Roper's King's Bench office. Closer inspection of Whitelocke's properties and assets suggest that he could have mustered £2500 on top of his legal income over this period, in the face of expenses of £9000 for Fawley, £240 for his reading, and an additional £315 for his

21 Aldolpus Ballard, *Chronicles of the Royal Borough of Woodstock. Compiled from the Borough Records and Other Original Documents* (Oxford 1896), p. 35; Eton College Records 27/267; *Liber Famelicus*, pp. 18, 19, 29, 44, 46, 59, 60, 76, 77. My calculations work upon Aylmer's assumption that the office of clerk of the rolls yielded around £4000 per annum. The badly perished front page of Whitelocke's assize book lists many of the clients represented by Whitelocke on the assizes, including St John's College and Thomas Mostin.

22 Aylmer, *The King's Servants*, p. 331, and cf. Jones, *Politics and the Bench*, where it is suggested that the attorney-general could expect to earn £6,000 per annum in the same period.

knighthood and associated expenses upon his promotion to the Chester judgeship.[23]

The *Liber Famelicus* indicates that Whitelocke extended substantial loans – running, on occasion, into thousands of pounds – to friends and associates, and receipts from later transactions suggest that he, in turn, borrowed substantial sums of money from family and friends. Whitelocke must have borrowed heavily to repay his debts between 1616 and 1620, and comments written below his financial accounts make it clear that his income was stretched to the limit over this time. Totalling his expenses for 1620, Whitelocke noted that although he had spent £3040. 10s. 2d. over the previous two years, he had earned only £2931. 7s. 4d. in the same period. Adding (apparently with alarm) that he had also acquired £9000 in land over the last four years, he vowed to keep more careful record of his financial transactions thereafter, and if 'the profits of my office and my expenses togeather matches thereafter it will be well'. In the end judicial promotion, rather than his crude book-keeping, ensured his ongoing solvency.[24]

After his appointment as a judge, Whitelocke benefited from a new range of financial incentives, and his Chester judgeship proved particularly lucrative. Whitelocke's yearly income from Chester, calculated by him at £1175. 3s. 9d. in 1623, bettered his subsequent earnings as Justice of the King's Bench, which he assessed at £974. 10s. for the year ending Michaelmas term 1627, and at £1002. 10s. during his last full year on the bench. Whitelocke was ever careful to extract the maximum financial benefits from his office, declining to relinquish his Chester office for the more prestigious King's Bench until after he had ridden the 1624 assize circuits, which gained him

---

23 Prest, 'Counsellors' Fees and Earnings in the Age of Sir Edward Coke', p. 174; *Liber Famelicus*, pp. 22, 23, 46, 53, 70-73, 84, 105; Works, vol. 4, pp. 100-102; Longleat Papers, vol. 5, fol. 170, and see Powell, thesis.

24 *Liber Famelicus*, pp. 29-30, 44; Longleat Papers, vol. 2, fol. 88, 89v; BL Additional MS 53725, fol. 134; cf. Jones, *Politics and the Bench*, p. 37.

£356. 9s. and £336. 5s. 3d. respectively, with a further £100. 7s. for work at Ludlow.[25]

From 1625, as Charles I sought to raise revenue to fight in Europe, Whitelocke's financial security was threatened in a dispute between the judges and the Crown over non-payment of wages. After he had totalled his profits for Easter term 1625, Whitelocke noted that the daily wage of 8s. 5 3/4 d. provided for a Justice of King's Bench furnished a yearly total of £154. 19s. 8d., emphasising that judges in King's Bench and Common Pleas received a further £94. 3s. 2d. for each assize circuit in twice-yearly instalments 'payd... *the day after Easter term and the day after Michaelmas term*'. Whitelocke's stated yearly profit of £771. 12s. 1d. for 1625 was in fact a projected figure, as it included the sum of £94. 3s. 2d. 'Due to me of my last yeares wages at Mich. 1625 where is payable the day after Mich. term'.[26]

Subsequent lists of profits show that from 1625 to 1628 this circuit fee (which comprised more than half of the Crown's yearly payment to Whitelocke) was halved. In Easter term 1626, Whitelocke stated that he had received no instalment of the circuit wage, which was eventually paid during his Autumn assize circuit. He did not receive a second payment in 1626, and, although he was paid following Easter term 1627, the delayed payment of his fee at Michaelmas term 1627 led him to note that the fee was 'not payd', a note that he crossed out. Even with this £188. 6s. 4d. Crown fee for both circuits in 1627, Whitelocke was making less from his salary than he had done during his time in Chester.[27]

Noting that official salaries were 'sometimes in arrears', Jones has suggested that an ongoing dispute between the judges and the Crown

---

25 BL Additional MS 53725, fols 148, 151-2, 175, 189.

26 Jones, *Politics and the Bench*, p. 37; BL Additional MS 53725, fols 164-5; *Liber Famelicus*, p. 104. Whitelocke's italics are omitted from Bruce's edition.

27 BL Additional MS 53725, fols 169, 170, 173, 175. It should be noted, however, that Sir Thomas Chamberlain was now having trouble forcing the Crown to pay the wages that Whitelocke assured him were his due as Chief Justice of Chester; CSPD 1625-1626, p. 60.

over non-payment of wages stands 'as striking indication of bad blood and dubious practices in high quarters'. Whitelocke certainly felt little sympathy towards the earl of Marlborough, given the thankless task by Charles I of raising new revenue to fight the war with Spain, noting that the Crown fee for assize work, 'whiche for memory of man had been alwayes payd the last day of Ester term and Michaelmas term, or the day after at the farthest, was unpayd the end of this Michaelmas term, 1627'. Along with Justices Jones, Croke and Serjeant Harvey, Whitelocke demanded an explanation from Treasurer Marlborough, who, Whitelocke recounted, 'gave sleeveless and cunning answeares, but craftely and deceitfully, underhand, did abuse the judges withe delayes'.[28]

The judges then reminded the treasurer of statutory requirements which bound him to pay them even in times of civil war, by recourse to funds derived from duties imposed upon the cities of London, Bristol and Kingston-on-Hull. Whitelocke recounted that Marlborough's response was to offer payment to those judges to whom he was personally in debt from his time as chief justice of King's Bench. As Whitelocke was not among this group, he must have been pleased that Sir Robert Pye refused the offer, 'that none ought to be preferred or singled out from ther fellowes'. If Marlborough expected a man as fiercely conscious of his rights as Whitelocke to accept this state of affairs, he was badly mistaken. Along with Jones and Dodderidge, he drew up a writ of *liberate*, based upon the statute of 18 Henry VI, to force the treasury to pay his fee, condemning Marlborough as an 'old dissembler, that had been on of our owne company, [but] used us worse than any man before him'.[29]

The Lord Keeper's intervention put a stay to proceedings, but it did not assure the judges of their circuit fee, which was again missing from Whitelocke's income for Hilary term. In a 'wonder' arising

---

28 Lockyer, *Early Stuarts*, p. 244; Jones, *Politics and the Bench*, p. 37; *Liber Famelicus*, p. 108; BL Additional MS 53725, fol. 176. Bruce has misread 'cumming' for 'cunning'.

29 BL Additional MS 53725, fol. 176; *Liber Famelicus*, pp. 108-9.

from the 1628 circuit, he noted that for the first time ever (to the best of his knowledge) all Crown circuit wages were suspended, forcing the judges 'ether to deceave the whole kingdom, whome by their summons they had called togeather [i.e., abandon the assizes], or spend their owne money in the king's service'. Whitelocke went on to detail the exact allowances provided for the 'Justice of Assize in their circuits', which comprised a daily fee of £3. 1s. per judge primarily to pay for his legal entourage, and usually allowed a judge to pocket slightly over £100 each. Yet as Whitelocke rode the Northern circuit in 1628, he was denied the king's fee of £67. 2s.[30]

A one-off payment of £40 in 'compensation' from his old friend Bishop Richard Neile of Durham pushed Whitelocke's profit up to £128. 9s. 8d., £28 more than he had earned in the previous year. Yet Whitelocke was at a loss to understand the government's policy and appears insensitive to the financial crisis caused by the war, blaming 'these monstrous enormityes in the state' upon the 'crooked dealing' of the treasurer. There was little Whitelocke could do if he wanted to retain his position upon the bench but comply with the king's personal requests for money, such as a loan of £20 that he was asked to provide on 13 February 1628 with promise of repayment within one year. After 1628, Crown wages would be paid on time, calming strained relations; it is open to speculation whether the king's need for judicial support in the wake of the troubled 1628 parliament caused this change of policy.[31]

III

Between 1607 and 1616, James Whitelocke projected his increasing wealth and status through property acquisitions in the capital and in the country. The birthplaces of his children indicate that, early in his

---

30 *Liber Famelicus*, pp. 109-10; BL Additional MS 53725, fol. 178

31 *Liber Famelicus*, p. 109; BL Additional MS 53725, fols 175, 179. I have found no mention of European affairs in any of Whitelocke's papers.

career, Whitelocke employed the extensive Bulstrode family properties as a base in the country and in London. In the capital, Whitelocke lived for many years in the Fleet Street mansion of his mother-in-law Cecilia Croke, an arrangement written into the marriage covenant with his wife. As the *Liber Famelicus* refers to 'my house in Fleet Street' in a note of the birth of his daughter Dorothy in September 1610, as distinct from earlier references to 'the Fleet Street house', it seems possible that management of the property had been handed over to Whitelocke after his mother-in-law's marriage to Sir John Brown, an Essex gentleman, in 1608. At one stage, the house was rented to Sir John Walter, until Whitelocke took up possession himself again in 1613. As an active member of his inn of court, James Whitelocke also maintained professional chambers at the Middle Temple as an office and for private use during his stays in the capital.[32]

Away from London, Whitelocke acquired properties from just north of Oxford to the Buckinghamshire/Berkshire borderlands in the south, spreading across a region divided by the Chiltern hills, and concentrating upon three towns with which he had life-long professional associations: Oxford, Windsor, and Woodstock. Whitelocke first acquired land near Whitechurch, to the north-east of Oxford, from his cousin William Whitelocke. In 1607, he purchased a farm near Witney, a few miles north-west of Oxford and within easy reach of Woodstock, where he had recently been appointed recorder. From 1611 until his acquisition of Fawley Court in 1616, pretensions to a gentry lifestyle led Whitelocke to settle his family in the manor of Clewer House, just beyond Windsor. Rented from Andrew Windsor, who leased the property from the Crown, Clewer established White-

32 *Collectanea Topographica and Genealogica*, ed. J.B. Nichols, 8 vols (London 1834-1843), vol. 5, p. 369; *Liber Famelicus*, pp. 15, 16, 17, 18, 19, 20, 25, 32; *Diary*, p. 45. Bulstrode was born at the Fleet Street address on 6 August 1605, Mary in Buckinghamshire on 6 October 1606, Cecilia in London on 10 March 1607, Joan on 6 August 1609 at Hedgely Bulstrode in Buckinghamshire, Dorothy on 15 September 1610 in Fleet Street.

locke along the River Thames and about halfway between his usual business destinations of Oxford and London.[33]

It was in this region, with Woodstock thirty miles to the west and London forty to the east, that Whitelocke made his most significant acquisition, purchasing Fawley Court in 1616. Whitelocke's manor house of Fawley, located at the southern extremity of Desborough hundred along the banks of the Thames, lies in ruins between Sir Christopher Wren's magnificent new manor and the river. It remains a visible symbol of Whitelocke's connections with the country and the centre, forming a point of contact between London, Oxford's colleges, the Oxford assize circuit, and the Buckinghamshire gentry community.[34]

Gift-giving has been primarily examined by historians of early modern society as an expression of power relations between patrons and clients. A purely social dimension to this form of exchange should not be overlooked; the *Liber Famelicus* first mentioned gifts so that Bulstrode Whitelocke might 'see these frendly kindnesses doon to me, which ar not so usual to those that ly in London as to those in the countrye, and that he may endeavour to live worthye of the like'. Gifts given to James Whitelocke (mostly at Christmas) ranged from spoons to geese, from a whole doe sent by a client to a jar of olives given by a cousin. St John's College sent Whitelocke a pair of gloves in 1615. Clients and associates such as Sir Francis Leigh, Richard Martin and Richard Vaux regularly sent presents to Whitelocke at Christmas.[35]

---

33 *Liber Famelicus*, pp. 2, 21, 25; *Diary*, p. 45.

34 Cf. G. Lipscomb, *The Histories and Antiquities of the County of Buckingham*, 4 vols (London 1847), vol. 3, p. 559; T. Langley, *The History and Antiquities of the Hundred of Desborough* (London 1797), p. 194.

35 Peck, *Court Patronage and Corruption*, p. 19; Felicity Heal, 'The Idea of Hospitality in Early Modern England', *Past and Present* 102 (1984), pp. 66-93; S.N. Eisenstadt, & L. Roniger, 'Patron-Client Relations as a Model of Structuring Social Exchange', *Comparative Studies in Society and History* 22 (1980), pp. 42-77; *Liber Famelicus*, p. 32, 45, 49.

In 1613, Whitelocke received venison from several patrons, including Sir Edward Zouche, Sir Henry Neville and Sir Francis Leigh, the size and form of the gifts deliberately impressing the status of the giver upon the recipient. Richard Jones, Whitelocke's landlord at Clewer House, and Richard Martin, a friend from the Middle Temple, sent smaller gifts of geese and pork while family members such as Richard Whitelocke and cousins William, Thomas and John sent gifts ranging from a 'fat turkeye' to a 'keg of sturgeon'. In that year, Whitelocke's mother-in-law Cecilia, always generous to her son-in-law, sent him geese, rabbits, a turkey pie and no less than eighteen puddings.[36]

Gifts given by James Whitelocke suggest that his interests in this form of exchange centred upon patronage. In 1614, he sent three Christmas presents. The first, a portion of sturgeon, went to Sir Julius Caesar, the new master of the rolls in Chancery whose support was of vital importance to Whitelocke. Sir John Croke, whose patronage had probably become of greater importance to Whitelocke since the death of David Williams two years earlier, received a sugar loaf and a turkey, while a swan and two turkeys went to Sir Edward Coke, chief justice of the King's Bench. While Croke might be taken as family, Whitelocke obviously had professional interests in mind as he considered his allocation of presents that winter.[37]

Nevertheless, there is always the danger of oversimplifying such transactions and ignoring a complex dynamic of mutual association and benefit. Returning from circuit work for Eton and Merton Colleges in August 1615, Whitelocke dispatched a salmon to Sir Edward Coke, who stressed his social superiority with the larger gift of half a buck, and invited Whitelocke to dine with him and other gentlemen of the county at Coke's Stoke Park estate. Whitelocke had already experienced some favour at the hands of Lady Coke, when she offered him a place for the parliament of 1614. Now, as White-

---

36 *Liber Famelicus*, p. 32.
37 *Liber Famelicus*, p. 45.

locke dined with leading figures in the county community, he increased his public profile and continued the process of acceptance into the ranks of a social elite as his wealth and influence continued to grow. Coke would subsequently ask Whitelocke to defend his legal interests, in a case involving copyholds, while the chief justice locked horns with Chancellor Ellesmere at Westminster.[38]

After his promotion to the judiciary, Whitelocke's status in the counties was assured, and he quickly benefited from the produce of patronage, receiving Christmas presents in 1621 ranging from coal and wood to a small farmyard's worth of poultry, meat and other foodstuffs 'easilye valued' at £50 by the recipient. Arriving in Chester to begin his circuit in April 1621, Whitelocke and his puisne were greeted by 'a great number of gentlemen of worthe'; the hospitality of local officials such as Sir Thomas Brereton, was such, he recounted, that although they had spent twice their allocated circuit fee 'our presents in Flint and Denbighe... wear so large that we defaced the whole charge of the circuit, and saved the king's allowances'. Whitelocke further noted the hospitality extended by the towns of Whitechurch and Ruthin, which had organised dances, a Latin oration, and a banquet in his honour.[39]

IV

Noting an array of overlapping national, regional, and local, occasional and permanent, and ecclesiastical and secular courts, Prest has remarked that it 'is straining language to speak of an early modern English legal *system*'. Whitelocke's professional life was regulated by the assizes, held during Lent Vacation from late February to early March and Trinity Vacation from late July to early

---

38 *Liber Famelicus*, pp. 44-50. Other guests included Henry Lord Danvers, later early of Danby, Sir Henry Drewry, Sir William Boyer and Sir William Clark, the son of Sir William Clark of Hitcham.

39 *Liber Famelicus*, pp. 89-93.

August, separate circuits for the colleges of Eton, Merton, Westminster and St John's, and by the four legal terms of Easter, Trinity, Michaelmas, and Hilary. A notebook of cases he compiled during his work on assizes finds him in the city of Oxford on 23 February 1608, from where he followed Justices David Williams and Sir Christopher Yelverton around the Oxford assize at sessions in Abingdon (25 February), Gloucester (29 February), Monmouth (3 March), Hereford (7 March), 'Wigorn' (Worcester) (10 March), Bridegnorth (14 March) and Stafford (17 March).[40]

Whitelocke's assize book shows that he was involved either as assisting counsel (in which case he marked his 'help' next to the name of the plaintiff or defendant), or more often as primary counsel, in between a quarter and a half of the cases arising from the Oxford assizes. The cases in his notebook concern a range of cases including false imprisonment, assault and battery, breach of contract, and forfeiture on payment of bonds. Cases of debt, and litigation arising from a variety of property disputes were particularly common. While most suits received only a short summary, others such as a complex financial dispute in *Lance v. Philips* at the Monmouth assizes in 1607 received a lengthy record, which included the authorities used to argue the case in court as well as details of the final sentence. Among Whitelocke's papers are also a number of bonds for drawing up conveyances. Soliciting was another routine aspect of legal work, and the kind of role that Whitelocke's influence could be expected to play with the judges is suggested in a letter from William Brampton to Richard Whitelocke, written in 1607, asking Richard to persuade his

40 Prest, 'Lawyers', pp. 64-5 and cf. Brooks, 'The Common Lawyers in England', pp. 56-57; Prest, *Rise of the Barristers*, p. 27; Assize book, fols 92, 93, 95, 97, 99, 102, 105. The Oxford assizes lasted an average of twenty-eight days. Easter term ran for seventeen days after Easter, Trinity for nineteen days after Whitsunday, Michaelmas ran from October 17 to November 28, and Hilary from January 23 to February 20.

brother to move Sir John Croke to accept common bail for George Cely, arrested for debt.[41]

Detailed notes of a range of cases arising from the sessions suggest that, given the ongoing nature of much of the litigation pursued in the courts, Whitelocke may have used his assize notebook to follow the progress of his clients' interests from year to year. A scoring, marking and cross-referencing of particular cases in his assize book suggests the way in which he tracked his clients' interests in a range of collateral actions. As Whitelocke's assize notebook built up a handy reference source by noting the records used to support various arguments in court along with the final outcome, it helped him to provide competent legal advice to his clients.[42]

The assizes prompted an enforced migration for Whitelocke, but his role as steward for the colleges of St John's, Eton, and Westminster would have made for a transient lifestyle anyway. The *Liber Famelicus* records 'progresses' made at the conclusion of circuit work in the summers of 1614, 1615, 1616 and 1617, with the provost and bursars of Eton College and the subwarden of Merton College, to inspect college properties and preside over manorial courts in Surrey, Kent, Suffolk, Norfolk, Cambridge, Bedford and Hertford. As well as ensuring the legality of college contracts and 'keeping court' for the colleges, Whitelocke gave legal advice to the fellows of the colleges in the course of his duties. On occasion, these colleges did become involved in legal disputes, as in a 1613 cause in Chancery between John King, bishop of London, and the College of Westminster, Whitelocke played a key role as Westminster's legal adviser, boasting that in this instance Chancellor Ellesmere had

41 Assize book, fol. 97; Longleat Papers, vol. 1, fols 50, 190, 194.

42 For example, fol. 92, *Edwin Kendall v. Wiliam Trelling*: '*vide infra* for instructions Oxon assizes last'; fol. 121, *George Craddock v. John Wakering*: '*supra* March 1607'. Cf. Barnes, 'Star Chamber Litigants', pp. 15, 22-3; Jones, *Politics and the Bench*, p. 37.

granted the defence insufficient time to prepare a case, 'yet by my extraodinarye paines [we] wear ready at the heering'.[43]

As recorder of Woodstock, Whitelocke acted as the salaried justice of the borough, advising the mayor and aldermen during local sessions of the peace. Preserving the rights and privileges of the borough was his foremost consideration, both in casual litigation and in parliament. The type of advice required of him as recorder is demonstrated in reply to an inquiry form the borough of Leicester in 1601. Whitelocke advised the mayor and aldermen that he had been in correspondence with the attorney general of the Duchy who, as a judge in the court where their protest was lodged, could not 'give a resolution of successe in our cause', but had suggested that the right of the borough to prosecute traders from other towns was best defended by recourse to a statute of Phillip and Mary, 'out of the preamble of which I mean to derive matter for our purpose'. He also offered his opinion on a number of points raised by the borough in a petition to Queen Elizabeth, such as increasing the toll on 'those who passed beside your towne', asking for further information on these issues. If this letter is any indication, an ability to lobby successfully in the courts, as well as a thorough grounding in the *minutiae* of local customary law, was the mark of a successful borough lawyer.[44]

---

43 *Liber Famelicus*, pp. 33, 43-4, 47, 49-50, 57, 59. Other details of Whitelocke's role are scarce. Eton College has a record of his appointment as Steward of Manors (Eton College Records 60/300, p. 101) which gives an idea of the perquisites of his office, such as provision of food and horses while on college business. Bodleian MS Wood F 28, fol. 214 lists St John's College lands, mostly manners and parsonages, held in Oxfordshire, while Bodleian MS Tanner 338 notes donations and endowments in a financial audit carried at by St John's in 1611. See also D.R. Hainsworth, 'The Estate Steward' in *Professions in Early Modern England*, pp. 155-6.

44 Woodstock Town Hall, MS B79/1, fol. 60; J.S. Baker, 'Criminal Courts and Procedure at Common Law 1550-1800' in *Crime in England*, p. 30; *Liber Famelicus*, p. 19; Hall Papers, vol. 3, no. 162, 'James Whitelocke to John Clark, 7 December 1601'; reprinted in *Records of the Borough of Leicester: Being a series*

Like many other lawyers, Whitelocke followed the machinery of royal justice between the provinces and the courts of Westminster Hall, a barrister's 'largest and most lucrative sphere of employment'. At Westminster, Whitelocke moved between those courts in which he could gain the right of audience, and at various stages of his career he practised in the courts of King's Bench, Chancery, Requests, Star Chamber and Constable. The sixteen percent Whitelocke took from the proceeds of Sir John Harrington's share in 'Roper's Office' from 1612 to 1616 was only part of the attraction, as the job guaranteed Whitelocke a permanent presence in the Court of King's Bench.[45]

For a barrister who had not attained the rank of serjeant-at-law, the second great centre of litigation and profit at Westminster was the Court of Chancery. Whitelocke was active in this court early in his career and with the support of Sir Julius Caesar, master of the rolls, he continued to plead there after his falling out with Ellesmere. John Haywarde notes his appearance as counsel in a Star Chamber case of 12 November 1607 which suggests an occasional presence before his activities antagonised the Privy Council. After 1616 judicial patrons such as Sir Francis Bacon, Ellesmere's successor in Chancery, and Lionel Cranfield, Master of the Court of Requests from 1616 and the

---

of Extracts from the Archives of the Corporation of Leicester, 1509-1603, ed. Mary Bateson, (Cambridge 1905), pp. 440-1.

45 Cockburn, *History of English Assizes*, p. xi; Prest, *Rise of the Barristers*, p. 50; *Liber Famelicus*, pp. 27, 30, 76-7; John Haywarde, *Les Reportes del Cases in Camera Stellata*, pp. 338-41; Bodl. MS Smith 71, fol. 59; BL MS Cott. Jul. C.3, fol. 54; CUL MS Gg. 2.23, fol. 90. The courts of Exchequer, King's Bench, and Chancery required no formal association with lawyers, who pleaded in one court, or more frequently moved between courts, as the dictates of business demanded. Before the Restoration, these courts kept no official records of the counsellors pleading before them, who were only infrequently indented alongside the cases in which they pleaded. It is thus a haphazard business at best to trace the activities of one lawyer in the voluminous (and not always complete) court records; in a brief search I found only one record of Whitelocke appearing as counsel in the central courts, noted in ch. 2. Clendenin (*thesis*, p. 47) has shown that Whitelocke appeared in at least five causes each term in the central courts between 1600 and 1612.

Court of Wards from 1618, were more than ready to let bygones be bygones. After initially promoting, and then withdrawing support for Whitelocke's candidacy as recorder of London in 1618, Cranfield showed himself Whitelocke's 'verye honourable and worthye frend' in the Court of Wards 'in heering me in court before others.' On the verge of royal appointment, familiarity with a range of figures who doubled as government officials and judges in the courts of law ensured Whitelocke's success.[46]

V

Whitelocke's professional connections developed, in tandem, from two disparate points of influence: practice on the Oxford assize circuit, and associations with the University of Oxford. Whitelocke, Henry Yelverton, Thomas Coventry and John Walter – three men he called his 'speciall frends' – appear to have dominated legal work on the Oxford assize circuit for over a decade. In a legal arena where counsel regularly appeared before a single judge hearing *nisi prius* business, he was lucky to have the long-standing patronage of David Williams, who regularly rode the Oxford circuit from his appointment as Justice of King's Bench on 4 February 1604 until his death on 22 January 1613. Whitelocke tells us that after familiarising himself with the circuit Williams 'toke me into his favour, and caryed me the circuit with him, in whiche, by his favour, I fell into practice, and the like favour he did me in the King's Bench.'[47]

Another passage in the *Liber Famelicus* underlined the importance of William's favour on the circuit, noting the removal of his 'verye

46 *Liber Famelicus*, pp. 76-7; Hawarde, *Les Reportes*, p. 338.

47 Cockburn, *History of English Assizes*, pp. 142, 293; *Liber Famelicus*, pp. 30, 54; Prest, *Rise of the Barristers*, p. 28. Yelverton became Attorney-General in 1617 and a judge of the Common Pleas in 1625, Coventry Recorder of London (1616), Solicitor-General (1617), Attorney-General (1621) and Lord Keeper (1625-40), while Walter was eventually appointed Chief Baron of the Exchequer.

good frend', in summer 1610 and winter 1611, to Norfolk from Oxford 'where I had followed him sithence his first cumming into it' and adding just underneath (presumably with relief) that Williams returned to Oxford in 1611. During this brief hiatus, Whitelocke had the opportunity to appear before his uncle Sir John Croke, a man he found 'very kind and affable to all lawyers that practised before him, and all suitors that had to do withe him.' By the time of Williams' death in 1613, Whitelocke's reputation was apparently strong enough to ensure his continued success. His continuing good relations with the assize judges was shown when Justices Warburton and Croke recommended him as a Justice of the peace for Oxfordshire and Buckinghamshire in May 1618.[48]

Beyond associations built through the common law, Whitelocke maintained strong, complementary ties developed through his years of studying the civil law at Oxford. Peregrinations to London during his years as a scholar of St John's Oxford had the benefit of exposing him to college business and in 1601 he was appointed as college steward, a post he held until his appointment as chief justice of Chester in 1620. Over this time, contacts that he had established as a student proved indispensable to his wider advancement. His appointment as recorder of Woodstock in 1606, for example, may have been partially due to the influence of the high steward, Sir Henry Lee, who was a tenant of St John's.[49]

Levack has suggested that 'the association of the civil lawyers with the ecclesiastical hierarchy – whether Arminian, orthodox, or moderately pro-Puritan – was the most distinctive feature of their professional life', and Whitelocke's ties with the emerging Arminian faction are striking in the years from 1610 to 1620. The networks of ecclesiastical patronage built up by Whitelocke suggest that his reputation spread upon the recommendation of John Buckeridge and

48 *Liber Famelicus*, pp. 19, 62, 76; Cockburn, *History of English Assizes*, pp. 268-70. Croke served continuously on the circuit until his death in 1619.

49 Prest, *Rise of the Barristers*, p. 144; *Liber Famelicus*, p. 15, 19; Stevenson & Salter, *Early History of St. John's*, p. 193; History of Parliament Trust.

William Laud, drawing further retainers from other members of the 'Durham House Group' such as Richard Neile and John Howson. On 7 May 1610 Whitelocke was appointed joint steward of Westminster College through the 'favour and frendship' of Richard Neile, who was at that time serving as dean of the college and bishop of Westminster. In 1616, he became sole steward of the college, and Neile's favour may have also gained him the understewardship of the court of St Martin's-le-grand in London. In 1617, John Buckeridge awarded a lifetime annuity of 60s. per annum to Whitelocke for legal counsel, and in 1620 John Howson provided an additional retainer for counsel of 40s. for life.[50]

Professional relations cemented personal associations between Whitelocke and his church patrons: in 1612 Whitelocke lent Buckeridge £400 upon his appointment to Rochester 'to shew my love unto him, and how far from covetousness he had lived'. As an invited guest to Whitelocke's 1619 law reading at the Middle Temple, Buckeridge contributed £5 to the cost of the reader's feast. Whitelocke's relationship with William Laud also appears to have been highly cordial, at least until the early 1620s. In a curious passage in the *Liber Famelicus*, Whitelocke recounted that his 'loving friend and ancient collegue', now archdeacon of Huntingdon, had told him on 7 November 1619 that he was then forty-six years of age. In 1619, Whitelocke admitted his son Bulstrode to St John's College, Oxford,

> where Dr Laud his father['s] great friend, and President of the College, took the charge and care of his education, and appointed a worthy and learned person to be his Tutor, Dr Parson a physitian, butt the President also took a strict account of his study and behaviour.

In Buckinghamshire, his good relations with Richard Neile, who acted as a Crown intermediary while serving as bishop of Lincoln

50 Levack, *Civil Lawyers*, p. 160; *Liber Famelicus*, pp. 19, 53, 57, 60. For the associations developing between Howson, Laud, Buckeridge and Neile over these years see Tyacke, *Anti-Calvinists*, pp. 107-8.

from 1614 to 1617, reinforced a strong claim to the local commission of the peace.[51]

Whitelocke's parliamentary reputation, which centred on his claims for the common law, lie in contrast with associations built up as an Oxford civilian. His parliamentary career, which began with selection as MP for Woodstock on 6 December 1609, confirmed his rising status in Oxfordshire. Whitelocke noted that he was returned 'in the place of Sir Richard Lea', who died in office on 22 December 1608, thus forcing a bye-election for the borough in which the high steward, to Whitelocke's advantage, was Sir Henry Lee. In 1614, Whitelocke's growing parliamentary and legal reputation prompted a number of patrons to support his election to the House of Commons. When Sir Phillip Herbert, steward of Woodstock manor, pressed another candidate for the borough, Sir Edward Coke's wife, Lady Hatton, used her influence in the borough of Corfe Castle (Isle of Purbeck, Dorset) to secure Whitelocke a place. Her decision was made (Whitelocke tells us) 'without my privity, for I was absent in the circuit when she sent my name, and when I came to her to take notice of it, and to thank her, she tolde me she did it least an honest man sholde be left out'. Another powerful supporter was Sir Robert Killigrew, who offered Whitelocke the seat of Helston in Cornwall. Although Whitelocke declined his offer, he used his good relations with Killigrew to nominate his brother-in-law Henry Bulstrode for the place, while negotiating with the corporation to retain his seat in Woodstock. By the 1620s, when Whitelocke was again nominated as MP for Woodstock, he was approaching his fifties, and a man of considerable standing in county and professional circles.[52]

---

51 *Liber Famelicus*, pp. 26, 73, 77; *Diary*, p. 47; Peck, *Court Patronage and Corruption*, p. 82.

52 While the forthcoming History of Parliament Trust biography suggests a direct connection between Lee's patronage and Whitelocke's appointment, Whitelocke himself considered it 'ever usual' for the recorder to represent the borough. Williams, *Parliamentary History of the county of Oxford*, pp. 198-9; *Liber Famelicus*, pp. 19, 40-1, 84; Moir, *Addled Parliament*, pp. 50-1.

Mark Kishlansky has stressed the essential homogeneity of county society, pointing to shared 'notions of honor, standing and deference' which helped to 'regulate and absorb conflict between and within loosely defined status groups.' Whitelocke's advancement through the ranks of the county community suggests some of the problems that could arise when ambiguities over prestige and property did exist. After buying a farm in 1607 near Witney in Oxfordshire, Whitelocke was drawn into dispute over the property rights of some woodlands formerly in the hands of the Pope family. Attempts to settle the issue by selling the lands back to Sir William Pope were met, Whitelocke suggests, with 'skorne' by the magnate, leading Whitelocke (in a calculated assertion of his property rights) to chop down over a thousand trees for sale. This he 'had no sooner doon but Sir William Pope took possession of the wood by force, entrenched up the gates, kept thear a garrison, and committed many outrages, as by the proceedings in court do there appeer'.[53]

At the Oxford assizes in 1608 Pope initiated a string of suits against Whitelocke, but must have perceived his weakness in a legal forum and brought none of his suits to trial. For his part, Whitelocke testified to Justices Williams and Yelverton of 'the outrages' perpetrated by Pope, emphasising his scant regard for public order and the authority of law. The judges obviously listened with a sympathetic ear; Pope was stripped of local office and put into the custody of the sheriff, in a stage-managed demonstration of their authority. Whitelocke recounted that

> when he arrose up in his place upon the benche, making accoumpt to answear the accusation, thear as he stood, he was commanded by the court to go to the bar, and justice Yelverton told him he was fitter to leade the rebells in Northampton... then to sit thear as a justice of the peace.

53 Kishlansky, *Parliamentary Selection*, p. 12; Stone, *Crisis of the Aristocracy*, p. 223 (and cf. Brooks, 'Litigants and Attorneys', pp. 49-50).

Pope retired to lick his wounds, and his retainers handed back possession of the woods – but only until the assize justices had vacated the county. At this point the magnate sought to reassert himself by 'new mischeefs', assembling two hundred carts to take away Whitelocke's wood, while a formal complaint was made to the Crown about his disgrace at the hands of the socially inferior assize justices.[54]

The petition Pope presented in Star Chamber is typical of the theatrical accounts constructed by the early modern gentry as they sought redress at the hands of the king. As Pope's story unfolds across a broad vellum canvas, it paints an implausible picture of a giant conspiracy to destroy his position in the county society. The preamble explains Pope's claim to the contested land, originally acquired by Sir Thomas Pope following Henry VIII's dissolution of the monasteries. In his version, Richard Brian's sale of the lease to Whitelocke flew in the face of an agreement already made between Pope and Brian's deceased father. Employing devious legal fictions, the usurper Whitelocke now supposedly tried to intimidate Pope with a gang of hired thugs 'assembled, arrayed and weaponed in most warlike manner'. A Machiavellian figure of some ability by Pope's reckoning, Whitelocke then put out a range of bribes to defame him as a string of false suits were brought against him at the Oxford assizes.[55]

Despite a colourful and indignant tone, this petition obviously held little water. As Whitelocke was quick to point out, if Pope had a solid case against him he would have pushed his claim at the assizes, and, by forcing the Crown to choose between his personal honour and the authority of its delegated representatives, he did himself little service. Whitelocke was heartened to note that the Council 'upon hearing

54 *Liber Famelicus*, pp. 22-3; Cockburn, *History of English Assizes*, p. 164; Anthony Fletcher, *Reform in the Provinces: The Government of Stuart England* (New Haven 1986), pp. 50-1. Fletcher confuses Whitelocke with Williams in this instance.

55 PRO STAC 8/281/24.

committed the knighte with great disgrace to the Fleet, and acquited the judge to his great honor, as by thear order entred in the counsell book dothe appeer'.[56]

As political protagonists, Pope personified the old gentry values while Whitelocke represented newer ways and means emerging in county society over the later decades of the sixteenth century. In 1607, Whitelocke had prepared a legal memorandum in support of Samuel West, an attorney-at-law who made the mistake of suing one of Pope's servants. According to Whitelocke, Pope sent for West to settle the issue, locked him in a room and beat him severely. While Pope's stature in the county gave him a feeling of social superiority which led him to be dismissive of the law, Whitelocke, on the other hand, relied upon his legal associations for his stature in the county. Unfortunately for Pope, Whitelocke's attitudes and legal attributes were neatly aligned with the wishes of a monarchy anxious to assert greater control over county affairs. By challenging Justice Williams, Pope implied an *a priori* right to overturn the actions of the government, and quickly ran foul of the Privy Council. Doubtless chastened by the experience, he turned to negotiation, and his dispute with Whitelocke was finally settled in 1609 with his legal acquisition of the contested lands, as Whitelocke's property interests shifted to Buckinghamshire.[57]

Whitelocke's friendly associations with the Bulstrode family, the local Justices of Assize and the bishop of Lincoln underlined his standing in Buckinghamshire, and as recommendations for county government were furnished by the local bishops, judges, and leading gentry he had good reason to expect promotion to local office. The lord lieutenant of the county from 1607 to 1616 was, however, Lord

---

56 *Liber Famelicus*, p. 23. This order, and another assuring Williams that the case would not be prejudicial to his judicial status, are preserved in the Longleat Papers, vol. 1, fols 51, 52.

57 Stone, *Crisis of the Aristocracy*, pp. 223-4, 234-42; Longleat Papers, vol. 1, fol. 50v; *Liber Famelicus*, p. 23; cf. Cockburn, *History of English Assizes*, pp. 153-170.

Ellesmere, who had the final say on any county appointments by virtue of his office as Chancellor and was also was responsible for revising recommendations for county government. Ellesmere's animosity toward Whitelocke apparently discouraged any nomination before 1616 and by the time of the Chancellor's death Whitelocke's appointment to county office was overdue.[58]

On 27 November 1617 Sir Henry Montagu, 'being justice of assise in Bukinghamshire', along with 'sum of the principall gentlemen of the countrye', recommended Whitelocke to Sir Francis Bacon as a suitable candidate for the county commission of the peace. With Buckingham's support, Whitelocke served thereafter on commissions of the peace for Buckinghamshire and Oxfordshire, acting as recorder for a special commission granted to the Dean of Westminster, and was placed 'fourth esquire' in the county. By acting as an mediator in local disputes and discharging public duties such as the quarter session charge, Whitelocke rehearsed for the day when he gained high legal office. With Buckingham's continued favour, Whitelocke achieved permanent crown employment as a judge in 1620. His promotion testifies to the strength of his local political base, his ability, and a new political world in which Buckingham was preeminent.[59]

VII

As the Crown's foremost legal representatives in the localities, the Justices of Assize provided, during their twice-yearly visits to the shires, 'a rare, indeed unique, occasion of direct contact between the centre and the locality'. As historians have increasingly realised, any distinction between the judges' 'judicial' and 'administrative' functions distorts the nature of the arrangements by which government was facilitated within and across the counties, a task in which the judges

58 *Diary*, p. 64; Peck, *Court Patronage and Corruption*, pp. 82-3; *Liber Famelicus*, p. 54; Cockburn, *History of English Assizes*, p. 142, 153-7; *Works*, vol. 6, p. 211.
59 *Liber Famelicus*, pp. 60, 62, 63, 69-70.

played an important role. Recently, as social historians have placed law enforcement within a broader social and political context, the rulings of provincial administrators have been re-examined as expressions of social power and control. Given our imperfect understanding of the relationship between the judges, the Crown and the provinces in the early Stuart period, James Whitelocke's judicial correspondences with the centre and with local administrators are equally significant.[60]

Between 1620 and 1632 Whitelocke played an important role in provincial government, taking up semi-permanent residence in Chester from 1620 until 1624, and thereafter riding the Oxford circuit with Justice Jones in 1625, the Midland circuit with Baron Bromley in 1626, the North with Justice Yelverton in 1627 and 1628, and returning to Jones and the Oxford circuit from 1629 until the year of his death. At Chester and on the assizes, Whitelocke listened to, presided over and redirected causes, and promoted Crown directives for the maintenance of local government through the assizes. Routine Crown directives about such matters as ale house regulation, the upkeep of bridges and the oversight of recusants were conveyed through private and public instruction to local officials.[61]

Whitelocke's commitment to his duties belies Anthony Fletcher's picture of a generally passive and poorly motivated judiciary in the 1620s, suggesting a vigorous response to local affairs with an eye to

---

60 Sharpe, *Personal Rule of Charles I*, p. 424; cf. Sharpe, *Crime in Early Modern England*, p. 23; *An Ungovernable People*, ed. Brewer & Styles, p. 13; Wrightson, 'Two concepts of order', p. 26; L.L. Peck, *Northampton: patronage and policy at the court of King James* (London 1982), p. 88; Fletcher, *Reform in the Provinces*, p. 44. Fletcher and Peck underestimate the importance of the assize judges.

61 Cockburn, *History of English Assizes*, Appendix 1, pp. 270-1. For Whitelocke's personal record of business as chief justice of Chester see PRO CHES 21/3. Other records of court business (mostly dealing with court work, but including charges against recusants and correspondence with the centre) are reprinted in HMC *5th Report* Appendix, p. 312; HMC *8th Report* Appendix, pt 1, no. 630 a; HMC *11th Report* VII, p. 213; HMC Cowper II, p. 68; Longleat Papers, vol. 2, fols 181, 182, 199 and vol. 3, *passim*.

government objectives. Indeed, his correspondence on such matters as bridge maintenance reflects far more upon the inertia of local administrators than any lack of commitment on the part of the judges. In response to a petition sent from a village in Denbigh, which requested direction from local Justices of the Peace to assist the repair of a dilapidated bridge, Whitelocke ordered the Justices to certify at the Court of Great Sessions what steps they had taken to repair the bridge in question. Other petitions showed a concern for the wider community, reflecting the reluctance of local administrators and villagers to enforce parliamentary statutes promulgated by Westminster; here Whitelocke could only admonish his subordinates to carry out their duties, under the threat of removal from office and possible prosecution. In a typical petition which survives in Whitelocke's papers, Tobias Ewbancke claimed that Robert Brandling, high sheriff of Northumberland, 'persecuteth many unjust and vexatious suits against the petitioner and terifies and threatens his servants', through 'uncivill and unchristian speeches (as will appeare by Affadavits hereunto annexed)'. Petitions such as this, urging 'that a warrant be issued to bring Brandling before the Court', illustrate how Whitelocke's importance as a means of mediation and arbitration was emphasised by the authority he held over the whole system.[62]

Historians have pointed to the 'participatory' nature of the arrangements which facilitated law enforcement in early modern England. Standing at the apex of the county legal system, Whitelocke had considerable influence over its workings – but relied extensively upon information which filtered up from the parish to the county level

---

62 Fletcher, *Reform in the Provinces*, pp. 49-52, 119, 164; Longleat Papers, vol. 2 fol. 72v; PRO CHES 21/3, fol. 60; Morrill, *The Cheshire Grand Jury 1625-1629: A Social and Administrative Study* (Leicester 1976), p. 28; T.C. Curtis, 'Quarter Sessions Appearances and their Background: A Seventeenth-Century Regional Study' in *Crime in England 1550-1800*, ed. J.S. Cockburn (London 1977), pp. 144-7, 154; Earl Marshal's Papers (fols 33, 34) at Arundel Castle, reproduced in *A Catalogue of the Earl Marshal's Papers at Arundel Castle*, ed. F.W. Steer (London 1964).

through the urging of the JPs, sheriffs, constables and private individuals of the shire. Through a range of petitions presented to Whitelocke, one can see the mediating role played by the judges at the shire, hundred and village level. Personal petitions received by Whitelocke usually asked for his intercession or clemency in legal cases already under way – early release from the county prison in a minor offence, re-direction of a stalled case for settlement at the next assizes, reduction of sentence on the promise of good behaviour. Elizabeth Slavery, for example, urged Whitelocke to release eleven-year-old Richard Radson, held in the Gloucester county jail for perjury, as he had been intimidated into making a false confession. More prominent figures were equally ready to influence Whitelocke by any means available: in 1627, for example, Ralph Bormington wrote to Sir John Coke, asking Coke (whose ruling Whitelocke was thought willing to accept) to help him furnish bail.[63]

Other petitions reflected more on Whitelocke's political influence in the provinces. In 1624, for example, Sir Roger Mostyn was petitioned by the Wynn family to 'procure Sir James Whitelocke's letter to the justice of the peace of their county in the behalf of Jack Mostyn' for election to the county of Anglesey; while Mostyn's son was returned, Whitelocke's response to this request is uncertain. Throughout Whitelocke's career, other suitors used whatever leverage they could acquire by way of political influence or kinship ties to gain his support. In 1623 the earl of Bridgewater asked that his cousin Piers Holland 'may find your courteous acceptance' as the 'partaker of your lawful and just favours', qualifying his open solicitation of Whitelocke with the remark that it 'never was my breeding... to loose

63 Morrill, *Cheshire Grand Jury*, pp. 24-8, 45; Sharpe, *Crime in Early Modern England*, p. 23; Keith Wrightson, *English Society 1580-1680* (London 1982), pp. 155-73; C.B. Herrup, *The Common Peace: Participation and the Criminal Law in Seventeenth-Century England* (Cambridge 1987); Longleat Papers, vol. 1, fol. 286; HMC Cowper I, p. 307, (Coke MS), 19 May 1627 and see, for example, HMC *13th Report* IV, p. 261 (Dovaston MS fol. 105v); Longleat Papers, vol. 1, fols 283, 284; vol. 2, fol. 53; vol. 24, fols 201-4.

my labour in going about to draw partiality or undue respect from a learned and religious judge'. The thin line between petition and solicitation in this request stresses the delicacy of Whitelocke's position in an age when even the greatest figures of the law were open to attack for abuse of office.[64]

While historians have viewed James I's provincial administration with caution, they have also noted the strenuous efforts made by Charles I and his Privy Council to increase the efficiency of the judicial apparatus in the counties. Whitelocke's correspondence in the years 1620-1632 suggests that the supposed *laissez faire* of the Jacobean reign may have reflected King James' instinctive perception of the art of the possible, while Charles' interventions lent a random uncertainty to provincial affairs. Orders and counter-orders to the judges of assize evidence the king's intention to instruct and supervise them in their supposed role as auxiliaries in the pursuit of Crown policy. Reeve, for example, has noted that despite Charles's leniency towards Catholics, Sir Robert Heath's appointment as attorney-general was 'in fact marked by a more stringent application of the laws against recusants'. On 20 December 1625, Heath instructed the Justices for Buckinghamshire to proceed against local recusants, urging that 'neither Lord nor Lady nor any other be spared or winked at'. Yet in July 1626, Heath instructed Whitelocke to allow an indictment against Sir Francis Smith for recusancy to lapse until the following year, writing also to the justices of assize in Lincolnshire in the same month to order that Lord Dunbar, personally cited by the Commons in their petition on the stronger enforcement of recusancy laws, be spared from prosecution for recusancy at Charles's insistence.[65]

---

64 J.K. Gruenfelder, *Influence in Early Stuart Elections, 1604-1640* (Columbus 1981), p. 105; HHL Ellesmere MS 6472; *Diary*, p. 60; Prest, 'Judicial Corruption', pp. 66-95.

65 Cockburn, *History of English Assizes*, pp. 231-4; L.M. Hill, 'County Government in Caroline England' in *Origins of the English Civil War*, p. 77; Sharpe, *Personal Rule of Charles I*, pp. 412-48; and cf. Derek Hirst, 'The Privy Council and

In this haphazard manner, the importance of the judges to the government's political program increased. By 1627, as the government found conventional sources of revenue inadequate under the strained circumstances of war, Whitelocke was asked to help implement more controversial government directives. After the judges had revealed their limited support for Crown policy by refusing to endorse the legality of the Forced Loan, members of the Privy Council took the unusual step of riding the circuit as 'lords itinerant' for the first time. Thereafter, the Council sought closer supervision of the judges' conduct by appointing them to joint commissions with members of the Privy Council and selected clerical dignitaries. On 1 June 1627, Whitelocke was appointed to one such commission, to consider the 'manning and maintayning of six sufficient shipps of warr for the guardings... of the coasts of this realme from the Thames mouth to the farthest Northeast point of the same', by raising funds from recusant fines extracted from the northern counties and a 'voluntary composition' upon all coal shipments leaving Newcastle or Sunderland.[66]

Council attempts to monitor judicial administration in the provinces crystallised in an order of 31 January 1631. This order appointed six councillors to each of six regions drawn along assize boundaries, and required the local justices 'to give an accompt monthly' to the judges, 'so that they may, in the beginning of every Tearme, give up the same to the Lords and other Commissioners'. Councillors were assigned to 'take accompt' of the judges, and if

---

Problems of Enforcement in the 1620s', *Journal of British Studies* 18 (1978), pp. 46-66; L.J. Reeve, 'Sir Robert Heath's Advice for Charles I in 1629', *Bulletin of the Institute of Historical Research* 59 (1986), p. 217; Longleat Papers, vol. 2, fol. 199; vol. 3, fols 47, 52; *Historical Collections*, vol. 1, pp. 391-396. See also Whitelocke's record of the House of Commons' 1628 petition against recusants, Longleat Papers, vol. 3, fol. 181 (reprinted in *Historical Collections*, vol. 1, p. 516).

66 Reeve, 'Sir Robert Heath's Advice', p. 217; Hirst, 'Privy Council', p. 59; *Acts of the Privy Council, January to August 1626*, p. 313.

necessary to 'call unto them... for better assistance'. James Whitelocke, along with Justice Jones, was required to administer the Oxford circuit under the guiding hand of the Lord Keeper, the earl of Bridgewater, the earl of Carlisle, the earl of Banbury, Viscount Dorchester and Viscount Falkland.[67]

Correspondence from the sheriffs of Berkshire, Stafford, Gloucester, Shropshire, and Worcester to Justices Jones and Whitelocke between 1631 and 1633 suggests how this system worked in practice. Certificates were requested from the local Justices of the Peace and the Mayors on such matters as poor relief, the regulation of corn prices and market regulations; they were then endorsed by the county sheriffs and passed on for the inspection of the judges, who presented an overall report for the circuit to the Privy Councillors.[68]

It appears that the king's grandiose vision for provincial administration underestimated the resistance of local officials to growing supervision from the centre: a letter of 23 June 1631 from Sir Ralph Dutton to Justices Jones and Whitelocke enclosed 'the only certificate received' for the month, a report on the regulation of market prices prepared by the Justices of Gloucester. As was usual, Whitelocke offered no thoughts on these 'new counsels', doing his duty as his independence was brought increasingly into question.[69]

VIII

Fletcher has rightly argued that for 'newer men [in the counties] there was no quicker way of achieving identification with the gentry community of the county than by an energetic role in government'. In his charge to the justices of assize in Star Chamber in 1602, Lord Ellesmere noted in sharper fashion the importance of county office

---

67 *Acts of the Privy Council 1630/31*, p. 215.

68 *Calendar of State Papers Domestic 1631-1633*, pp. 31, 37, 45, 47, 50, 53, 69, 74, 88, 91.

69 *Calendar of State Papers Domestic 1631-1633*, p. 88.

for men with the 'ambitious humour of gaining reputation amongst their neighbours'. Whitelocke's rise in the county community is best understood by exploring this interdependence of professional expertise and social position. As many tasks at the level of local administration were customarily delegated to men with active legal experience and because such offices carried with them a degree of social distinction, Whitelocke's professional abilities placed him from the outset in a relatively advantageous position. As well as its financial benefit, appointment to local office conferred social honour upon its incumbent, reinforcing the prestige of the position in a society preoccupied with questions of position and place.[70]

Throughout his career, Whitelocke was quick to seize upon those natural advantages offered by his training as a lawyer. Acquisition of local administrative positions was achieved through conventional exploitation of familial and friendship ties, supported by demonstrated legal ability. The voluntary patronage of David Williams and numerous high-ranking clerics, the continuing support of St John's College, and a successful marriage into an established county family were all of invaluable assistance while his career was still in its infancy. Yet much credit for his rise to prominence still goes to James Whitelocke. It is worth remembering, in light of his success, that Whitelocke was not born to succeed any more than the hundreds of other young untitled Elizabethans who clamoured for status and wealth. Whitelocke's legacy to his children of the manor and lands at Fawley, and his elevation to high office under the Crown, were more than just the achievement of driving personal dreams, for they were probably never conceived as such. Placing the Whitelocke family into

70 Fletcher, *Reform in the Provinces*, p. 42; Folger MS X.d. 337 (unfol.), Star Chamber Charge, 14 Feb. 1602, quoted in Cockburn, *History of English Assizes*, p. 156; Kishlansky, *Parliamentary Selection*, pp. 41-4.

the highest ranks of the county community, they were the most notable 'memorialls for posterity' that James Whitelocke could leave his family as a basis for future prospects and future generations.

Conclusion

Voice and silence in James Whitelocke's *Liber Famelicus*

This book has sought, through James Whitelocke, to illuminate a mind formed in the study of civil law and refined in the practice of English common law. Our understanding of Whitelocke's fears and confidences over a long career in the law are bound largely to the *Liber Famelicus*, the notebook in which he recorded his achievements, observations and feelings for posterity. Close to political controversy throughout his life, a variety of other public and private documents attest to his engagement with and achievement within early Stuart society. These records attest to the grounds of controversy throughout Whitelocke's public life – Jacobean parliamentary disagreements over taxation in which he was personally involved, arguments between civil and common lawyers which resulted in the dismissal of Sir Edward Coke and the impeachment of Sir Francis Bacon, the constitutional tensions brought to bear by the Forced Loan and other fiscal measures employed in the reign of Charles I, and, towards the end of his life, the growing religious discord created by Arminian designs for reforming the Church. In its assertions, and in its silences, the *Liber Famelicus* reveals the coherence, confusion and contradictions at work in James Whitelocke's inner, mental world.

Written over twenty-three years, the *Liber Famelicus* draws upon record-keeping techniques developed by James Whitelocke in his training at university and the inns of court. At once a notebook, account book and journal, it defies easy classification, and may be related to other notebooks maintained by common lawyers of the period as a record of their professional and personal journeying. Compiled as a series of notes and observations rather than a coherent narrative, Whitelocke wrote within days, or sometimes months, of the events he described. Its anecdotal quality provides a vitality which is sometimes missing in accounts written from the safer vantage of hindsight, and one gets the impression that while the *Liber Famelicus* was erratically kept, Whitelocke made good use of it when his own interests were spurred by events, at least until the 1620s. Beyond its candid nature, noteworthy in an age of rigorous self-censorship, its entries cover the entire span of Whitelocke's life, from recollections of an Elizabethan childhood, to a final record of professional receipts in the year of his death.

We have seen that Whitelocke progressed from school to university, and from there to the inns of court and chancery, achieving high judicial office in the last decade of his life. At the end of his life, his son recalled that Whitelocke's

> reason was clear and strong, and his learning deep and general; he had the Latin tongue... he understood the Greek very well, and the Hebrew... exactly knowing in the history of his own country... and was most conversant in the studies of antiquity and heraldry: he was not excelled in the knowledge of his profession of the common law of England, wherein his knowledge of the civil law (whereof he was a graduate in Oxford) was a help to him: his learned arguments both at the bar and the bench will confirm this truth.

It is important to see that Whitelocke's outlook was not determined by the boundaries of his knowledge, which encompassed a classical and theological education, a grounding in continental law, and a formation in English law and custom, but by the psychological assurances that held his world together. As Whitelocke's contemporary John Selden remarked, 'When men comfort themselves with philosophy, 'tis not because they have gott two or three sentences, but because they have digested these sentences, and made them their own'. Law and religion formed the twin pillars of the lexicon from which Whitelocke drew such sentences as he made his own. The public and private record of his life, in its successes and its failings, reflects his search for a *via media* between emerging tensions that threatened, in his lifetime, the coherence of the Stuart world order.[1]

I

As the profession to which Whitelocke had 'ever' aimed from his youth, the common law was to provide a crucible in which Whitelocke's political and social views were fired and refined over his life. Whitelocke's recollection of Sir Edward Coke's request that, as 'one of his owne coat', he escort the chief justice around Windsor after a sermon in 1615 reflects one of the many ways in which he and other English lawyers, proud of their traditions and overtly sensitive to criticism, affirmed social and professional solidarity.[2]

Although Whitelocke's legal training allowed him to move fluidly between the narrowly English traditions exalted in the common law, and broader European traditions upheld by his university education, he maintained a characteristically English appreciation of European culture, in which respect for Western literature, to which he laid claim intellectually, was coupled with a basic suspicion of foreign ways. As his family's continental adventures had led to much misery in Whitelocke's eyes, it is not surprising that when his son asked for permission to travel abroad, he was redirected to visit the antiquities of his own country. Psychologically, Whitelocke was always inclined to feel safer

1 *Table Talk of John Selden*, ed. S.W. Singer (London 1847), p. 93; Whitelock, *Memorials* (Oxford 1853), vol. 1, p. 50.

2 *Liber Famelicus*, pp. 13-14, 48, 74-76, 78-86, 95-99, which includes examples of Whitelocke's careful descriptions of the dress code, ceremonies and speeches of the common law; and cf. Baker, 'Inns of Court and Legal Doctrine', p. 274; Bouwsma, 'Lawyers in Early Modern Culture', pp. 309, 315-17; Prest, *Rise of the Barristers*, pp. 258-60; *idem*, 'Lawyers', pp. 68-9; Lemmings, 'Ritual and Law', pp. 3-20; W.R. Prest, 'The Art of Law and the Law of God: Sir Henry Finch (1558-1625)' in *Puritans and Revolutionaries: Essays in Seventeenth-Century History Presented to Christopher Hill*, ed. David Pennington & Keith Thomas (Oxford 1978), p. 101.

on home soil. Thus, although he demonstrated his intellectual confidence before some 'foreigners... of quality' through an assize charge he delivered in Latin for their benefit, Whitelocke was at pains to inform these 'strangers and scholars of the ability of our judges, and the cause of our proceedings in matters of law and justice'.[3]

Godfrey Goodman, bishop of Gloucester from 1624 to 1640, remarked that to be a lawyer 'was indeed to be a governor of one's country'. As an agent of the king's law, James Whitelocke occupied, by virtue of his office, an important and relatively independent position in society. In a series of judicial charges drafted over his career, Whitelocke suggested the binding role of law in his understanding of the interrelation of cosmic and social order. The common law of England was, he assured one jury, 'drawne from the law of God, of Nature, of nations'. Working deductively from God's commandment that 'thou shalt not covett thy neighbours house, nor his oxe nor his asse nor any thing that is his', Whitelocke instructed another jury that formal definition of this principle in society came from the 'lawes of the Kingdom' in courts erected for this purpose. Crime was, to Whitelocke's way of thinking, a manifestation of sin, and must be met as such with a response appropriate to the demands of a righteous creator. And so, because

> state and commonwealthe shall flourishe where vice and vicious persons are suppressed, this ought to move you with all diligence to find out the secret practices of persons ill affected whoe... give themselves to worke all manner of wronge and oppression to the great contempt both of God and his ordinance.[4]

It is not surprising to find that as overseer of this social order Whitelocke had his enemies. Shortly after his father's death, Bulstrode moved to punish members of the local community who

---

3 *Diary*, p. 51.

4 Godfrey Goodman, *The Court of King James I*, 2 vols (London 1839) vol. 1, p. 294; Longleat Papers, vol. 21, fols 100-165; Powell, 'Sir James Whitelocke' pp. 18-31; Sharpe, *Crime in Early Modern England*, p. 12; C.B. Herrup, 'Law and Morality in Seventeenth-Century England', *Past & Present* 106 (1985), p. 111, *idem*, *Common Peace*, p. 193.

criticised Whitelocke for his severity during his time as a judge. Despite this, James Whitelocke's emphasis on the rights of property and the need for order accurately reflected 'the common ground between the values of the legal elite, the gentry and the local men of middling status' by encouraging an obedience to God and state that ensured social peace. Sir Richard Hutton reflected that Whitelocke's concern 'for observing order and regularity' in which he was 'held to be more severe than necessary', was 'well excused in this loose and insolent age where many offend in a capital fashion with greediness'. As a lawyer and a landowner, James Whitelocke employed the 'rhetoric of magistracy' not just to legitimate his own position in society, but to uphold a delicate social order that relied as much upon psychological as physical structures to keep its components in place.[5]

II

It was once a commonplace to associate law and religion as ingredients that fused to produce political 'opposition' in early Stuart England. Revisionists have rightly dismissed such a notion: in keeping with the political sensibilities of the day, Whitelocke conceived of a natural order upheld through the power of the king, ideally expressed with consent and counsel of parliament. Any open resistance to the king would bring such a world to the point of collapse. This is not to dismiss, however, Whitelocke's exposure to overlapping and competing constitutional traditions of varied political emphasis. One tradition, employed by the king, bishops such as Richard Bancroft and Richard Neile, and civil law theorists such as John Cowell, played selectively upon continental and native theological traditions, drawing parallels between royal and sacred power and mystifying the king's

5 *Diary*, p. 68; Herrup, 'Law and Morality', p. 108; *Diary of Sir Richard Hutton*, p. 91 (Law French); Richard Cust & Peter Lake, 'Sir Richard Grosvenor and the Rhetoric of Magistracy', *Bulletin of the Institute of Historical Research* 54 (1981), p. 40.

prerogative. Whitelocke, in contrast and in keeping with his training in the common law, drew upon another tradition that placed greater emphasis on the contractual obligation between the monarch and his subjects.[6]

The coherence and currency of Whitelocke's own brand of constitutional thought remains open to question. Paul Christianson has argued that a 'common-law' political theory, in which Whitelocke's own thoughts played a significant role, can be traced back to Thomas Hedley's speech on impositions in the parliament of 1610. These shallow roots seem unconvincing. In contrast to continental theories which placed majesty firmly in the hands of the prince, Brian Tierney suggests the 'fusing' of two highly developed medieval theories in seventeenth-century English political theory, in which the king as the head of church and state possessed unique powers, but was still required to rule with the counsel and consent of the political nation. In 1610 Whitelocke urged the king to consider parliamentary counsel so that political consensus might be upheld. Twenty years later, he punished individual parliamentarians for destroying consensus, as a new generation of MPs made a desperate cry for their counsel to be considered. Here one must acknowledge the fundamental dilemma Whitelocke faced along with all other proponents of 'mixed monarchy' in the early seventeenth century: the system permitted neither

---

6 Hill, *Society and Puritanism*, pp. 162, 302-7, 330-42, 349-53; *idem*, *Intellectual Origins*, ch. 5; Prest, *Inns of Court*, pp. 209-19; *idem*, *Rise of the Barristers*, pp. 226-7; Nicholas Tyacke, 'Puritanism, Arminianism and Counter-Revolution' in *Origins of the English Civil War*, p. 140; J.D. Eusden, *Puritans, Lawyers, and Politics in Early Seventeenth-Century England* (New Haven 1958), *passim*; David Little, *Religion, Order and Law: A Study in Pre-Revolutionary England* (Oxford 1970), pp. 39-53; Sommerville, *Politics and Ideology*, pp. 105-8; *idem*, 'Richard Hooker, Hadrian Saravia, and the Advent of the Divine Right of Kings', *History of Political Thought* 4 (1983), pp. 229-45; Burgess, *Politics of the Ancient Constitution*, pp. 139-78.

the king nor his parliamentary representatives simply to arrogate the rights of the other.[7]

In his search for consensus, Whitelocke swayed toward conjoined royal and parliamentary sovereignty, and then recoiled as parliamentary unrest over government policies threatened to unravel the principle of mixture. Bulstrode Whitelocke recalled that, as he began his own parliamentary career in 1626, his father 'gave him good counsell concerning his demeanour in Parlement', asking him to sit apart from vocal critics of the Crown, to follow 'his own conscience and judgement', and 'not to be engaged in any party or faction whatsoever'. Always one to seek a remedy rather than a dispute in cases of political friction, a personal attack on the monarch was for Whitelocke unthinkable, as he assumed that the existing system worked to the best interests of all.[8]

In instances where royal or parliamentary conduct threatened harmony, Whitelocke is silent. Careful to avoid open discussion of 'great mysteries of policie and government' in public or in private, Whitelocke found the role of an 'historiographer' of parliamentary controversies untenable, directing readers of his *Liber Famelicus* to more candid remarks on other events in parliament and state prepared in separate accounts, now lost. If Whitelocke had maintained a consistent level of political commentary throughout the *Liber Famelicus*, his observations on events in the 1620s would be invaluable. As

7 Paul Christianson, 'Royal and parliamentary voices on the ancient constitution, c. 1604-1621' in *Mental World*, pp. 71-95; Tierney, *Religion, Law, and the Growth of Constitutional Thought*, 1150-1650 (Cambridge 1982), pp. 83, 106-8; cf. G.L. Harriss, 'Medieval doctrines in the debates on supply, 1610-1629' in Sharpe (ed.), *Faction and Parliament*, pp. 74-6; J.S. Roskill, 'Perspective in English Parliamentary History' in *Historical Studies of the English Parliament*, ed. E.B. Fryde & E. Miller, 2 vols. (Cambridge 1970), vol. 2, pp. 296-323. It could be argued that the theoretical framework of the arguments of the early Stuart period attempted to force the king to obey the coronation oath of Edward II (retained in its essentials until 1688) which obliged the king to 'grant and preserve good laws and customs' and 'to observe laws to be chosen by the people or community'.

8 *Diary*, p. 53.

Prest has observed, however, his 'vivid account of his life and times becomes quite cryptic soon after his promotion to the judiciary'. Although Whitelocke was prepared to criticise government officials in the epitaphs scattered throughout his journal, he had always shied away from criticism of the king. Whitelocke was called in 1628 to rule whether a remark that Charles I was 'as unwise a king as ever was' constituted treason in *Hugh Pine's Case*. As Charles repeatedly emphasised the relationship between his own will and government policy throughout the 1620s, Whitelocke knew that criticism was a delicate business where the person of the king was involved. An absence of political commentary creates deep silences in the *Liber Famelicus* after 1624, the year in which Whitelocke returned from Chester to take up his appointment to the King's Bench. Although these silences are frustrating to the historian they are instructive, particularly in light of his son's testimony that James Whitelocke felt himself to be the victim of deeply unfortunate circumstances during this final period of his life.[9]

In James Whitelocke's mind, there could be no irreconcilable conflict of interest between the king's legal prerogatives, and the judges' imperative to 'do equal law, and execution of right, to all his subjects, rich and poor'. Mercifully, Whitelocke was never required to take sides in the bloody wars that proved this assumption unfounded. For this reason, attempts to define Whitelocke's views in terms of 'royalist' or 'anti-absolutist' sentiment are inappropriate, as they force frameworks of definition upon Whitelocke which tell us little about the political assumptions that held his world together.

---

9 *State Trials*, vol. 2, col. 481; vol. 3, cols 359-68; *Liber Famelicus*, p. 41; Prest, 'Politics and Profession' p. 163; Cust, *Forced Loan*, pp. 224-8; Whitelock, *Memorials* (1732), p. 39. For the issue of silence in political commentaries of the 1620s and 1630s cf. Cust, *Forced Loan*, p. 187; Reeve, *Charles I*, p. 91; Hirst, 'Privy Council', pp. 50-51; C.M. Hibbard, *Charles I and the Popish Plot* (Chapel Hill 1983), pp. 89, 232; Judith Richards, '"His Nowe Majestie" and the English Monarchies: the Kingship of Charles I before 1640', *Past & Present* 113 (1986), pp. 72-3.

James Whitelocke suggests, in his voices and his silences, that new methods of government were tearing at the internal fabric of his mental world, pointing to a psychological impasse afflicting constitutional thought in the reign of Charles I.[10]

III

Beyond law, religion provided the second great pillar of order in Whitelocke's moral and mental world. His personal reflections upon his spiritual journey through life, most fully recorded in the will he personally prepared in the year of his death, reflect a Calvinist hope 'for eternall rest after my travayle in this restless life', concluding that in his worldly 'pilgrimage... I have plentifully tasted of God's blessinge'. It is notable that while Bulstrode Whitelocke referred to his mother as one 'called by some a Puritan' in his memoirs, he remembered his father simply as 'one that truley feared God'. In an undated prayer thanking God for deliverance 'from the perils of this last night' Whitelocke remembered God's 'blessings in my wife, my children, my friends, my fortunes'. As Whitelocke received many 'blessings' from high-church 'friends' who had openly supported his career since his days as a university scholar, he may well have felt that these clerics were best left to face God with their own consciences.[11]

In recent years, the shifting doctrinal emphasis of the early Stuart era has come under great scrutiny. Nicholas Tyacke and Peter White, in particular, have debated the level of disunity within the established

10 *Statutes at Large*, ed. O. Ruffhead, 10 vols (London 1786), vol. 1, pp. 239, 241; Sir John Davies, *Les Primer Report des Cases et Matters en Ley* (1628), 'Preface Dedicatory'.

11 Longleat Papers, vol. 24, fol. 157; PRO PROB 11/162/113; *Diary*, pp. 44, 63, 66. See J.D. Alsop, 'Religious Preambles in English Wills as Formulae', *Journal of Ecclesiastical History* 40 (1989), pp. 19-27; C. Marsh, 'In the name of God? Will-making and faith in early modern England' in *The records of the nation: the Public Record Office, 1838-1988*, ed. G.H. Martin & P. Spufford (Woodbridge 1990), pp. 61-6.

church and the toleration or rejection of 'anti-Calvinist' dogma in the 1620s and 1630s. Whitelocke's approach may serve as an archetype of the '*via media* between extremes' suggested by White, in which moderate Calvinism cannot necessarily be equated with anti-Arminianism, even in the decade before the outbreak of war. Yet Whitelocke's attempts to embrace religious consensus evidence the strain placed upon even the most moderate Calvinists by the increasingly vigorous imposition of an Arminian design for the English Church.[12]

Historians have long noted the 'antipathy of Puritans and common lawyers to prerogative justice', finding also that 'professional and careerist considerations would tend to produce a dislike of Puritanism among the vast majority of civil lawyers who found their most spectacular career opportunities in the ecclesiastical courts... so detested by common lawyers'. Whitelocke's scattered public and private comments suggest that he stood, at times, uneasily between ecclesiastical and common lawyers as they argued over their juridical powers and limitations. His thinly-veiled attack upon Archbishop Bancroft in an emotional session of the 1610 parliament, in which he advised 'any churchmen' who might 'endeavour by application of the text of Scripture, to overthrow the antient law and liberties of the kingdom' to be admonished by the 'ill success' of Cardinal Wolsey, avoided direct criticism of his own ecclesiastical patrons. It was to cause him some considerable embarrassment in the brief parliament of 1614,

---

12 Tyacke, 'Puritanism, Arminianism and Counter-revolution', pp. 119-143; Peter White, 'The Rise of Arminianism Reconsidered', *Past and Present* 101 (1983), pp. 34-54; Tyacke, *Anti-Calvinists*; Tyacke and White, 'Debate: The rise of Arminianism reconsidered', *Past & Present* 115 (1987), pp. 201-229; Peter Lake, 'Calvinism and the English Church 1570-1635', *Past and Present* 114 (1987), pp. 32-76; Peter White, *Predestination, Policy and Polemic. Conflict & Consensus in the English Church from the Reformation to the Civil War* (Cambridge 1992); Peter Lake, 'Predestinarian Propositions' (book review), *Journal of Ecclesiastical History* 46 (1995), pp. 110-123.

when Richard Neile took over Bancroft's role as a champion of prerogative rights and suggested that those (including Whitelocke) who had questioned the legality of impositions were guilty of breaking the oath of allegiance. While Whitelocke's was nominated to and served a committee established to punish Neile, he is conspicuously absent from the parliamentary record of comments made by member of this committee.[13]

In the 1620s, as the Arminian vision for a church of revitalised dignity and power gained royal sanction, Whitelocke's moderate appeal for the rights of the clergy, articulated most fully in his 1619 reading on benefices, was put to the test as his Arminian patrons gathered benefices for their financial benefit. Recording a loan of £400 he made to John Buckeridge upon his appointment as bishop of Rochester, Whitelocke noted Buckeridge's accumulation of livings in Kent, London, and Windsor, suggesting 'how far from covetousnes he had lived'. Such comment may suggest a view that in this case 'episcopal pluralism was caused by necessity rather than greed'; it may, however, reflect a hollow attempt to defend his friend from the imputation that he was manipulating the laws of *commendam* for personal profit. Whitelocke's eirenic views on the plurality of benefices, which promoted him as a friend of the clergy in 1619, may have hardened in the face of reality in 1621 as William Laud insisted on retaining a college benefice for his personal profit upon his resignation from the presidency of St John's. Laud's refusal to relinquish the parsonage of Crick, Northamptonshire, which had been acquired by Sir William Craven in 1613 'for the good of St. John's', led to a tripartite legal challenge to Laud from Whitelocke and his clerk Gavin Champineys, Sir Oliver and Lady Anna Cromwell, and the Company of Merchant Taylors. While the outcome of this

13 Ashton, *English Civil War*, p. 105; Usher, *Rise and Fall of the High Commission*, pp. 121-235; Sommerville, *Politics & Ideology*, p. 120; *State Trials*, vol. 2, col. 485; *Proceedings in Parliament 1614*, p. 346; History of Parliament Trust.

litigation is unknown, it underlines the unhappy effects, at a personal level, of Laud's push to improve the status and wealth of the clergy.[14]

Tyacke has argued that the 1620s, 'taken as a whole, saw a dramatic shift in official Church of England teachings', as James I's policy of balancing the aspirations of Calvinist bishops with those of an increasingly coherent Arminian party was abandoned by Charles I, ushering in a new period of influence for Neile, Laud and their supporters. Russell has concluded that the religious disharmony which beset Charles's reign

> was in the area where religious conviction and political power met, and in the area where they were so closely involved together that it is not even a meaningful question to ask which is which.

The difficulty of James Whitelocke's position, in his last decade of life, was that his religious convictions could not be convincingly integrated into the base of his political power.[15]

The sixteen bishops mentioned in the *Liber Famelicus* cover a full spectrum of Calvinists and 'anti-Calvinists' and it is notable that while Whitelocke followed the progress of Laud, Buckeridge and Neile, he also kept an eye on the fortunes of such prominent Calvinist bishops as John King, George Abbot, John Davenport and John Williams. Whitelocke's first contact with John Williams was in November 1617, when the new Lord Keeper promoted him to the Buckinghamshire commission of the peace. Thereafter, cordial

---

14 *Liber Famelicus*, p. 26; Lockyer, *Early Stuarts*, p. 111; Carlton, *Archbishop William Laud*, p. 29; Steig, *Laud's Laboratory*, p. 100; Hugh Trevor Roper, *Archbishop Laud 1573-1645* (London 1940), p. 57; H. Bell, *Archbishop Laud and Priestly Government* (London 1905), p. 29; *History, Topography, and Directory of Northamptonshire*, ed. Francis Whellan (London 1874), p. 345; Thomas Mason, *Serving God and Mammon* (Newark, Delaware 1985), p. 32; Court Minutes of the Merchant Taylors' Company, 24 March 1623, quoted in H.B. Wilson, *The History of Merchant Taylors' School*, 2 vols (London 1812-1814), vol. 1, p. 211.

15 Tyacke, *Anti-Calvinists*, p. 106; Russell, *Causes of the English Civil War*, p. 62.

relations were extended between the two, so that Williams lodged at Whitelocke's home at Fawley Court on his way to visit the king at Woodstock in September 1621. In 1624, it was Williams that persuaded his 'assured loving frend' to accept office in King's Bench and relinquish his preferred role as chief justice of Chester.[16]

It appears that Whitelocke's support for his Arminian patrons became increasingly strained in the last decade of his life, as the textbook tempests of university theology gave way to genuine political debate about an appropriate course for the Church of England to follow. The first strong test of his loyalties came in an assize ruling which attempted to calm tensions in Bishop Neile's 'model diocese' of Durham. In 1628, Peter Smart, a prebend who had been excluded from Durham cathedral for preaching against the Arminian ecclesiology of Bishop Neile and his followers, brought charges against the chapter at the August assizes, initiating 'the greatest religious controversy of the century in the North of England'. Serving as the senior justice of assize in the region, Whitelocke encouraged the jury to reject Smart's indictment, which argued that the communion table was placed the wrong way and that the creed was sung and lights and tapers were used during the service.[17]

Both Neile and Laud would have been pleased with John Cosin's report that Whitelocke

> rejected the indictments in open court, letting the country know that he knew no law whereupon they should be grounded; and adding, that the man deserved no small punishment who, in this unwonted sort, had gone about to disgrace the Church, and dishonour the solemnity of God's service there where himself had been an eye and ear witness that all things were done in decency and order.

---

16 Tyacke, *Anti-Calvinists*, pp. 21-2, 46, 92; *Liber Famelicus*, pp. 60, 89, 96; The *Liber Famelicus* includes references to George Abbot, Lancelot Andrewes, John Buckeridge, John Davenant, William Day, Theophilus Field, John Howson, John King, William Laud, Richard Neile, Rowland Searchfield, Giles Thompson, John Thornborough, Robert Tounson, John Williams, and George Wright.

17 Trevor Roper, *Catholics, Anglicans and Puritans*, pp. 70-1; John Hoffman, 'The Arminian and the Iconoclast', *The Historical Magazine of the Protestant Episcopal Church XLVIII* (1979), p. 301.

Whitelocke's endorsement of high-church ceremonial stand in sharp contrast to the findings of his old friend Henry Yelverton, who encouraged a 1629 jury to prefer the indictments rejected by Whitelocke, adding that he 'objected to organ-playing, which he termed whistling', ordering that church-goers 'must stand only at the Apostle's Creed', and concluding that he had always been 'accounted a Puritan, and he thanked God for it, and so he would die'. In light of Whitelocke's support for Bishop Neile, it is significant that when his circuit fees were withheld in 1628, as a desperate financial measure on the part of the Crown, Neile provided him with £40 in 'compensation' for circuit work in Durham.[18]

Whitelocke's desultory involvement in a second religious *cause célèbre* of the late 1620s demonstrates that by this time any opposition to the 'anti-Calvinist' party at Court was tantamount to political opposition to the Crown. Early in 1629, ten Jesuits were seized at Clerkenwell College, only to be released at a King's Bench hearing held before Whitelocke and his associates on the bench. The decision met with popular outrage and charges were laid in parliament that, while 'plain treason was prov'd at the trial', the judges of King's Bench had refused to read papers providing important evidence for the prosecution. Replying to Sir Thomas Hoby's imputation that he had ignored his declared intention 'to doe right to all' at the trial, Whitelocke replied lamely, through Sir Miles Fleetwood, that although he was present for two days of the trial 'it was late before he returned from dinner... and the evidence [had been] given before his

18 *Calendar of State Papers Domestic 1628-1629*, p. 259; *The Correspondence of John Cosin, D.D., Lord Bishop of Durham*, ed. G. Ormsby, 2 vols, Sturtees Society 52 & 55 (1868 & 1870), vol. 1, pp. 145-6; *Calendar of State Papers Domestic 1629-1632*, p. 15; Trevor Roper, *Catholics, Anglicans and Puritans*, p. 74; BL Add. MS 53725, fol. 179. The irony is that Whitelocke may actually have done Smart and his followers a favour had he ended the case. When Smart subsequently pursued their claims before the Court of High Commission he was forced to recant, deprived of his canonry, fined £400, and then imprisoned for twelve years. Smart's fate stresses the increasingly charged religious atmosphere of the Caroline era.

return'. He further informed parliament that he knew of 'no evidence of papers read after his coming to the Sessions'. Whitelocke's casual standards of participation during this important court case are highly unconvincing. His answers evade the real issue: Charles I had personally commanded the judges to bail the priests in an order sent via the earl of Dorset. Whitelocke's final years in office were spent attempting to avoid further controversy as new and unwelcome changes threatened not just his professional integrity, but his private beliefs.[19]

Events surrounding the consecration of Whitelocke's private chapel in 1631 suggest that visible and invisible manifestations of belief could not be separated in the minds of their Arminian and Calvinist advocates. Significantly, it was not his Arminian patrons who were asked to consecrate this monument to Whitelocke's private beliefs, but rather John Williams, who had elsewhere defended an austere ecclesiological style as Arminian criticism of Calvinist practices grew louder in the 1620s, and Robert Wright, bishop of Bristol. Being no puritan, Williams was treated to a display of organ music and song, which led him to remark that 'no subject in Christendom had better musicke then Judge Whitelocke had in his house'.[20]

---

19 Gardiner, *History of England*, vol. 8, p. 57; Sir Thomas Crew, *The Proceedings and Debates of the House of Commons, In the Sessions of Parliament, begun the Twentieth of January, 1628* (London 1707), p. 104; *Commons Debates for 1629*, ed. Wallace Notestein (Minneapolis 1921), pp. 153, 216, 218, 154, and cf. p. 82, in which Barrington is reported as saying that 'he had come late on the first day, and therefore understood not the business, and the second day was not there at all'.

20 *Liber Famelicus*, pp. 110-11; Tyacke, *Anti-Calvinists*, p. 209; Heal & Holmes, *The Gentry*, p. 369; *Diary*, p. 65; BL Add. MS 53726, fol. 69. Cf. Pauline Croft, 'The Religion of Robert Cecil', *Historical Journal* 34 (1991), pp. 787-90; Ian Atherton, 'Viscount Scudamore's "Laudianism": The Religious Practices of the First Viscount Scudamore', *Historical Journal* 34 (1991), pp. 569-70; Lake, 'Calvinism and the English Church', pp. 74-5.

Unfortunately, Williams's accommodating outlook contrasted with the aggressive stance taken by some of the other clerics assembled for the occasion, who objected to the chapel on three grounds:

> 1. That the pulpit was placed even with the Communion Table. 2. That the Altar was not rayled in. 3. That there were no Images nor Crucifixes in the Walles or windowes...

James Whitelocke's response to this embarrassing criticism was characteristically mute. Refusing to be drawn into debate, he avoided taking issue with the Arminians on questions he 'thought not fitt to answear'.[21]

Peter White has challenged the assumption that the 'essence of conflict' over religion, in the two decades before civil war, came with the usurpation of Calvinist doctrine at court by an increasingly favoured Arminian faction. James Whitelocke's example makes the point that for many Englishmen, the discomfort of Arminianism was not encountered so much in what was said about Calvinistic practices, but what was done to obstruct them. Whatever his misgivings, Whitelocke could accommodate the soteriological position of his Arminian friends, respecting their right to search for their own salvation. As the Arminian drive to modify church practices became more assertive, he struggled to accommodate 'reforms' undertaken by Laud and his associates, such as the improvement of clerical status through the accumulation of benefices. The discomfort of Whitelocke's position came home once and for all in the 1630s through a Laudian campaign to reconfigure private and public places of worship.[22]

In this sense, the confidence of those junior clerics who felt it appropriate to criticise Whitelocke's private chapel at Fawley Court underlines the catastrophic damage done by Laudian reforming zeal to religious harmony. The last mention of William Laud in the *Liber*

---

21 *Liber Famelicus*, p. 111; *Diary*, p. 65.

22 White, 'The Rise of Arminianism Reconsidered', pp. 34-5. Cf. William Lammont, 'The Puritan Revolution: a historiographical essay' in *Varieties of British Political Thought*, pp. 124-5.

Famelicus noted Laud's consecration as bishop of St David's in November 1621. Although it sounds suspiciously like wisdom after the event, Bulstrode Whitelocke's *Memorials* suggest that his father had privately thought William Laud 'too full of fire, though a just and good man', and that he worried in his later years that the archbishop's 'want of experience in state matters, and his too much zeal for the Church, and heat, if he proceeded in the way he was then in, would set this nation on fire'. James Whitelocke's death in 1632 allowed him to maintain a compromising stance that would have been almost untenable by the late 1630s, when the heat of the Laudian establishment was more powerfully felt.[23]

IV

As this book draws to a close, it is fitting to return to the *Liber Famelicus*. Fairly assessed by its original editor, John Bruce, as 'a register of the enlargement of his family, and his professional advancement', his first words in such a journal 'for posteritye' suggest his belief that he would achieve his public and personal goals. In light of the seemingly wasteful lives of his older brothers, it was a growing sign of God's blessing upon himself, his wife and children. The *Liber Famelicus* is appropriately named, as family, both nuclear and extended, formed the touchstone of James Whitelocke's private world, and at the end of his life it was to family that Whitelocke returned.[24]

---

23 *Liber Famelicus*, p. 90; Whitelocke, *Memorials* (Oxford 1853), vol. 1, p. 99 (and cf. pp. 36, 75). No one can say what James Whitelocke would have made of Laud's eventual fate, but it seems a fitting epilogue to note that his son refused to take part in the prosecution of his father's old friend, declaring that 'it was not fit for me to appear in it against one to whom I had been beholden for my education'. By 1645, such moderation had become powerless to spare Laud from the scaffold, or to prevent the religious fire prophesied by James Whitelocke before his death.

24 *Liber Famelicus*, p. vi; Collins, *From Divine Cosmos to Sovereign State*, pp. 20-1.

Reflecting upon a marriage which had proved so fortunate, James Whitelocke remembered his wife Elizabeth, who died on 28 May 1631, as

> a woman most dedicated to her husband, most faithful, most careful in the management of her affairs, most long-suffering in adversity, and God-fearing, religious, devoted to God, and charitable to the poor, far beyond all the women whom I know. She was buried in the church of Fawley, where I await a place by her side.

At her passing, Whitelocke 'sadly asked, is my wife dead?', breaking down 'into abundance of tears, and sighs and bitter mourning for her death'. It appears that from this time James Whitelocke may have lost the inclination if not the will to live. Telling his servants 'how uncomfortable his condition was without her', he predicted his own passing as they wrapped her body for burial. The year that followed was, for him, time to finish off business and say goodbye to friends and colleagues.[25]

Retiring to Fawley Court from Serjeants' Inn, Whitelocke settled the details of his estate 'with as much composure of mind as att other times', drafting a will which passed on to his family the fruits of his labours. In the will, which was made in the form of a gift to Bulstrode (to avoid the assessment of his estate by the Prerogative Court of Canterbury), his son took possession of Fawley and a half share in the adjoining manor of Fillet's Court. Bulstrode also received £4500 as well as 'plate and household goods'. Bulstrode, as executor of the will, was to keep the other £2500 of Whitelocke's estate aside for his sister Cecilia's marriage portion, with an allowance of £60 per annum for her maintenance until her marriage. £10 a quarter was bequeathed to his other daughter Elizabeth, whose husband Sir Thomas Mostyn received the gift of Whitelocke's posy ring. A final sum of £100 was

---

25 *Diary*, p. 63. The original Latin inscription, open to inspection in Fawley Church, is found in the *Liber Famelicus*, p. 101 and the *Diary*, p. 63. For an photography of the monument see Geoffrey Tyack, *Fawley Buckinghamshire: A short history of the Church and Parish* (Fawley 1986), p. 6.

set aside for the building of a monument to Whitelocke and his wife at Fawley Church.[26]

In the preface to his *Second Report*, published in the year of Whitelocke's marriage to Elizabeth Bulstrode, Sir Edward Coke advised a generation of young lawyers to 'cast their eyes upon the sages of the law', who had achieved 'honesty, gravity, and integrity' by virtue of their learning 'and by the goodness of God hath obtained a greater blessing and ornament than by any other profession to their family and prosperity'. Thirty years later, his self-styled epitaph would ascribe to Whitelocke many of the qualities to which Coke referred, reflecting back on forty years of dedication to the law. For a man who had started his legal education with less that £100 to his name, the wealth that James Whitelocke had amassed by the end of his life lent some credence to Coke's claims. More importantly for Whitelocke, perhaps, was the psychological assurance that this prosperity gave him of God's continuing favour in the world to come.[27]

Surveying the trappings of his father's success, Bulstrode proudly declared that James Whitelocke had 'by the blessing of God uppon his industry raysed his own fortune and his family'. His father had been, Bulstrode felt, 'a most laborious student all his dayes, of a most just and courteous nature, and of a spirit most invincible and industry indefatigable'. Anyone who has tried to read James Whitelocke's surviving legal memoranda would have to agree that his industry was exceptional. If one can forgive Whitelocke for the venom he reserved for those who might threaten his path to prosperity in the worldly kingdom of the early Stuarts, his son's judgement seems apt.[28]

---

26 *Diary*, pp. 66-7; PRO PROB 11/162/113.

27 Sir Edward Coke, *Second Part of the Reports of Sir Edward Coke* (London 1602), 'Preface', and cf., for example, Henry Philipps, *A treatise enumerating the most illustrious families of England, who have been raised to honour and wealth by the profession of the law* (1686).

28 *Diary*, pp. 66-7; *Contemporaries of Bulstrode Whitelocke*, p. 428. Whitelocke's landholdings are listed in PRO C142/481/36.

At ease with the thought of death (his son Bulstrode later recounted), Whitelocke 'expressed fully his assurance of the love of God to him, and of his eternall happines through the merits of Christ, and so recommending his soul to God... his breath expired on the 22nd day of June 1632'. Among the goods of his deceased father's estate, Bulstrode received the key to a cabinet in which James Whitelocke left a small, private legacy to the world among 'divers papers of consequence'. As well as the epithets James Whitelocke had composed for a monument that his son would shortly erect to honour his parents at Fawley Church, into Bulstrode's care passed 'his liber famelicus, a short story of his own life, written by himself'. This investigation opened with the words that James Whitelocke penned as his opening remarks in the *Liber Famelicus* twenty-one years before his death. It should close at this point, as the text was passed on to his son and from there into history.[29]

---

29 *Diary*, pp. 66-7; Longleat Papers, vol. 6, fols 28, 29. Notices of Whitelocke's death by fellow judges are found in *Diary of Sir Richard Hutton*, p. 91, *Les Reportes de William Jones* (London 1675), p. 299.

Select Bibliography

Manuscript Sources

The Marquess of Bath's Collection, Longleat House:

Whitelocke Papers, vols. 1-5 (1562-1633); vols. 21, 24, 26 (miscellaneous); Parcel 9 (miscellaneous legal note books)

British Library:

Additional MS 53725 *Liber Famelicus*

Additional MS 24481, fols. 62-75v (J. Hunter's extracts from the *Liber Famelicus*, 19th century)

Additional MS 53726 Bulstrode Whitelocke's 'Annals of his own life Dedicated to his Children' (1605-1634)

Hargrave MS 198 'Lectura Jacobi Whitlock Armigeri in Medio Templo 2 Augusti 1619 super Statutum 21 Hen 8 cap. 13 de facultatibus beneficiorum' (reading on benefices)

Hargrave 91, fols. 196-295v (reading on benefices)

Hargrave 237, fols. 5-95v (reading on benefices; Bartholomew Hall's copy. Turn volume upside down and read from back to front)

Hargrave MS 91, fols. 296-319v 'Conceits sur le stat de 32 Hen 8 ca 5 c. 13' (list of points taken from 1619 reading)

Harley MS 4176, fols. 16-18 'Of the Antiquite, Use, and Ceremonie of Lawful Combats in England' (discourse on combats)

Stowe MS 596, fols. 35-39 (discourse on combats)

Additional MS 25247, fols. 93-95 (discourse on combats)

Cottonian MS Faustina E.v, fols. 51-52 'Of the antiquite, use, and privilege of places for students & professors of the common lawes of England' (autograph)

Additional MS 36,082, fols. 105-176v 'The Question whether the kinge without assent of Parliament may sett Imposicions uppon the wares & goods of Merchaunts exported and imported out of and into the realme' (1610 speech on impositions)

Stowe MS 298, fols. 89-140v (1610 speech on impositions)

Lansdowne MS 160, fol. 83 'The whole proceeding at Whitehall ag. Mr Whitlock & Sr Robt. Mansell by the P.C. assisted by the Judges an. 1613 touching some contempts' (1613 prosecution; Sir Julius Caesar's notes)

Additional MS 4149, fols. 173-176v (copy of counsel record against Whitelocke and Mansel, incorrectly dated to 1609)

Harley MS 583, fols. 48-52 (Whitelocke's 1621 charge to Chester Grand Jury)

Cottonian Julius C.3, fol. 54 (letter from Whitelocke to Sir Robert Cotton, asserting the right of common lawyers to plead before the Earl Marshal's court; dated in margin 1609?)

Cottonian MS Titus F. iv, fols. 11-15 (Sir Francis Bacon suggests Whitelocke as potential reporter in review of common law, 1614)

Cambridge University Library:

MS Ll .3.12, fols. 326-477 (reading on benefices)

MS Ee .6.3, fols. 192-225v (notes on Whitelocke's reading in Law-French; includes discussions "after dinner" by Hadsor, Hoskins and Trist expounding questions of law raised by Whitelocke during the reading)

MS Oo .6.114, fols. 106-114 'The Antiquitye, Varyetye,and Reason of Mottoes, or words with armes of Noblemen and Gent. in England' (draft and two autograph copies)

MS Dd .2.25 (1610 speech on impositions)

MS Ff .3.17, fols. 75v ff. (1610 speech on impositions; Sir John Davies' copy)

MS Dd .5.7 (autograph record of cases in inns of chancery, c. 1599-1600)

MS Dd .9.20 (autograph academic commonplace book)

MS Dd .8.48 (autograph reports of cases in Queen's Bench and other courts, 39-42 Eliz.)

MS Dd .3.69 (autograph law commonplace book)

MS Gg .2.23, fol. 90 (Whitelocke listed as pleader before Justice Williams in King's Bench)

Bodleian Library:

MS Dep. d 804 (transcript of *Liber Famelicus* belonging to John Whitelocke [1757-1833])

MS Dep. d 746 (reading on benefices)

MS Rawlinson C. 207, fols. 62-96v (notes on 1619 reading)

MS Rawlinson C. 207, fols. 245-270 (paper book includes notes on Whitelocke's reading)

MS Ashmole 1150 (1), fols. 1-83 (reading on benefices)

MS Ashmole 856, fols. 149-153 (discourse on combats)

MS Tanner 278, fols. 141-142v (discourse on combats)

MS Tanner 85, fols. 16-38 (discourse on combats)

MS Smith 71, fol. 59 (copy of letter to Sir Robert Cotton)

MS Wood F.28, fols. 204-214 (papers relating to St. John's College)

MS Tanner 338, fols. 373-381 (papers relating to St. John's College)

Lincoln's Inn Library:

MS Miscellaneous 486 (8) (reading on benefices)

MS Law 14. Ii (reading on benefices)

MS Maynard 79, fols. 329-380 (reading on benefices)

MS Maynard 52 (4) (1610 speech on impositions)

Inner Temple Library:

MS Petyt 537.14, fols. 187v-213v (records examined and noted by Whitelocke in the case of impositions)

MS Miscellaneous 19, fols. 241-266v (record of Eliot's case; Whitelocke's judgement fols. 265-266v)

Middle Temple Library:

Uncataloged MS copy of reading on benefices; Muniment's Room

Minutes of the Parliament of the Honourable Society of the Middle Temple, vol. D 4 (1551-1610), vol. C3 (1610-1626)

Guildhall Library:

Merchant Taylors' Company Court Minute Book; Microfilm 326-328 (1595-1630)

Journal of the Court of Aldermen of the City of London, Report 33, 34.

Lambeth Palace Library:

Gibson MS 936, no. 249 (2 fols.) (draft submission for Whitelocke's release from prison in 1613 by Sir Francis Bacon)

College of Arms, London:
Vincent MS 43, fols. 26-42 (discourse on combats)

Public Record Office:
STAC 8/231/24 (Pope's petition against Whitelocke in Star Chamber, 1609)
CHES 21/3 (Chester Crown Book of judges' legal memoranda, 15 James I - 12 Charles I; Whitelocke's notes are in fols. 49-107)
E2/2 (Exchequer appearance books; lists Whitelocke as attorney Eliz. 39)
CHES 28/8, 28/9 (Prothonotary's papers of court proceedings; 14 James I -1 Charles I)
C 33/100-138 (Chancery decree & order books, 1600-1620. Indexed by PRO Index 1478-1516 [A and B books])
C 66/1956 (Chancery Patent Rolls, Whitelocke (& Heath) to clerkship of enrollments in King's Bench)
C 66/2220 (Whitelocke's commission as Justice of Denbigh & Montgomery)
C 66/2324 (Whitelocke's commission as Justice of King's Bench)
C 142/481/36 (Whitelocke's landholdings)
16/147/74 (Dorchester to Hyde)
PROB 11/62, Q. 113 (Whitelocke's will)

Woodstock Record Office:
Woodstock Borough MS B79/1, fol. 60 (notice of Whitelocke's recordership)

Eton College:
Eton College Records 27/267 (Whitelocke's appointment, and fees and as steward)
Eton College Records 60/300

Trinity College Dublin:
MS 853 (4) (reading on benefices)
MS 733 (3) (reading on benefices)

Edinburgh University Library:
Laing MS II.645/1, fols. 34-38 (discourse on combats)

University College of North Wales:

Mostyn MS 7294 (marriage negotiations with Mostyn)

Clwyd Record Office:

Mostyn MS D/M/3608 (articles of marriage between Sir Roger Mostyn and Elizabeth Whitelocke)

Harvard Law School:

MS 1077 (reading on benefices)

MS 1083, fol. 50v (judgement in King's Bench)

William Andrews Clark Memorial Library:

Selden-Hale Collection MS 586 (reading on benefices)

University of Pennsylvania Law School:

MS 1206 (reading on benefices)

Henry E. Huntington Library:

Ellesmere MS E 6472 (letter from Bridgewater to Sir James, 1621)

PRINTED SOURCES:

Historical Manuscripts Commission:

3rd Report

5th Report Appendix

8th Report Appendix Part I

8th Report II, Appendix Part III (p. 15, Bulstrode Whitelocke's

'Historie of the Parliament of England' incorrectly attributed to James; original is BL MS Stowe 300)

10th Report Appendix IV

11th Report Part VII

13th Report Part IV

Cowper I

Cowper II

De L'Isle and Dudley vol. V

Downshire IV

Portland IX

Salisbury (Cecil) XXII

Calendar of State Papers Domestic

Calendar of State Papers Venetian

Acts of the Privy Council

Journal of the House of Commons

Journal of the House of Lords

Statutes of the Realm

Archaeologica: or Miscellaneous Tracts, relating to Antiquity, London, Society of Antiquaries, 1770.

The Soveraigns Prerogative and the Subjects Privilege, comprised in several Speeches, Cases, and Arguements of Law Discussed between the Late King Charles And the most Eminent Persons of both Houses of Parliament, London, 1658.

Bacon, N., *An Historical and Political Discourse of the Laws and Government of England*, 4th ed., London, 1688.

Baildon, W.P. (ed.), *The Records of the Honourable Society of Lincoln's Inn: the Black Books* (2 vols.), London, Society of Lincoln's Inn, 1897-1902.

Baker, J.H. (ed.), *The Reports of Sir John Spelman* (2 vols.), London, Selden Society 93 & 94, (1976 & 1977).

(ed.), *The Order of Serjeants at Law: A chronicle of creations, with related texts*, London, Selden Society Supplementary Series 5,1984.

Ballard, A., *Chronicles of the royal borough of Woodstock, compiled from borough records and other original documents*, Oxford, 1896.

Barnes, T.G. (ed.), *Somerset Assize Orders 1629-1640*, Somerset Record Society 65 (1959).

Bateson, M. (ed.), *Records of the Borough of Leicester: Being a series of Extracts from the Archives of the Corporation of Leicester, 1509-1603* (3 vols.), Cambridge, Cambridge University Press, 1905.

Bede, *The history of the church of England* (trans. T. Stapleton), Antwerp, 1565.

Birch, T. (ed.), *The Court and Times of James the First. Illustrated by Authentic and Confidential Letters, From Various Public and Private Collections* (2 vols.), London, Henry Colburn, 1848.

(ed.), *The Court and Times of Charles the First* (2 vols.), London, Henry Colburn, 1848.

Bland, D.S., (ed.), *Early Records of Furnival's Inn: Edited from a Middle Temple manuscript*, Newcastle upon Tyne, Department of Extra-Mural Studies, 1957.

Bossewell, J., *Workes of armorie, deuyded into three bookes*, London, 1597.

Bracton, H., *Henrici de Bracton de legibus & consuetudinibus Angliae*, London, 1569.

Lord Braybrooke (ed.), *The Autobiography of Sir John Bramston, K.B., of Skreens, in the Hundred of Chelmsford*, London, Camden Society Old Series 32, 1845.

Bruce, J. (ed.), *Liber Famelicus of Sir James Whitelocke, a Judge of the Court of King's Bench in the Reigns of James I and Charles I*, London, Camden Society Old Series 70, 1858.

(ed.), *The Diary of John Manningham, of the Middle Temple, and of Bradborne, Kent, Barrister-at-Law 1602-1603*, London, Camden Society Old Series 91, 1868.

Buc, G., *The Third Universitie of England. Or a Treatise of the Foundations of all the Colleges, Avncient Schooles of Priviledge etc.*, appended to J. Stow, *The Annales, or General Chronicle of England*, London, 1615.

Cardwell, E. (ed.), *Documentary Annals of the Reformed Church of England; Being a Collection of Injunctions, Declarations, Orders, Articles of Inquiry, Etc., from the Year 1546 to the Year 1716* (2 vols), Oxford, Oxford University Press, 1844.

Carr, C. (ed.), *Pension Book of Clement's Inn*, London, Selden Society 78, 1960.

Clark, M.A. (ed.), *Register of the University of Oxford* (4 vols.), Oxford, Clarendon Press, 1887-9.

Clarke, A.W.H. (ed.), *The Parish Register of St. Dunstan in the East, London 1558-1654*, London, Harleian Society vol. 69, 1939.

Coke, E., *The Fourth Part of the Institutes of the Laws of England concerning the Jurisdiction of Courts*, London, 1767.

The Twelfth Part of the Reports of England, London, 1655.

Cowell, J., *Institutiones juris Anglicani*, London, 1605.

Crew, T., *The proceedings and debates of the House of Commons, in the sessions of Parliament, begun the twentieth of January, 1628 and ended by dissolution the tenth of March following...*, London, 1707.

Davies, *Jus imponendi Vectigalia; or the Learning touching the Customs, Tonnage, Poundage, and Impositions on Merchandizes &c., asserted*, London, 1656.

De Villiers, E. (ed.), 'The Hasting Journal of the Parliament of 1621', *Camden Miscellany* 20, London, Camden Society, 1953.

Dugdale, W., *Origines Juridiciales*, London, 1663.

Dyer, J., *Abridgement des reportes signior Dyer*, London, 1590.

Erasmus, *On Copia of Words and Ideas* (trans. D.B. King and H.D. Rix), Milwaukee, University of Milwaukee Press, 1963.

Fortescue, J., *The commendation of the laws of England* (trans. R. Mulcaster), London, 1590.

Foster, E.R. (ed.), *Proceedings in Parliament 1610* (2 vols.), New Haven, Yale University Press, 1966.

Foster, J., *Alumni Oxonienses: The Members of the University of Oxford* (4 vols.), London, 1891.

Fulbecke, W., *A Direction or Preparatiue to the study of the Lawe: Wherein is shewed, what things ought to be obseured and used of them that are addicted to the study of the Law, and what on the contrary part ought to be eschued and auoyded*, London, 1600.

Fuller, N., *The Sovereign's Prerogative and the Subjects' Privileges discussed, &c, in the 3rd and 4th year of King Charles I*, London, 1657.

Fuller,T., *The history of the worthies of England: who for parts and learning have been eminent in the several counties: together with an historical narrative of the native commodities and rarities in each county,* London, 1662.

Gardiner, S.R. (ed.), *Parliamentary debates in 1610; edited from a member of the House of Commons*, London, Camden Society Old Series 81, 1862.

(ed.), *Notes of the Debates in the House of Lords officially taken by Henry Elsing, clerk of the parliaments A.D. 1624 and 1626*, London, Camden Society New Series 24, 1879.

Gibson, E. (ed.), *Reliquiae Spelmanniae. The Posthumous Works*, London, 1727.

Goodman, G. (ed.), *The Court of King James I* (2 vols.), London, Richard Bentley, 1839.

Groombridge, M.J. (ed.), *Calendar of Chester City Council Minutes 1603-1642*, Blackpool, Record Society of Lancashire and Cheshire 106 (1956).

Hart, E.P. (ed.), *Merchant Taylors' School Register 1561-1934* (2 vols.), London, Eastern Press, 1936.

Haywarde, J., *Les Reportes del Cases in Camera Stellata 1593 to 1609* (ed. W.P. Baildon), London, 1894.

Hearne, T. (ed.), *A Collection of Curious Discourses Written by Eminent Antiquaries Upon Several Heads in our English Antiquities* (2 vols.), London, 1771.

Hill, L.M. (ed.), *The Ancient State, Authoritie, And Proceedings of the Court of Requests by Sir Julius Caesar*, Cambridge, Cambridge University Press, 1975.

Hinde, W., *The Office and Use of the Morall Law of God in the dayes of the Gospell*, London, 1623.

Holdsworth, R., 'Directions for a Student in the Universitie', Emmanuel College MS 48 in Fletcher, *The Intellectual Development of John Milton*, vol. 2, Appendix 2, pp. 623-655.

Holles, J., 'A summary of what was done in the Parliament begun the 5 of April, 1614 &c' HMC Portland IX, pp. 132-139.

Hopkinson, H.L., *Report on the Ancient Records in the possession of the Guild of Merchant Taylors of the Fraternity of St. John the Baptist in the City of London*, London, Waterlow & Sons, 1915.

Hopwood, C.H. (ed.), *Middle Temple Records* (3 vols.), London, Published by order of the Masters of the Bench, 1904.

Howell, T.B. (ed.), *A Complete Collection of State Trials* (34 vols.), London, 1809-1828.

Hughey, R. (ed.), *The Correspondence of Lady Katherine Paston 1603-1627*, Norfolk Record Society 14 (1941).

Jansson, M. (ed.), *Proceedings in Parliament 1614 (House of Commons)*, Philadelphia, American Philosophical Society 172 (1988).

Jessop, A. (ed.), *The Lives of the Right Hon. Francis North, Baron Guilford; the Hon. Sir Dudley North; and the Hon. and Rev. Dr. John North* (3 vols.), London, 1890.

Jones, W., *Les Reportes de William Jones*, London, 1675.

Jovius, P., *The worthy tract of Paulus Jouius* (trans. S. Daniel), London, 1585.

Keeler, M.F., M.J. Cole & W.B. Bidwell (eds.), *Proceedings in Parliament: Commons Debates 1628* (6 vols.), New Haven, Yale University Press, 1977-1983.

King, H.C., *Records and Documents concerning Serjeant's Inn, Fleet Street,* London, Richard Flint & Company, 1922.

Lamoine, G. (ed.), *Charges to the Grand Jury 1689-1803*, Camden Society 4th Series 43 (1992).

Langley, T., *The History and Antiquities of the Hundred of Desborough, and Deanery of Wycombe, in Buckinghamshire; including the Borough Towns of Wycombe and Marlow, and Sixteen Parishes*, London, 1797.

Livy, T., *The Romane Historie* (trans. P. Holland), London, 1598.

MacGreath, H.F. & H.A.C. Sturgess (eds.), *Register of Admissions to the Honourable Society of the Middle Temple* (3 vols.), London, The Honourable Society of the Middle Temple, 1949.

Martin, C.T. (ed.), *Minutes of the Parliament of the Middle Temple* (4 vols.), London, Printed for the Masters of the Bench, 1904-5.

McClure, N.E. (ed.), *The Letters of John Chamberlain* (2 vols.), Philadelphia, Princeton University Press, 1939.

McIllwain, C.H. (ed.), *The Political Works of James I: Reprinted from the Edition of 1616*, Cambridge (Mass.), Harvard University Press, 1918.

Monro, C. (ed.), *Acta Cancellariae; or, selections from the Records of the Court of Chancery*, London, William Benning and Co., 1847.

Nicholas, E., *Proceedings and Debates of the House of Commons in 1620 and 1621* (2 vols.), Oxford, 1766.

Nichols, J.G. (ed.), *Collectanea Topographica and Genealogica* (8 vols.), London, 1834-1843.

Notestein, W., *Commons Debates for 1629: critically edited and an introduction dealing with parliamentary sources for the early Stuarts*, Minneapolis, University of Minnesota Press, 1921.

'The winning of the initiative by the House of Commons', *Proceedings of the British Academy* 11 (1924-5), pp. 125-75.

Oliphant, J. (ed.), *The Educational Writings of Richard Mulcaster (1532-1611)*, Glasgow, James Maclehose & Sons, 1903.

Ormerod, G. (ed.), *The History of the County Palatine and City of Chester* (3 vols., rev. T. Helsby), London, 1875-82.

Ornsby, G. (ed.), *The Correspondence of John Cosin, D.D., Lord Bishop of Durham*, 2 vols, London, Sturtees Society 52 & 55 (1868 & 1870).

Parsons, R., *An Answere to the Fifth Part of the Reportes Lately set forth by Syr Edward Coke, knight, the Kinges Attorney generall*, St. Omer, 1607.

Plutarch, *Lives of the Noble Grecians and Romanes together with that grave and learned philosopher Plutarke of Chaeronea. Translated out of Greeke into French by James Amyot: and out of French into Englishe by Thomas North*, 5 vols., London, 1572 (reprinted by the Nonesuch Press, London, 1929-1930).

Prest, W.R. (ed.), *The Diary of Sir Richard Hutton 1614-1639*, London, Selden Society Supplementary Series 9, 1991.

Relf, F.H. (ed.), *Notes of the Debates in the House of Lords officially taken by Robert Bowyer and Henry Elsing, clerks of the Parliaments, A.D. 1621, 1625, 1628*, London, Camden Society New Series 42, 1929.

Relf, F.H. & H. Simpson (eds.), *Commons Debates in 1621*, New Haven, Yale Historical Publishing, 1935.

Ridley, T., *A View of the Civile and Ecclesiastical Law*, Cambridge, 1607.

Robinson, C.J. (ed.), *A Register of Scholars Admitted into Merchant Taylors' School, from AD 1562 to 1874, Compiled from Authentic Sources and Edited with Biographical Notices*, London, 1882.

Robinson, F.J. (ed.), *The Works of Geoffrey Chaucer*, 2nd ed., London, 1957.

Rushworth, J., *Historical collections of private passages of state, weighty matters in law, remarkable proceedings in five Parliaments* (8 vols.), London, 1659-1701.

Rymer, T., *Foedera Conventiones, Literae et cujuscunque generis Acta Publica, inter Reges Angliae* (10 vols.), London, 1745.

Selden, J., *Historie of Tithes*, London, 1618.

Singer, S.W. (ed.), *Table Talk: being the discourses of John Selden esquire, or his sense of various matters of weight and high consequence &c*, London,1847.

Sorien, R.P. (ed.), *The Diary of John Manningham of the Middle Temple 1602-1603*, Hanover New Hampshire, University of New England, 1976.

Spalding, R. (ed.), *The Diary of Bulstrode Whitelocke 1605-1675*, New York & London, The British Academy, 1990.

Spedding, J., R.L. Ellis & D.D. Heath (eds.), *The Works of Sir Francis Bacon, Baron of Verulam, Viscount St. Alban, and Lord High Chancellor of England* (7 vols.);

Spedding, J. (ed.), *The Letters and Life of Francis Bacon: Including All His Occasional Works* (7 vols.; vols. 7-14 of *Works*), London, Longman & Co., 1858-1874.

Spingarn, J.E. (ed.), *Critical Essays of the Seventeenth Century*, 3 vols. Oxford, Oxford University Press, 1908-1909.

Steer, F.W. (ed.), *A Catalogue of the Earl Marshal's Papers at Arundel Castle*, London, Harleian Society, 1964.

Sturgess, H.A.C. (ed.), *Register of Admissions to the Honourable Society of the Middle Temple from the Fifteenth Century to the year 1944* (5 vols.), London, printed for the Honourable Society of the Middle Temple, 1949.

Tanner, J.R. (ed.), *Constitutional Documents of the Reign of James I*, 2nd ed., Cambridge, Cambridge University Press, 1962.

Taylor, A., *The Epistle of the Lord to his Bride*, London, 1623.

Thorne, S.E. & J.H. Baker (eds.), *Readings and Moots at the Inns of Court in the Fifteenth Century* (2 vols.), London, Selden Society 71 & 105, 1954 & 1989.

Vives, J., *On Education [De tradendis disciplinis]* (trans. F. Watson), Cambridge, Cambridge University Press, 1913.

Winwood, R., *Memorials of Affairs of State in the Reigns of Queen Elizabeth and King James &c.* (3 vols.), London, 1725.

Whitelocke, B., *Memorials of the English Affairs: or, An Historical Account of what passed from the Beginning of the Reign of King Charles the First, to King Charles the Second his happy Restauration*, London, 1732.

Whitelocke, J., *A learned and necessary argument to Prove that each Subject hath a Propreity in his Goods &c*, London, 1641.

Williamson, J.B. (ed.), *The Middle Temple Bench Book, being a Register of the Middle Temple from the Earliest Records to the Present Time with Historical Introduction*, 2nd ed., London, for the Masters of the Bench, 1937.

Wilson, J.P. (ed.), *The Complete Works of William Shakespeare*, London, 1980.

Wood, A., *Athenae Oxonienses: An exact history of all the writers and bishops who have had their education in the University of Oxford* (5 vols., ed. P. Bliss), London, 1813-20.

Woodbine, G.E. (ed.), *De legibus et consuetudinibus angliae* (4 vols., rev. and trans. S.E. Thorne), Cambridge Mass., Harvard University Press, 1968-1977.

Yale, D.E.C. (ed.), Hake, E., *Epieikeia: a dialogue on equity in three parts*, New Haven, Yale University Press, 1953.

Yates, J.B. (ed.), 'The Rights and Jurisdiction of the County Palatine of Chester, The Earls Palatine, The Chamberlain, and Other Officers', *Chetham Miscellany* 37 (1856), pp. 14-34.

SECONDARY SOURCES:

Adamson, J.S.A., 'The Diary of Sir Richard Hutton 1614-1639 with related texts' (book review), *Cambridge Law Journal* 51 pt 3 (1993), pp. 550-552.

Allen, J.W., *A History of Political Thought in the Sixteenth Century*, London, Methuen, 1928.

Alsop, J.D., 'Religious Preambles in Early Modern English Wills as Formulae', *Journal of Ecclesiastical History* 40 no. 1 (1989), pp. 19-27.

Amussen, S.D., 'Gender, Family and the Social Order, 1560-1725' in Fletcher & Stevenson (eds.), *Order and disorder in early modern England*, pp. 196-217.

Ashman, P.M., 'Heraldry and the Law of Arms in England', *Journal of Legal History* 9 no. 1 (1988), pp. 50-86.

Ashton, R., *The English Civil War: Conservatism and Revolution* 1603-1649, 2nd ed., London, Weidenfield & Nicholson, 1989.

Atherton, I.J., 'Viscount Scudamore's 'Laudianism': The Religious Practices of the First Viscount Scudamore', *Historical Journal* 34 no. 3 (1991), pp. 567-596.

Aylmer, G.E., *The King's Servants: The Civil Service of Charles I 1625-1642*, revised ed., London, Routledge & Kegan Paul, 1974.

Baker, D., *Sanctity and Secularity: The Church and the World*, London, Basil Blackwell, 1973.

Baker, H., *The race of time: three lectures on Renaissance historiography*, Toronto, Toronto University Press, 1967.

Baker, J.H., 'The Dark Age of English Legal History' in Jenkins (ed.), *Legal History Studies*, pp. 1-27 (reprinted in *Legal Records and the Historian*, pp. 435-460).

'The Inns of Court and Legal Doctrine' in Charles-Edwards *et al.* (eds.), *Lawyers and Laymen*, pp. 274-286.

(ed.), *Legal Records and the Historian*, London, Royal Historical Society, 1978.

An Introduction to English Legal History, 3rd ed., London, Butterworths, 1990.

The Legal Profession and the Common Law: Historical Essays, London, Hambledon Press, 1986.

(ed.), *Manual of law French*, 2nd ed., London, Scolar Press, 1990.

Baker, J.H., & S.F.C. Milsom (eds.), *Sources of English Legal History: Private Law to 1750,* London, Butterworths, 1986.

Bakhtin, M.M., *Rabelais and his World* (trans. H. Iwolski), Bloomington, Indiana University Press,1984.

Barbu, Z., *Problems of Historical Psychology*, London, Routledge & Kegan Paul, 1960.

Barnes, T.G., 'Star Chamber Litigants and their Counsel, 1596-1641' in Baker (ed.), *Legal Records and the Historian*, pp. 7-28.

Somerset 1625-1640: A County's Government During the Personal Rule, Cambridge Mass., Harvard University Press, 1961.

Barraclough, G., 'The Earldom and County Palatine of Chester', *Transactions of the Historical Society of Lancaster and Cheshire* 103 (1951), pp. 23-57.

Bateson, M. (ed.), *Borough Customs* (2 vols.), London, Selden Society vols. 18 & 21 (1904, 1906).

Beaven, A.B., *The Aldermen of the City of London: Temp. Henry III–1908. With notes on the parliamentary representation of the city, the aldermen and the livery companies, the aldermanic veto, aldermanic baronets and knights, &c*, London, Fisher & Company, 1908.

Bell, H., *Archbishop Laud and Priestly Government*, London, Fisher & Company, 1905.

Bellot, H.H., 'The Jurisdiction of the Inns of Court over the Inns of Chancery', *Law Quarterly Review* 26 (1910), pp. 384-399.

Berman, H.J., *Law and Revolution: The Formation of the Western Legal Tradition*, Cambridge Mass., Harvard University Press, 1983.

Bindoff, S.T., J. Hurstfield & C.H. Williams (eds.), *Elizabethan Government and Society: Essays presented to Sir John Neale*, London, Athelone Press, 1961.

Bland, D.S., 'Learning Exercises and Readers at the Inns of Chancery in the 15th and 16th Centuries', *Law Quarterly Review* 95 (1979), pp. 244-252.

Bloch, M., *The Historian's Craft* (trans. P. Putnam), Manchester, Manchester University Press, 1967.

Bolgar, R.R., *The Classical Heritage and its Beneficiaries*, Cambridge, Cambridge University Press, 1954.

Bossy, J., 'Godparenthood: The Fortunes of a Social Institution in Early Modern Christianity' in Van Greyerz (ed.), *Religion and Society in Early Modern Europe*, pp. 194-201.

Bouwsma, W.J., 'Lawyers in Early Modern Culture', *American Historical Review* 78 no. 2 (1973), pp. 303-328.

'Anxiety and the Formation of Early Modern Culture' in Malament (ed.), *After the Reformation*, pp. 215-246.

John Calvin: A Sixteenth-Century Portrait, Oxford, Oxford University Press, 1988.

Bowen, C.D., *The Lion and the Throne: the life and times of Sir Edward Coke 1552-1634*, London, Hamish Hamilton, 1957.

Bowker, M., *The Henrician Reformation: the Diocese of Lincoln under John Longland 1521-1547*, Cambridge, Cambridge University Press, 1981.

Braddock, R., 'The Rewards of Office Holding in Tudor England', *Journal of British Studies* 14 no. 2 (1975), pp. 29-47.

Brauer, J.C., 'Types of Puritan Piety', *Church History* 56 no. 1 (1987), pp. 39-58.

Brewer, J. & J. Styles (eds.), *An Ungovernable People: The English and their law in the seventeenth and eighteenth centuries*, London, Hutchinson, 1980.

Brinkworth, E.R.C., 'The Laudian Church in Buckinghamshire', *Birmingham University Historical Journal* 5 no. 1 (1955), pp. 31-59.

Brooks, C.W., 'Litigants and Attorneys in the King's Bench and Common Pleas 1560-1640' in Baker (ed.), *Legal Records and the Historian*, pp. 41-59.

'The Common Lawyers in England, c. 1558-1642' in Prest (ed.), *Lawyers in Early Modern Europe and America*, pp. 42-64.

Pettyfoggers and Vipers of the Commonwealth: The 'Lower Branch' of the Legal Profession in Early Modern England, Cambridge, Cambridge University Press, 1986.

'The Place of Magna Carta and the Ancient Constitution in Sixteenth-Century English Legal Thought' in Sandoz (ed.), *The Roots of Liberty*, pp. 57-88.

Brooks, C.W. & K. Sharpe, 'History, English Law and the Renaissance', *Past & Present* 72 (1976), pp. 133-142.

Buck, A.R., 'The Politics of Land Law in Tudor England, 1529-1540', *Journal of Legal History* 11 no. 2 (1990), pp. 200-217.

Burgess, G., 'On Revisionism: An Analysis of Early Stuart historiography in the 1970s and 1980s', *Historical Journal* 33 no. 3 (1990), pp. 609-627.

'The Impact on Political Thought: Rhetorics for Troubled Times' in Morrill (ed.), *The Impact of The English Civil War*, pp. 67-83.

The Politics of the Ancient Constitution: An Introduction to English Political Thought, 1603-1642, London, Macmillan, 1992.

Butt, J., 'The Facilities for Antiquarian Study in the Seventeenth Century', *Essays and Studies* 24 (1938), pp. 64-79.

Cam, H.M. (ed.), *Selected Historical Essays of F.W. Maitland*, Cambridge, Cambridge University Press, 1957.

Chafe, W.L., 'Language and consciousness', *Language* 50 no. 1 (1974), pp. 111-133.

Charles-Edwards, T.M., M.E. Owen & D.B. Walters (eds.), *Lawyers and Laymen: Studies in the History of Law presented to Professor Dafydd Jenkins*, Cardiff, University of Wales Press, 1986.

Charlton, K., 'Liberal Education and the Inns of Court in the Sixteenth Century', *British Journal of Educational Studies* 9 no. 1 (1960), pp. 25-38.

Education in Renaissance England, London, Routledge & Kegan Paul, 1965.

Christianson, P., 'The Causes of the English Revolution: A Reappraisal', *Journal of British Studies* 15 no. 2 (1976) pp. 40-75

'The Peers, the People, and Parliamentary Management in the First Six Months of the Long Parliament', *Journal of Modern History* 49 no. 4 (1977) pp. 575-599.

'Political Thought in Early Stuart England', *Historical Journal* 30 no. 4 (1987), pp. 955-970.

'Royal and parliamentary voices on the constitution, c. 1604-1621' in Peck (ed.), *Mental World of the Jacobean Court*, pp. 71-95.

'Ancient Constitutions in the Age of Sir Edward Coke and John Selden' in Sandoz (ed.), *The Roots of Liberty*, pp. 89-146.

Clark, P., *English Provincial Society from the Reformation to the Revolution: Religion, Politics and Society in Kent 1500-1640*, Hassocks, Harvester Press, 1977.

Cliffe, J.T., *The Yorkshire Gentry From the Reformation to the Civil War*, London, Athelone Press, 1969.

The Puritan Gentry: The Great Puritan Families of Early Stuart England, London, Routledge & Kegan Paul, 1984.

Clode, C.M., *The Early History of the Guild of Merchant Taylors of the Fraternity of St. John the Baptist* (2 vols.), London, Harrison & Sons, 1888.

Memorials of the Guild of Merchant Taylors of the fraternity of St. John the Baptist in the city of London, London, Harrison & Sons, 1875.

Cockburn, J.S., 'Seventeenth-century clerks of assize – some anonymous members of the legal profession', *American Journal of Legal History* 13 no. 4 (1969), pp. 315-332.

A History of English Assizes 1558-1714, Cambridge, Cambridge University Press, 1972.

'Trial by the Book? Fact and Theory in Criminal Process 1558-1625' in Baker (ed.), *Legal Records and the Historian*, pp. 60-79.

'Early modern assize records as historical evidence', *Journal of the Society of Archivists* 5 (1975), pp. 215-231.

(ed.), *Crime in England 1550-1800*, London, Methuen, 1977.

Collins, S.L., *From Divine Cosmos to Sovereign State: An Intellectual History of Consciousness and the Idea of Order in Renaissance England*, Oxford, Oxford University Press, 1989.

Collinson, P., *The Religion of Protestants: The Church in English Society 1559-1625 (The Ford Lectures 1979)*, Oxford, Clarendon Press, 1982.

Cogswell, T.E., 'Coping with revisionism in early Stuart history', *Journal of Modern History* 62 no. 3 (1990), pp. 538-551.

'A low road to extinction? Supply and redress of grievances in the parliaments of the 1620s', *Historical Journal* 33 no. 2 (1990), pp. 283-303.

Cope, E.S., *Politics Without Parliaments 1629-1640*, London, Unwin & Allen, 1987.

'The Bishops and Parliamentary Politics in Early Stuart England', *Parliamentary History* 9 pt. 1 (1990), pp. 1-14.

Corcoran, S. (ed.), *Law and History in Australia: A Collection of Papers presented at the 1989 Law and History Conference*, Adelaide, Adelaide Law Review Association, 1991.

Costello, W.T., *The Scholastic Curriculum at Early Seventeenth-Century Cambridge*, Cambridge Mass, Harvard University Press, 1958.

Costin, M.A., *The History of St. John's College Oxford 1598-1860*, Oxford, Clarendon Press, 1958.

Coward, B., 'The Lieutenancy of Lancashire and Cheshire in the Sixteenth and Early Seventeenth Centuries', *Transactions of the Historic Society of Lancashire and Cheshire* 119 (1976), pp. 39-64.

Cragg, G.R., *Freedom and Authority: A Study of English Thought in the Early Seventeenth Century*, Philadelphia, The Westminster Press, 1975.

Cressy, D., *Education in Tudor and Stuart England*, London, Edward Arnold, 1975.

'Educational Opportunity in Tudor and Stuart England', *History of Education Quarterly* 16 no. 3 (1976), pp. 303-306.

'Kinship and Kin Interaction in Early Modern England', *Past & Present* 113 (1986), pp. 38-69.

Croft, P., 'Fresh Light on Bate's Case', *Historical Journal* 30 no. 3 (1987), pp. 523-540.

'The Religion of Robert Cecil', *Historical Journal* 34 no. 4 (1991), pp. 773-796.

Croke, A., *The genealogical history of the Croke family, originally named Le Blount* (2 vols.), Oxford, 1823.

Croll, M.W., *Style, Rhetoric and Rhythm*, Princeton, Princeton University Press, 1966.

Cross, C., D. Loades & J.J. Scarisbrick (eds.), *Law and government under the Tudors*, Cambridge, Cambridge University Press, 1988.

Cumberlege, G., *The Corporation of London: Its Origin, Constitution Powers and Duties,* London, Corporation of London, 1950.

Curtis, M., *Oxford and Cambridge in Transition 1558-1642*, Oxford, Clarendon Press, 1959.

Curtis, T.C., 'Quarter Sessions Appearances and their Background: A Seventeenth-Century Regional Study' in Cockburn (ed.), *Crime in England*, pp. 135-154.

'Explaining Crime in Early Modern England', *Criminal Justice History* 1 (1980), pp. 117-137.

Cussons, J.E., *History of Hertfordshire* (3 vols.), London, Stephen Austin & Sons, 1870-1881.

Cust, R.P., 'Charles I, the Privy Council, and the Forced Loan', *Journal of British Studies* 24 no. 2 (1985), pp. 208-235.

'News and Politics in Early Seventeenth-Century England', *Past & Present* 112 (1986), pp. 60-90.

The Forced Loan and English Politics 1626-1628, Oxford, Clarendon Press, 1987.

'Politics and the Electorate in the 1620s' in Cust & Hughes (eds.), *Conflict in Early Stuart England*, pp. 134-167.

'Charles I, the Privy Council and the Parliament of 1628', *Transactions of the Royal Historical Society*, 6th series no. 2 (1992), pp. 25-50.

Cust, R.P. & A. Hughes (eds.), *Conflict in Early Stuart England: studies in religion and politics 1603-1642*, London, Longman, 1989.

Cust, R.P. & P.G. Lake, 'Sir Richard Grosvenor and the Rhetoric of Magistracy', *Bulletin of the Institute of Historical Research* 54 no. 129 (1981), pp. 40-53.

Daly, J., 'The Idea of Absolute Monarchy in Seventeenth-Century England', *Historical Journal* 21 no. 2 (1978), pp. 227-250.

'Cosmic Harmony and Political Thinking in Early Stuart England', *Transactions of the American Philosophical Society* 69 pt. 7 (1979), pp. 1-41.

Dawson, J.P., 'Coke and Ellesmere Disintered: The Attack on Chancery in 1616', *Illinois Law Review* 36 (1941), pp. 127-152.

The Oracles of the Law, Ann Arbor, University of Michigan Law School, 1968.

Dean, D.M. & N.L. Jones (eds.), *The Parliaments of Elizabethan England*, London, Basil Blackwell, 1990.

Dean, J., *Middle Temple Hall: Four Centuries of History*, London, Society of the Middle Temple, 1970.

Dollimore, J. & A. Sinfield (eds.), *Political Shakespeare: New essays in cultural materialism*, Manchester, Manchester University Press, 1985.

Draper, F.W.M., *Four Centuries of Merchant Taylors' School 1561-1961*, London, Oxford University Press, 1962.

Dubrow, H. & R. Strier (eds.), *The Historical Renaissance: New Essays on Tudor and Stuart Literature and Culture*, Chicago, University of Chicago Press, 1988.

Eccleshall, R., *Order and Reason in Politics: Theories of Absolute and Limited Monarchy in Early Modern England*, Oxford, Oxford University Press, 1978.

Eisenstadt, S.N. & L. Roniger, 'Patron-Client Relations as a Model of Structuring Social Exchange', *Comparative Studies in Society and History* 22 no. 1 (1980), pp. 42-77.

Elton, G.R., 'Studying the History of Parliament', *British Studies Monitor* 2 no. 1 (1971), pp. 4-14.

'The Rule of Law in Sixteenth-Century England' in Slavin (ed.), *Tudor Men and Institutions*, pp. 265-294.

'A High Road to Civil War?' in *Studies in Tudor and Stuart Politics and Government,* vol. 2, pp. 164-182.

'Tudor Government: The Points of Contact' in *Studies in Tudor and Stuart Politics and Government* vol. 3, pp. 3-57.

Studies in Tudor and Stuart Politics and Government (3 vols.), Cambridge, Cambridge University Press, 1974-1983.

Emerson, C. & M. Holquist (eds.), *Speech genres and other late essays* (trans. V.W. McGee), Austin, University of Texas Press, 1986

Eusden, J.D., *Puritans, Lawyers, and Politics in Early Seventeenth-Century England*, New Haven, Yale University Press, 1958.

Evans, J., *A History of the Society of Antiquaries*, Oxford, Society of Antiquaries, 1956.

Everitt, A., *The Community of Kent and the Great Rebellion 1640-60,* Leicester, Leicester University Press, 1966.

Change in the Provinces: The Seventeenth Century, Leicester, Leicester University Press, 1969.

The Local Community and the Great Rebellion, London, The Historical Association, 1969.

Farnell, J.E., 'The Social and Intellectual Basis of London's Role in the English Civil Wars', *Journal of Modern History* 49 no. 4 (1977), pp. 641-660.

Ferguson, A.B., *Clio Unbound: Perception of the Social and Cultural Past in Renaissance England*, Durham (NC), Duke University Press, 1979.

Figgis, J.N., *The Divine Right of Kings*, 2nd ed., Cambridge, Cambridge University Press, 1914.

Fildes, V. (ed.), *Women as Mothers in Pre-Industrial England: essays in memory of Dorothy McLaren*, London, Routledge, 1990.

Fisher, R.M., 'The Reformation in microcosm? Benchers at the Inns of Court, 1530-1580' in Jack (ed.), *Rulers, religion and rhetoric in Early Modern England*, pp. 33-61.

Fitzhugh, T.V.H. (ed.), *The Dictionary of Genealogy*, rev. ed., Sherborne, Alphabooks, 1988.

Flemion, J.S., '"A Savings to Satisfy All": The House of Lords and the Meaning of the Petition of Right', *Parliamentary History* 10 pt. 1 (1991), pp. 27-44.

Fletcher, A., 'National and Local Awareness in the County Communities' in Tomlinson (ed.), *Before the English Civil War*, pp. 151-174.

Fletcher, A., *A County Community in Peace and War: Sussex 1600-1660*, London, Longman, 1975.

Reform in the Provinces: The Government of Stuart England, New Haven, Yale University Press, 1986.

Fletcher, A. & J. Stevenson (eds.), *Order and Disorder in Early Modern England*, Cambridge, Cambridge University Press, 1985.

Fletcher, H.F., *The Intellectual Development of John Milton* (2 vols.), Urbana, University of Illinois Press, 1956.

Fletcher, J.M., 'Change and resistance to change: a consideration of the development of English and German universities during the sixteenth century', *History of Universities* 1 (1981), pp. 1-36.

Foss, E., *The Judges of England; with sketches of their lives, and miscellaneous notices connected with the courts of Westminster, from the time of the conquest* (10 vols.), London, Longman, Brown, Green, Longmans & Roberts, 1857.

A Biographical Dictionary of the Judges of England: From the Conquest to the Present Time 1066-1870, London, John Murray, 1870.

Foster, A., 'The function of a bishop: the career of Richard Neile, 1562-1640' in O'Day & Heal (eds.), *Continuity and change*, pp. 33-55.

'Church Policies of the 1630s' in Cust & Hughes (eds.), *Conflict in Early Stuart England*, pp. 193-223.

Foster, E.R., 'Procedure in the House of Lords During the Early Stuart Period', *Journal of British Studies* 5 no. 2 (1966), pp. 56-73.

'Printing the Petition of Right', *Huntington Library Quarterly* 38 (1974/5), pp. 81-84.

'Petitions and the Petition of Right', *Journal of British Studies* 14 no. 1 (1974), pp. 21-45.

The House of Lords 1603-1649: Structure, Procedure, and the Nature of its Business, Chapel Hill, University of North Carolina Press, 1983.

Foster, F.F., 'Merchants and Bureaucrats in Elizabethan London', *Guildhall Miscellany* 4 no. 3 (1972), pp. 149-160.

Fox, L. (ed.), *English historical scholarship in the sixteenth and seventeenth centuries: a record of the papers delivered at a Conference arranged by the Dugdale Society to commemorate the tercentenary of the publication of Dugdale's Antiquities of Warwickshire*, London, Oxford University Press, 1956.

Fryde, E.B. and E. Miller (eds.), *Historical Studies of the English Parliament* (2 vols.), Cambridge, Cambridge University Press, 1970.

Fussner, F.S., *The Historical Revolution: English Historical Writing and Thought 1580-1640*, Westport, Greenwood Press, 1962.

Gardiner, S.R., *History of England from the Accession of James I to the Outbreak of the Civil War 1603-1642* (10 vols.), London, Longmans, Green & Co., 1883-1884.

Gleason, J.H., *The Justices of the Peace in England 1558 to 1640: A Later Eirenarcha*, Oxford, Clarendon Press, 1969.

Godwin, G., *The Middle Temple: the society and fellowship*, London, Staples Press, 1954.

Gordon, W.M. & T.D. Fergus (eds.), *Legal History in the Making: Proceedings of the Ninth British Legal History Conference*, London, Hambledon Press, 1991.

Grafton, A., 'Renaissance Readers and Ancient Texts: Comments on Some Commentaries', *Renaissance Quarterly* 38 no. 4 (1985), pp. 615-649.

Grafton, A. & L. Jardine (eds.), *From Humanism to the Humanities: Education and the Liberal Arts in Fifteenth and Sixteenth-Century Europe*, London, Duckworth, 1986.

Gray, C.M., 'Parliament, Liberty, and the Law' in Hexter (ed.), *Parliament and Liberty*, pp. 155-200.

Gray, H.H., 'Renaissance Humanism: The Pursuit of Eloquence' in Kristeller & Wiener (eds.), *Renaissance Essays*, pp. 199-216.

Greaves, R.L., *The Puritan Revolution and Educational Thought: Background for Reform*, New Brunswick, Rutgers University Press, 1969.

Greaves, R.L. & R. Zaller (eds.), *Biographical Dictionary of British Radicals in the Seventeenth Century* (3 vols.), Brighton, Harvester Press, 1982.

Green, T.A., *Verdict according to conscience: perspectives on the English criminal trial jury, 1200-1800*, Chicago, University of Chicago Press, 1985.

Greenblatt, S., 'Invisible Bullets: Renaissance Authority and its Subversion, Henry IV and Henry V' in Dollimore & Sinfield (eds.), *Political Shakespeare*, pp. 18-47.

'Psychoanalysis and Renaissance Culture' in Parker & Quint (eds.), *Literary Theory/Renaissance Studies*, pp. 210-224.

Shakespearean Negotiations: The Circulation of Social Energy in Renaissance England, Berkeley, University of California Press, 1988.

Greenleaf, W.H., *Order, Empiricism and Politics: Two Traditions of English Political Thought, 1500-1700*, London, Oxford University Press, 1964.

Gruenfelder, J.K., 'The Parliamentary Election at Chester, 1621', *Transactions of the Historic Society of Lancashire and Cheshire* 120 (1968), pp. 35-44.

'The Electoral Patronage of Sir Thomas Wentworth, Earl of Stafford, 1614-1640', *Journal of Modern History* 49 no. 4 (1977), pp. 557-574.

Influence in early Stuart elections, 1604-1640, Columbus, Ohio State University Press, 1981.

Guy, J.A., 'The Origin of the Petition of Right Reconsidered', *Historical Journal* 25 no. 2 (1982), pp. 289-312.

Hainsworth, D.R., 'The Estate Steward' in Prest (ed.), *The Professions in Early Modern England*, pp. 154-180.

Hall, G.D.G., 'Impositions and the Courts 1554-1606', *Law Quarterly Review* 69 (1953), pp. 200-218.

'An Assize Book of the Seventeenth Century', *American Journal of Legal History* 7 (1963), pp. 228-245.

Ham, R.E., 'The Four Shire Controversy', *Welsh History Review* 8 no. 4 (1977), pp. 381-399.

Hammer, C.I., 'Bolts and Chapel Moots at Lincoln's Inn in the 16th Century', *Journal of the Society of Public Teachers of Law* 11 (1970), pp. 24-28.

Harris, B.E., 'Palatine Institutions and County Government 1547-1680' in *V.C.H. Cheshire*, vol. 2, pp. 36-55.

Harriss, G.L., 'Medieval doctrines in the debates on supply, 1610-1629' in Sharpe (ed.), *Faction and Parliament*, pp. 73-104.

Hart, J.S., 'Provincial Politics and Government in Stuart England', *Journal of British Studies* 28 no. 3, (1989), pp. 304-311.

Justice upon Petition: The House of Lords and the Reformation of Justice 1621-1675, London, HarperCollins Academic, 1991.

Hawkins, M., 'The Government: Its Role and Its Aims' in Russell (ed.), *The Origins of the English Civil War*, pp. 35-65.

Heal, F., 'The Idea of Hospitality in Early Modern England', *Past & Present* 102 (1984), pp. 66-93.

Hospitality in early modern England, Oxford, Clarendon Press, 1990.

Herrup, C.B., 'Law and Morality in Seventeenth-Century England', *Past & Present* 106 (1985), pp. 102-123.

The Common Peace: Participation and the criminal law in seventeenth-century England, Cambridge, Cambridge University Press, 1987.

'The counties and the country: some thoughts on seventeenth-century historiography', *Social History* 8 no. 2, pp. 162-182.

Hexter, J.H., 'The education of the aristocracy in the Renaissance', *Journal of Modern History* 22 no. 1 (1950) pp. 1-20.

(ed.), *Parliament and liberty from the Reign of Elizabeth to the English civil war*, Stanford, Stanford University Press, 1992.

'Power Struggle, Parliament and Liberty in Early Stuart England', *Journal of Modern History* 50 no. 1 (1978), pp. 1-50.

'The Early Stuarts and Parliament', *Parliamentary History* 1 (1982), pp. 181-215.

Hibbard, C., *Charles I and the Popish Plot*, Chapel Hill, University of North Carolina Press, 1983.

Hill, C., *The Economic Problems of the Church: From Archbishop Whitgift to the Long Parliament*, Oxford, Clarendon Press, 1956.

Intellectual Origins of the English Revolution, Oxford, Oxford University Press, 1965.

Society and Puritanism in pre-Revolutionary England, London, Secker & Warburg, 1964.

Change and Continuity in Seventeenth-Century England, London, Weidenfield and Nicholson, 1974.

Hill, J.E.C., 'Parliament and the People in Seventeenth Century England', *Past & Present* 93 (1981), pp. 100-125.

Hill, L.M., 'County Government in Caroline England' in Russell (ed.), *The Origins of the English Civil War*, pp. 66-90.

Bench and Bureaucracy: The Public Career of Sir Julius Caesar, 1580-1636, Stanford, Stanford University Press, 1988.

Hinton, R.W.K., 'English Constitutional Theories from Sir John Fortescue to Sir John Eliot', *English Historical Review* 75 no. 296 (1960), pp. 410-467.

Hirst, D., *The Representative of the People? Voters and Voting in England under the Early Stuarts*, Cambridge, Cambridge University Press, 1975.

'Court, County, and Politics before 1629' in Sharpe (ed.), *Faction and Parliament*, pp. 105-137.

'The Privy Council and Problems of Enforcement in the 1620s', *Journal of British Studies* 18 no. 1 (1978), pp. 46-66.

'Parliament, Law and War in the 1620s', *Historical Journal* 23 no. 2 (1980), pp. 455-461.

'The Place of Principle' in Rabb & Hirst, 'Revisionism Revised', pp. 79-99.

Holdsworth, W.S., *A History of English Law* (3 vols.), 3rd. ed., London, Methuen & Co., 1923.

Hollinger, D.A., 'T.S. Kuhn's Theory of Science and Its Implications for History', *American Historical Review* 78 no. 2 (1973), pp. 370-393.

Holmes, C., 'The County Community in Stuart Historiography', *Journal of British Studies* 19 no. 2 (1980), pp. 54-73.

Seventeenth Century Lincolnshire, Lincoln, Society for Lincolnshire History and Archaeology, 1980.

Holquist, M. (ed.), *The dialogic imagination: Four essays by M.M. Bakhtin* (trans. C. Emerson & M. Holquist), Austin, University of Texas Press, 1981.

Howell, W.S., *Logic and Rhetoric in England, 1500-1700*, Princeton, Princeton University Press, 1956.

Hughes, A., 'The King, the Parliament, and the Localities during the English Civil War', *Journal of British Studies* 24 no. 2, (1985), pp. 236-263.

Politics, Society and Civil War in Warwickshire, 1620-1660, Cambridge, Cambridge University Press, 1987.

'Local History and the Origins of the English Civil War' in Cust & Hughes (eds.), *The Causes of the English Civil War*, pp. 224-253.

The Causes of the English Civil War, London, Macmillan, 1991.

Hutchinson, J., *A Catalogue of Notable Middle Templars, with Brief Biographical Notices*, London, for the Masters of the Bench, 1902.

Ives, E.W. & A.H. Manchester (eds.), *Law, Litigants and the Legal Profession (British Legal Conference 1979)*, London, Royal Historical Society, 1983.

Jack, S.M. (ed.), *Rulers, religion and rhetoric in early modern England: A Festschrift for Geoffrey Elton from his Australasian Friends*, Sydney, Paragon, 1988.

James, M., *Family, Lineage, and Civil Society: A Study of Society, Politics, and Mentality in the Durham Region, 1500-1640*, Oxford, Clarendon Press, 1974.

Society, Politics & Culture: Studies in early modern England, Cambridge, Cambridge University Press, 1986.

Jenkins, D. (ed.), *Legal History Studies: papers presented to the Legal History Conference, Aberystwyth, 18-21 July 1972*, Cardiff, University of Wales Press, 1975.

Jensen, J.V., 'The Staff of the Jacobean Privy Council', *Huntington Library Quarterly* 40 no. 1 (1976/7), pp. 11-44.

Jones, F., *The Princes and Principality of Wales*, Cardiff, University of Wales Press, 1969.

Jones, G., *History of the Law of Charity 1532-1827*, Cambridge, Cambridge University Press, 1969.

Jones, N.L., 'An Elizabethan Bill for the Reformation of the Ecclesiastical Law', *Parliamentary History* 4 (1985), pp. 171-189.

Jones, W.J., *The Elizabethan Court of Chancery*, Oxford, Clarendon Press, 1967.

'Ellesmere and Politics, 1603-1617' in Reinmuth (ed.), *Early Stuart Studies*, pp. 11-63.

Politics and the Bench: The Judges and the Origins of the English Civil War, London, George Allen & Unwin, 1971.

'The Exchequer of Chester in the Last Years of Elizabeth I' in Slavin (ed.), *Tudor Men and Institutions*, pp. 123-170.

'The Crown and the Courts in England 1603-25' in Smith (ed.), *The Reign of James IV and I*, pp. 177-194.

Judson, M.A., *The Crisis of the Constitution: an essay in constitutional and political thought in England 1603-1645*, New York, Octagon Books, 1964.

Kantorowicz, E.H., *The King's Two Bodies: A Study in Medieval Political Theology*, Princeton, Princeton University Press, 1957.

Kelley, D.R., *Foundations of modern historical scholarship: language, law and history in the French Renaissance*, New York, Columbia University Press, 1970.

'History, English Law and the Renaissance', *Past & Present* 65 (1974), pp. 24-51.

'Jurisconsultus perfectus: the lawyer as Renaissance man' in Schochet *et al.* (eds.), *Law, Literature and the settlement of regimes*, pp. 143-170.

Kendall, R.T., *Calvin and English Calvinism to 1649*, Oxford, Oxford University Press, 1979.

Kenyon, J.P., *The Stuart Constitution 1603-1688: Documents and Commentary*, Cambridge, Cambridge University Press, 1966.

The Stuart Constitution 1603-1688: Documents and Commentary, 2nd ed., Cambridge, Cambridge University Press, 1986.

The Civil Wars of England, London, Weidenfield & Nicholson, 1988.

Kinney, A.F., 'Sir Philip Sydney and the Uses of History' in Dubrow & Strier (eds.), *The Historical Renaissance*, pp. 293-314.

Kishlansky, M.A., 'The Emergence of Adversary Politics in the Long Parliament', *Journal of Modern History* 49 no. 4 (1977), pp. 617-640.

Parliamentary Selection: Social and Political Choice in Early Modern England, Cambridge, Cambridge University Press, 1986.

Kittleson, J.M. & P.L. Transue (eds.), *Rebirth, Reform and Resilience: Universities in Transition 1300-1700*, Columbus, Ohio State University Press, 1984.

Klein, W.E., 'Parliament, Liberty and the Continent in the Early Seventeenth Century: The Perception', *Parliamentary History* 6 no. 2 (1987), pp. 209-221.

Knafla, L.A., 'The Law Studies of an Elizabethan student', *Huntington Library Quarterly* 32 no. 3 (1969), pp. 221-240.

'The Matriculation Revolution and Education at the Inns of Court in Renaissance England' in Slavin (ed.), *Tudor Men and Institutions*, pp. 232-264.

Law and Politics in Jacobean England: The Tracts of Lord Chancellor Ellesmere, Cambridge, Cambridge University Press, 1977.

'"Sin of All Sorts Swarmeth": Criminal Litigation in an English County in the Early Seventeenth Century' in Ives & Manchester (eds.), *Law, Litigants and the Legal Profession*, pp. 50-67.

Kopperman, P.E., *Sir Robert Heath 1575-1649: Window on an Age*, London, Royal Historical Society, 1989.

Kretzmann, N., A. Kenny & J. Pinborg (eds.), *Cambridge History of Later Medieval Philosophy: From the Rediscovery of Aristotle to the Disintegration of Scholasticism*, Cambridge, Cambridge University Press, 1982.

Kristeller, P.O., *Renaissance Thought: the Classics, Scholasticism and Humanist Strains*, New York, Harper & Row, 1961.

Kristeller, P.O. & P.P. Wiener (eds.), *Renaissance Essays: From the Journal of the History of Ideas*, New York, Harper, 1968.

Lake, P.G., 'The Collection of Ship Money in Cheshire during the 1630s: A Case Study of Relations between Central and Local Government', *Northern History* 17 (1981), pp. 44-71.

Moderate Puritans and the Elizabethan Church, Cambridge, Cambridge University Press, 1982.

'Calvinism and the English Church, 1570-1635', *Past & Present* 114 (1987), pp. 32-76.

Anglicans and Puritans? Presbyterianism and English Conformist Thought from Whitgift to Hooker, London, Unwin Hyman, 1988.

Lamont, W.M., *Godly Rule: Politics and Religion, 1603-60*, London, MacMillan, 1969.

Larminie, V.M., *The Godly Magistrate: The Private Philosophy and Public Life of Sir John Newdigate 1571-1610*, Oxford, Dugdale Society Occasional Papers no. 28 (1982).

Lees, S. (ed.), *Dictionary of National Biography* (63 vols.), 1st ed., London, Smith, Elder & Co., 1885-1900.

Lemmings, D., 'Ritual and the Law in Early Modern England' in Corcoran (ed.), *Law and History in Australia*, pp. 3-20.

Levack, B.P., *The Civil Lawyers in England 1603-1641: A Political Study*, Oxford, Clarendon Press, 1973.

'The English Civilians, 1500-1750' in Prest (ed.), *Lawyers in Early Modern Europe and America*, pp. 108-128.

'Law and Ideology: The Civil Law and Theories of Absolutism in Elizabethan and Jacobean England' in Dubrow & Strier (eds.), *The Historical Renaissance,* pp. 220-241.

'The civil law, theories of absolutism, and political conflict in late sixteenth and early seventeenth-century England' in Schochet *et al.* (eds), *Law, Literature and the settlement of regimes*, pp. 29-48.

Levy, F.J., 'How Information Spread Among the Gentry, 1550-1640', *Journal of British Studies* 21 no. 2 (1982), pp.11-34.

Lipscomb, G., *The History and Antiquities of the County of Buckingham* (4 vols.), London, J. & W. Robins, 1831-1847.

Little, D., *Religion, Order, and Law: A Study in Pre-Revolutionary England*, New York, Harper and Row, 1970.

Lloyd, J.E., & R.T. Jenkins (eds.), *The Dictionary of Welsh Biography down to 1940, under the auspices of the Honourable Society of Cymmrodorion*, Oxford, Blackwell, 1959.

Lockyer, R., *Buckingham: The Life and Political Career of George Villiers, First Duke of Buckingham 1592-1628*, London, Longman, 1981.

The Early Stuarts: A political history of England 1603-1642, London, Longman, 1989.

Lovejoy, A.O., *The Great Chain of Being: A study of the History of An Idea*, New York, Harper, 1960.

Lytle, G.F., 'The Careers of Oxford Students in the Later Middle Ages' in Kittleson & Transue (eds.), *Rebirth, Reform and Resilience*, pp. 213-253.

'Religion and the Lay Patron in Reformation England' in Lytle & Orgel (eds.), *Patronage in the Renaissance*, p. 65-114.

Lytle, G.F. & S. Orgel (eds.), *Patronage in the Renaissance*, Princeton, Princeton University Press, 1981.

Macaffrey, W., 'Place and Patronage in Elizabethan Politics' in Bindoff *et al.* (eds.), *Elizabethan Government and Society*, pp. 95-126.

'Patronage and Politics under the Tudors' in Peck (ed.), *Mental World of the Jacobean Court*, pp. 21-35.

MacFarlane, A., *The Justice and the Mare's Ale: Law and Disorder in Seventeenth-Century England*, Cambridge, Cambridge University Press, 1981.

Maitland, F.W., *English Law and the Renaissance*, Cambridge, Cambride University Press, 1901.

The Constitutional History of England, Cambridge, Cambridge University Press, 1908.

'English Law, 1307-1600' in Cam (ed.), *Selected Historical Essays*, pp. 122-134.

Malament, B.C. (ed.), *After the Reformation: essays in honour of J.H. Hexter*, Manchester, Manchester University Press, 1980.

Mallet, C.E., *A History of the University of Oxford vol. II: The Sixteenth and Seventeenth Centuries*, London, Methuen & Co., 1924.

Marchant, J.R.V., 'The Middle Temple Records', *Law Quarterly Review* 21 (1905), pp. 346-356.

Marcus, L.S., *Childhood and Cultural Despair: A Theme and Variations in Seventeenth-Century Literature*, Pittsburgh, University of Pittsburgh Press, 1978.

Marsh, C., 'In the name of God? Will-making and faith in early modern England' in Martin & Spufford (eds.), *The records of the nation*, pp. 61-66.

Martin, G.H., & P. Spufford (eds.), *The records of the nation: the Public Record Office, 1838-1988*, Woodbridge, British Record Society, 1990.

Mason, Thomas, *Serving God and Mammon*, Newark, University of Delaware Press, 1985.

McConica, J., 'The social relations of Tudor Oxford', *Transactions of the Royal Historical Society*, 5th series no. 27 (1977), pp. 115-134.

'Scholars and Commoners in Renaissance Oxford' in Stone (ed.), *The University in Society*, vol. 1, pp. 151-181.

(ed.), *The History of the University of Oxford vol. III: The Collegiate University*, Oxford, Clarendon Press, 1986.

McGowan, A.P. (ed.), *The Jacobean Commissions of Enquiry, 1608 and 1618, Navy Records Society* 116 (1971).

McIllwain, C.H., *The High Court of Parliament and Its Supremacy: An Historical Essay on the Boundaries between Legislation and Adjudication in England*, New Haven, Yale University Press, 1910.

McKendrick, N. (ed.), *Historical Perspectives: studies in English thought and society, in honour of J.H. Plumb*, London, Europa Press, 1974.

Meekings, C.A.F., 'King's Bench Files' in Baker (ed.), *Legal Records and the Historian,* pp. 97-139.

Moir, T.L., *The Addled Parliament of 1614*, Oxford, Clarendon Press, 1958.

Momigliano, A., *Studies in Historiography*, London, Weidenfield & Nicholson, 1966.

Morrill, J.S., *Cheshire 1630-1660: County Government and Society during the English Revolution*, Oxford, Oxford University Press, 1974.

The Cheshire Grand Jury 1625-1629: A Social and Administrative Study, Leicester, Leicester University Press, 1976.

The Revolt of the Provinces: Conservatives and Radicals in the English Civil War 1630-1650, 2nd. ed., London & New York, Longman, 1980.

'The Religious Context of the English Civil War', *Royal Historical Society Transactions*, 5th series no. 34 (1984), pp. 155-178.

(ed.), *The Impact of the English Civil War*, London, Collins & Brown, 1991.

Neale, J.E., 'The Biographical Approach to History', *History* 36 no. 128 (1951), pp. 193-203.

Nederman, C.J., 'Bracton on Kingship Revisited', *History of Political Thought* 5 no. 1 (1984), pp. 61-77.

Notestein, W., *The Winning of the Initiative by the House of Commons*, London, the British Academy, 1924.

The House of Commons, 1604-1610, New Haven & London, Yale University Press, 1971.

Oakley, F., 'Jacobean Political Theology: The Absolute and Ordinary Powers of the King', *Journal of the History of Ideas* 19 no. 3 (1968), pp. 323-346.

O'Day, R., 'The Law of Patronage in Early Modern England', *Journal of Ecclesiastical History* 26 no. 3 (1975), pp. 247-260.

The English Clergy: The Emergence and Consolidation of a Profession 1558-1642, Leicester, Leicester University Press, 1979.

Education and Society 1500-1800: The social foundations of education in early modern Britain, London & New York, Longman, 1982.

O'Day, R. & F. Heal (eds.), *Continuity and change: Personnel and administration of the Church of England 1500-1642*, Leicester, Leicester University Press, 1976.

Ormerod, G., *The History of the County Palatine and City of Chester* (3 vols.), 2nd ed., (rev. T. Helsby), London, Routledge, 1875-1882.

Ong, W., *Ramus, Method, and the Decay of Dialogue*, Cambridge (Mass.), Harvard University Press, 1958.

Interfaces of the Word: Studies in the Evolution of Consciousness and Culture, Ithaca, Cornell University Press, 1977.

Orme, N., *Education and Society in Medieval and Renaissance England*, London, The Hambledon Press, 1989.

Parker, P., & D. Quint (eds.), *Literary Theory / Renaissance Texts*, Baltimore, Johns Hopkins University Press, 1986.

Pawlisch, H.S., 'Sir John Davies, The Ancient Constitution, and Civil Law', *Historical Journal* 23 no. 3 (1980), pp. 689-702.

Pearl, V., *London and the Outbreak of the Puritan Revolution: City Government and National Politics, 1625-1643*, Oxford, Oxford University Press, 1961.

Peck, L.L., 'Corruption at the Court of James I: The Undermining of Legitimacy' in Malament (ed.) *After the Reformation*, pp. 75-93.

'Court Patronage and Government Policy: The Jacobean Dilemma' in Lytle & Orgel (eds.), *Patronage in the Renaissance*, pp. 27-46.

Northampton: Patronage and Policy at the Court of James I, London & Boston, Allen & Unwin, 1982.

'"For a King not to be bountiful were a fault": Perspectives on Court Patronage in Early Stuart England', *Journal of British Studies* 25 no. 1 (1986), pp. 31-61.

Court Patronage and Corruption in Early Stuart England, Boston, Unwin Hyman, 1990.

(ed.), *The Mental World of the Jacobean Court, Cambridge*, Cambridge University Press, 1991.

Pennington, D., & K. Wrightson (eds.), *Puritans and Revolutionaries: Essays in Seventeenth-Century History Presented to Christopher Hill*, Oxford, Oxford University Press, 1978.

Plunkett, F.B.A., *Early English Legal Literature*, Cambridge, Cambridge University Press, 1958.

Pocock, J.G.A., *The Ancient Constitution and Feudal Law: A Study of English Historical Thought in the Seventeenth Century*, Cambridge, Cambridge University Press, 1957.

Politics, Language and Time: essays on political thought and history, London, Methuen, 1972.

The Ancient Constitution and Feudal Law: A Study of English Historical Thought in the Seventeenth Century: a reissue with a retrospect, Cambridge, Cambridge University Press, 1987.

Pollock, L., 'Younger sons in Tudor and Stuart England', *History Today* 39/6 (1989), pp. 23-29.

Powell, D.X., 'Sir James Whitelocke's advice to the Crown in 1627', *Historical Journal* 39 (1996), pp. 737-42.

'Why was Sir Francis Bacon Impeached? The Common Lawyers and the Chancery Revisited: 1621', *History* 264 (1996), pp. 511-26.

'James Whitelocke, Chief Justice of Chester 1620-1624', *Transactions of the Historic Society of Lancashire and Cheshire* 143 (1993), pp. 1-34.

'Why did James Whitelocke go to jail in 1613? "Principle" and political dissent in Jacobean England', *Australian Journal of Law and Society* 11 (1995), pp. 169-90.

Prest, W.R., 'The legal education of the gentry at the inns of court, 1560-1640', *Past & Present* 38 (1967), pp. 20-39.

'The Learning Exercises at the Inns of Court, 1590-1640', *Journal of the Society of Public Teachers of Law* 9 no. 3 (1967), pp. 302-313.

The Inns of Court Under Elizabeth I and the Early Stuarts 1590-1640, London, Longman, 1972.

'Counsellor's Fees and Earnings in the Age of Sir Edward Coke' in Baker (ed.), *Legal Records and the Historian*, pp. 165-184.

'The Dialectical Origins of Finch's Law', *Cambridge Law Journal* 36 pt. 2 (1977), pp. 326-352.

'The Art of Law and the Law of God: Sir Henry Finch (1558-1625)' in Pennington & Wrightson (eds.), *Puritans and Revolutionaries*, pp. 94-117.

'The English Bar, 1550-1700' in *Lawyers in Early Modern Europe and America*, pp. 65-85.

(ed.), *Lawyers in Early Modern Europe and America*, London, Croom Helm, 1981.

The Rise of the Barristers: A Social History of the English Bar 1590-1640, Oxford, Clarendon Press, 1986.

'Politics and Profession in early Stuart England: the diary of Sir Richard Hutton' in Jack (ed.), *Rulers, religion and rhetoric*, pp. 163-177.

'Judicial Corruption in Early Modern England', *Past & Present* 133 (1991), pp. 66-95.

'Predicting Civil War Allegiances: The Lawyers' Case Considered', *Albion* 24 (1992), pp. 225-236.

'Law, learning and religion: gifts to Gray's Inn library in the 1630s' in *Protestants, Property, Puritans: Godly People Revisited*, ed. S.M. Jack & B.A. Masters (*Parergon*, n.s. vol. 14 no. 1 (1996)), pp. 205-22.

Prestwich, M., *Cranfield: Politics and Profits under the Early Stuarts*, Oxford, Clarendon Press, 1966.

Price-Williams, D., 'Toward the idea of a cultural psychology: A superordinate theme for study', *Journal of cross-cultural psychology* 11 no. 1 (1980), pp. 75-88.

Public Record Office Current Guide (1991) vol. 1, 'Records of the Palatinate of Chester'.

Quintrell, B.W., 'Government in Perspective: Lancashire and the Privy Council, 1570-1640', *Transactions of the Historical Society of Lancashire and Cheshire* 131 (1981), pp. 35-62.

Rabb, T.K., 'The Role of the Commons' in Rabb and Hirst, 'Revisionism Revised', pp. 55-78.

Rabb, T.K. & D. Hirst, 'Revisionism revised: two perspectives on early Stuart parliamentary history', *Past & Present* 42 (1981), pp. 55-99.

Reinmuth, H.S. (ed.), *Early Stuart Studies*, Minneapolis, University of Minnesota Press, 1970.

Reeve, L.J., 'The Legal Status of the Petition of Right', *Historical Journal* 29 no. 2 (1986), pp. 257-277.

'Sir Robert Heath's Advice for Charles I in 1629', *Bulletin of the Institute of Historical Research* 59 no. 140 (1986), pp. 215-224.

'The Arguments in King's Bench in 1629 concerning the Imprisonment of John Selden and Other Members of the House of Commons', *Journal of British Studies* 25 no. 3 (1986), pp. 264-287.

Charles I and the Road to Personal Rule, Cambridge, Cambridge University Press, 1989.

Relf, F.H., *The Petition of Right*, Minneapolis, University of Minnesota Press, 1917.

Richards, Judith, '"His Nowe Majestie" and the English Monarchy: the Kingship of Charles I before 1640', *Past & Present* 113 (1986), pp. 70-96.

Richardson, R.C., *The Debate on the English Revolution Revisited*, 2nd ed., London, Routledge, 1988.

Richardson, W.C., *A History of the Inns of Court: With Special Reference to The Period of The Renaissance*, Baton Rouge, Claitor's Publishing, 1980.

Roberts, C., & O. Duncan, 'The Parliamentary Undertaking of 1614', *English Historical Review* 93 no. 368 (1978), pp. 481-498.

Roberts, P., 'Wales and England after the Tudor "union": Crown, principality and parliament, 1543-1624' in Cross *et al.* (eds.), *Law and government under the Tudors*, pp. 111-135.

Rodgers, C.P., 'Humanism, History and the Common Law', *Journal of Legal History* 6 no. 2 (1985), pp. 129-156.

Roskill, J.S., 'Perspectives in English Parliamentary History' in Fryde and Miller (eds.), *Historical Studies of the English Parliament*, vol. 2, pp. 296-323.

Russell, C.S.R., (ed.), *The Origins of the English Civil War*, London, Macmillan, 1973.

'Parliamentary History in Perspective, 1604-1629', *History* 61 no. 201 (1976), pp. 1-27.

'The Nature of a Parliament in Early Stuart England' in Tomlinson (ed.), *Before the English Civil War*, pp. 123-150.

Parliaments and English Politics 1621-1629, Oxford, Clarendon Press, 1979.

Unrevolutionary England, 1603-1642, London, The Hambledon Press, 1990.

The Causes of the English Civil War: the Ford Lectures delivered in the University of Oxford 1987-1988, Oxford, Clarendon Press, 1990.

'English Parliaments 1593-1606: One Epoch or Two?' in Dean & Jones (eds.), *The Parliaments of Elizabethan England*, pp. 191-213.

The Fall of the British Monarchies, 1637-1642, Oxford, Clarendon Press, 1991.

Russell, E., 'The influx of commoners into the University of Oxford before 1581: an optical illusion?', *English Historical Review* 92 no. 365 (1977), pp. 721-745.

Salmon, J.H.M., 'Stoicism and Roman Example: Seneca and Tacitus in Jacobean England', *Journal of the History of Ideas* 50 no. 2 (1989), pp. 199-225.

Sandoz, E. (ed.), *The Roots of Liberty: Magna Carta, Ancient Constitution, and the Anglo-American Tradition of the Rule of Law*, Columbia and London, University of Missouri Press, 1993.

Schmitt, C.B., *John Case and Aristotelianism in Renaissance England*, Ontario, McGill-Queens University Press, 1983.

Schochet, G.J., *Patriarchalism in Political Thought: The Authoritarian Family and Political Speculation and Attitudes Especially in Seventeenth-Century England*, Oxford, Oxford University Press, 1975.

P.E. Tatspaugh & C. Brobeck (eds.), *Law, Literature and the settlement of regimes*, Washington, Folger Shakespeare Library, 1990.

Schoeck, R.J., 'Rhetoric and Law in sixteenth-century England', *Studies in Philology* 50 (1953), pp. 110-127.

'The Elizabethan Society of Antiquaries and Men of Law', *Notes & Queries* 199 (1954), pp. 417-421.

Schwarz, M.L., 'James I and the Historians', *Journal of British Studies* 13 no. 2 (1974), pp. 114-134.

Seipp, D.J., 'The Structure of English Common Law in the Seventeenth Century' in Gordon & Fergus (eds.), *Legal History in the Making*, pp. 61-83.

'The Reception of Canon Law and Civil Law in the Common Law Courts before 1600', *Oxford Journal of Legal Studies* 13 (1993), pp. 388-411.

'Bracton, the Year Books, and the "Transformation of Elementary Legal Ideas" in the Common Law', *Law and History Review* 7 no. 1 (1989), pp. 175-217.

Sharpe, J.A., *Crime in Seventeenth-Century England: A County Study*, Cambridge, Cambridge University Press, 1983.

Crime in Early Modern England 1550-1750, London, Longman, 1984.

Sharpe, K.M., 'Parliamentary History 1603-1629: In or Out of Perspective?' in *Faction and Parliament*, pp. 1-42.

'A commonwealth of meanings: languages, analogues, ideas and politics' in *Politics & Ideas*, pp. 3-71.

'Crown, parliament and locality: government and communication in Early Stuart England' in *Politics & Ideas*, pp. 75-100.

Faction and Parliament: essays on early Stuart history, New York, Oxford University Press, 1978.

Sir Robert Cotton 1586-1631: history and politics in early modern England, Oxford, Oxford University Press, 1979.

'Archbishop William Laud', *History Today* 33/8 (1983), pp. 26-30.

'The personal rule of Charles I' in Tomlinson (ed.), *Before the English Civil War*, pp. 53-78.

Politics and Ideas in Early Stuart England: Essays and Studies, London, Pinter Publishers, 1989.

The Personal Rule of Charles I, London & New Haven, Yale University Press, 1992.

Sherzer, J., 'A discourse-centred approach to language and culture', *American anthropologist* 89 no. 2 (1987), pp. 295-309.

Shuger, D.K., *Habits of Thought in the English Renaissance: Religion, Politics, and the Dominant Culture*, Berkeley, University of California Press, 1990.

Shweder, R.A., *Thinking Through Cultures: Expeditions in Cultural Psychology*, Cambridge (Mass.), Harvard University Press, 1991.

Simon, J., *Education and Society in Tudor England*, Cambridge, Cambridge University Press, 1966.

'Dr. Cowell', *Cambridge Law Journal* 26 no. 2 (1968), pp. 260-276.

The Social Origins of English Education, London, Routledge & Kegan Paul, 1972.

Simpson, A.W.B., 'The source and function of the later year books', *Law Quarterly Review* 87 (1971), pp. 94-118.

Skeel, C.A.J., *The Council in the Marches of Wales: A Study in Local Government during the Sixteenth and Seventeenth Centuries*, London, Hugh Rees Ltd., 1904.

Skinner, Q., 'History and Ideology in the English Revolution', *Historical Journal* 8 no. 2 (1965), pp. 151-178.

'The Limits of Historical Explanations', *Philosophy* 41 (1966), pp. 199-215.

'Motives, Intentions and the Interpretation of Texts', *New Literary History* 3 no. 2 (1972), pp. 393-408.

'The Principles and Practice of Opposition: The Case of Bolingbroke versus Walpole' in McKendrick (ed.), *Historical Perspectives*, pp. 93-128.

The Foundations of Modern Political Thought (2 vols.), Cambridge, Cambridge University Press, 1978.

collected essays in Tully, J., *Meaning and Context: Quentin Skinner and his Critics*, Princeton, Princeton University Press, 1988.

Slack, P., *The Impact of Plague in Tudor and Stuart England*, London & Boston, Routledge & Kegan Paul, 1985.

Slavin, A.J. (ed.), *Tudor Men and Institutions: Studies in English Law and Government*, Baton Rogue, Louisiana State University Press, 1972.

Smith, A.G.R. (ed.), *The Reign of James IV and I*, London, Macmillan, 1973.

Smuts, R.M., *Court Culture and the Origins of a Royalist Tradition in Early Stuart England*, Philadelphia, University of Pennsylvania Press, 1987.

Sommerville, J.P., 'Richard Hooker, Hadrian Saravia, and the Advent of the Divine Right of Kings', *History of Political Thought* 4 no. 2 (1983), pp. 229-245.

Politics & Ideology in England 1603-1640, New York, Longman, 1986.

'Ideology, Property and the Constitution' in Cust & Hughes (eds.), *Conflict in Early Stuart England*, pp. 47-71.

'James I and the divine right of kings: English politics and continental theory' in Peck (ed.), *Mental World of the Jacobean Court*, pp. 55-70.

'Parliament, Privilege, and the Liberties of the Subject' in Hexter (ed.), *Parliament and Liberty*, pp. 56-84.

Spalding, R., *The Improbable Puritan: a life of Bustrode Whitelocke, 1605-1675,* London, Faber & Faber, 1975.

(ed.), *Contemporaries of Bulstrode Whitelocke*, New York, The British Academy, 1990.

Squibb, G.D., *The High Court of Chivalry: A Study of the Civil Law in England*, Oxford, Clarendon Press, 1959.

Stevenson, W.H. & H.E. Salter, *The Early History of St. John's College Oxford*, Oxford, Clarendon Press, 1939.

Steig, M.M., *Laud's Laboratory: The Diocese of Bath and Wells in the Early Seventeenth Century*, Lewisburg, Bucknell University Press, 1982.

Stigler, J.W., R.A. Shweder & G. Herdt, *Cultural psychology: Essays on comparative human development*, New York and Cambridge, Cambridge University Press, 1990

Stone, L., 'The Educational Revolution in England, 1560-1640', *Past & Present* 28 (1964), pp. 41-80.

The Crisis of the Aristocracy 1558-1641, Oxford, Clarendon Press, 1965.

'The Size and Composition of the Oxford Student Body 1580-1910' in *The University in Society*, vol. 1, pp. 3-110.

(ed.), *The University in Society* (2 vols.), Princeton, Princeton University Press, 1974.

The Family, Sex and Marriage in England 1500-1800, London, Weidenfeld & Nicolson, 1977.

Strathmann, E.A., 'Ralegh's *Discourse of Tenures* and Sir Roger Owen', *Huntington Library Quarterly* 20 (1956-7), pp. 219-232.

Swanson, R.N., 'Universities, graduates, and benefices in later medieval England', *Past & Present* 106 (1985), pp. 28-61.

Tanner, J.R., *English Constitutional Conflicts of the Seventeenth Century, 1603-1689*, Cambridge, Cambridge University Press, 1962.

Taylor, C., *Human agency and language: philosophical papers 1*, Cambridge, Cambridge University Press, 1985.

Taylor, C., *Sources of the self: The making of modern identity*, Cambridge, Cambridge University Press, 1989.

Thirsk, J., 'Younger sons in the seventeenth century', *History* 54 no. 182 (1969), pp. 358-377.

Thomas, G.W., 'James I, Equity and Lord Keeper John Williams', *English Historical Review* 91 no. 360 (1976), pp. 506-528.

Thompson, C., 'The Divided Leadership of the House of Commons in 1629' in Sharpe (ed.), *Faction and Parliament,* pp. 245-284.

Thorne, S.E., *Essays in English Legal History*, London, Hambledon Press, 1985.

Tierney, B., *Religion, Law, and the Growth of Constitutional Thought, 1150-1650*, Cambridge, Cambridge University Press, 1982.

Tomlinson, H. (ed.), *Before the English Civil War: Essays on Early Stuart Politics and Government*, London, Macmillan, 1983.

Trevor-Roper, H., *Archbishop Laud 1573-1645*, London, Macmillan & Co., 1940.

Catholics, Anglicans and Puritans: Seventeenth Century Essays, London, Martin Secker & Warburg, 1987.

Tuck, R., 'Power and Authority in Seventeenth-Century England', *Historical Journal* 17 no. 1 (1974), pp. 43-61.

Natural Rights Theories, Cambridge, Cambridge University Press, 1979.

Tully, J., *Meaning and Context: Quentin Skinner and his Critics*, Princeton, Princeton University Press, 1988.

Tyack, G., *Fawley Buckinghamshire: A short history of the Church and Parish*, Fawley Parochial Church Council, 1986.

Tyacke, N., 'Puritanism, Arminianism and Counter-Revolution' in Russell (ed.), *The Origins of the English Civil War*, pp. 119-143.

'The Rise of Arminianism Reconsidered', *Past & Present* 115 (1987), pp. 201-216.

Anti-Calvinists: the Rise of English Arminianism, c. 1590-1640, Oxford, Clarendon Press, 1987.

Tyacke, N. & White, 'The rise of Arminianism reconsidered', *Past & Present* 115 (1987), pp. 201-229.

Underdown, D.E., *Somerset in the Civil War and Interregnum*, Newton Abbot, David & Charles, 1973.

Usher, R.G., 'Nicholas Fuller: A Forgotten Exponent of English Liberty', *American Historical Review* 12 no. 4 (1907), pp. 743-760.

Van Greyerz, K. (ed.), *Religion and Society in Early Modern Europe, 1500-1800*, London, Allen & Unwin, 1984.

Victoria County History:

Buckinghamshire

Oxfordshire

Cheshire

Wagner, A., *Heralds of England: A History of the Office and College of Arms*, London, H.M.S.O., 1967.

Walzer, M., *The Revolution of the Saints: a study in the origins of radical politics*, Cambridge Mass., Harvard University Press, 1965.

Waswo, R., *Language and Meaning in the Renaissance*, Princeton, Princeton University Press, 1987.

Wertsch, J.V., *Voices of the Mind: A Sociocultural Approach to Mediated Action*, Cambridge (Mass.), Harvard University Press, 1991.

Weston, C.C. & J.R. Greenberg, *Subjects and Sovereigns: The Grand Controversy over Legal Sovereignty in Stuart England*, Cambridge, Cambridge University Press, 1981.

Whellan, F. (ed.), *History, Topography and Directory of Northamptonshire*, London, 1874.

White, S.D., 'Observations on Early Stuart Parliamentary History', *Journal of British Studies* 18 no. 2 (1979), pp. 160-170.

Williams, C.H., 'Early Law Readings', *Bulletin of the Institute of Historical Research* 3 no. 7 (1925), pp. 96-101.

Williams, P., *The Council in the Marches of Wales under Elizabeth I*, Cardiff, University of Wales Press, 1958.

Williams, P., 'The Activity of the Council in the Marches under the early Stuarts' in *The Welsh History Review* 1 no. 2 (1961), pp. 133-160.

'The Attack on the Council in the Marches 1603-1642', *Transactions of the Honourable Society of Cymmodorion* 1 (1961), pp. 1-22.

Williams, W.R., *The parliamentary history of the county of Oxford, including the city and university of Oxford, and the borough of Banbury, Burford, Chipping, Norton, Dadington, Witney, and Woodstock from... 1213-1899*, Brecknock, 1899.

Wilson, A., 'The ceremony of childbirth and its interpretation' in Fildes (ed.), *Women as Mothers in Pre-Industrial England*, pp. 68-107.

Wilson, D.H., *The Privy Councillors in the House of Commons 1604-1629*, New York, Octagon Books, 1971.

James VI and I, London, Jonathan Cape, 1972.

Wilson, H.B., *History of Merchant Taylors' School, from its foundation to the present time* (2 vols.), London, 1812-1814.

Wootton, D. (ed.), *Divine Right and Democracy: An Anthology of Political Writing in Stuart England*, London, Penguin, 1986.

Worden, B., 'The 'Diary' of Bulstrode Whitelocke', *English Historical Review* 153 no. 426 (1993), pp. 122-134.

Wormald, J., 'James VI and I, *Basilikon Doron* and *The Trew Law of Free Monarchies*: the Scottish context and the English translation' in Peck, *Mental World of the Jacobean Court*, pp. 36-54.

Wrightson, K., *English Society 1580-1680*, London, Hutchinson, 1982.

'Two concepts of order: justices, constables and jurymen in seventeenth-century England' in Brewer and Styles (eds.) *An Ungovernable People*, pp. 21-46.

Yates, F.A., *The Art of Memory*, 2nd ed., London, Ark Paperbacks, 1984.

Young, M.B., 'The Origins of the Petition of Right Reconsidered Further', *Historical Journal* 27 no. 2 (1984), pp. 449-452.

Zagorin, P., *Rebels & Rulers 1500-1660* (2 vols.), Cambridge, Cambridge University Press, 1982.

Zaller, R., *The Parliament of 1621: A study in constitutional conflict*, London, University of California Press.

Unpublished theses:

Burgess, P.G., 'Custom, Reason and the Common Law: English Jurisprudence 1600-1650' (University of Cambridge PhD, 1988).

Clendenin, T., 'The Common Lawyers in Parliament and Society: A Social and Political Study of the Common Lawyers in the First Jacobean Parliament' (University of North Carolina PhD, 1975).

Cooper, H.H.A., 'Promotion and Politics Among the Common-Law Judges of the Reigns of James I and Charles I' (Liverpool University MA, 1964).

Higgins, G.P., 'County Government and Society in Cheshire, c. 1590-1640' (Liverpool University MA, 1973).

Shaller, T.K., 'English Law and the Renaissance: the Common Law and Humanism in the Sixteenth Century' (Harvard University PhD, 1979).

Index